Bloom's Modern Critical Views

Bloom's Modern Critical Views

Bloom's Modern Critical Views

MARK TWAIN
Updated Edition

Edited and with an introduction by
Harold Bloom
Sterling Professor of the Humanities
Yale University

CHELSEA HOUSE
PUBLISHERS
An imprint of Infobase Publishing

Bloom's Modern Critical Views: Mark Twain, Updated Edition

©2006 Infobase Publishing

Introduction © 2006 by Harold Bloom

Chelsea House
An imprint of Infobase Publishing
132 West 31st Street
New York NY 10001

Library of Congress Cataloging-in-Publication Data
Mark Twain / [edited and with an introduction by] Harold Bloom.
    p. cm. — (Bloom's modern critical views)
  Includes bibliographical references and index.
  ISBN 0-7910-8569-4
  1. Twain, Mark, 1835-1910—Criticism and interpretation. 2. Humorous stories, American—History and criticism. I. Bloom, Harold. II. Series.
  PS1338.M2725 2006
  818'.409—dc22   2005028789

Chelsea House books are available at special discounts when purchased in bulk quantities for businesses, associations, institutions, or sales promotions. Please call our Special Sales Department in New York at (212) 967-8800 or (800) 322-8755.

You can find Chelsea House on the World Wide Web at http://www.chelseahouse.com

Contributing Editor: Amy Sickels
Cover design by Keith Trego
Cover photo © Bettman/CORBIS

Printed in the United States of America

Bang EJB 10 9 8 7 6 5 4 3 2 1

This book is printed on acid-free paper.

All links and web addresses were checked and verified to be correct at the time of publication. Because of the dynamic nature of the web, some addresses and links may have changed since publication and may no longer be valid.

Contents

Editor's Note

My introduction centers upon *Huckleberry Finn*, and emphasizes the secular sublimities of Twain's loving study of his own nostalgia for the freedom of storytelling.

Bernard DeVoto's overview of Twain's career usefully integrates life, work, and socio-historical context.

The poet-critic T.S. Eliot returns to his own St. Louis boyhood to celebrate *Huckleberry Finn* as a tribute to the River, which like Huck has no beginning and no end.

Pudd'nhead Wilson is defended by F.R. Leavis, who finds in it a "moral astringency," while the poet-novelist Robert Penn Warren formalistically analyzes both *Huckleberry Finn* and *A Connecticut Yankee in King Arthur's Court* as structures that reflect Twain's own creative anguish.

In an essay much in Twain's own ironic spirit, James M. Cox revisits *Life on the Mississippi*, and commends the book for its most problematic aspects.

Selfhood and reality, a Twainian dialectic, is seen by Susan Gillman as central to this greatest of American humorists, after which Shelley Fisher Fishkin speculates upon the influence of African-American vernacular voices upon Twain's language.

Innocents Abroad is the sphere in which Henry B. Wonham discovers Twain's triumphant employment of the art of the tall tale, while Neil Schmitz brings us into the place found for his humor by Twain in the Civil War, who attempted to exorcise the Confederate ghost of Sir Walter Scott.

John Carlos Rowe amiably gives us Post-Colonialist Twain, who prophesies in *A Connecticut Yankee* our ongoing imperialism: think what Twain would have made of our Iraqi adventure!

In a final essay, we return to Huck Finn with Joseph L. Coulombe, who gives us a Huck natural-all-too-natural.

HAROLD BLOOM

Introduction

I

> After supper she got out her book and learned me about Moses
> and the Bulrushers, and I was in a sweat to find out all about him;
> but by-and-by she let it out that Moses had been dead a
> considerable long time; so then I didn't care no more about him;
> because I don't take stock in dead people.

Huck Finn's American vision has this in common with Captain Ahab's or Walt Whitman's, that Huck too would strike the sun if it insulted him. The three best American books—*Huckleberry Finn, Moby-Dick, Leaves of Grass*—have in common also that they are each the most American of books. Twain's masterpiece is essentially comic, Melville's is tragic, Whitman's is beyond characterization or categorization, except that despite its humor and its Emersonian hopes for America, we remember it best for its dark shadows. *Huckleberry Finn*, shrewd and grim as it is sometimes compelled to be, remains unique in our national literature for its affirmative force. Fecund in its progeny—as diverse as Kipling's *Kim*, Eliot's *The Dry Salvages*, Hemingway's *The Sun Also Rises*, and Mailer's *Why Are We in Vietnam?*—the book is likely to go on engendering our strongest writers, with only *Leaves of Grass* as a rival in that role.

What is the secret of an appeal that affected Eliot and Faulkner, Hemingway and Joyce, with almost equal intensity? Is it because the book tells the truth? That was the judgment of Lionel Trilling, and I am not moved to dismiss such a judgment lightly. The book tells a story which most Americans need to believe is a true representation of the way things were, are,

1

and yet might be. Huck lives in a complex reality that nevertheless does not negate his freedom. Yet that freedom is also a solitude, and is purchased by a series of lies, noble in their intention, but lies nevertheless. Without a family, yet with a murderous father always apt to turn up again, Huck perpetually experiences a primal loneliness that he both welcomes and dreads:

> Miss Watson she kept pecking at me, and it got tiresome and lonesome. By-and-by they fetched the niggers in and had prayers, and then everybody was off to bed. I went up to my room with a piece of candle and put it on the table. Then I set down in a chair by the window and tried to think of something cheerful, but it warn't no use. I felt so lonesome I most wished I was dead. The stars was shining, and the leaves rustled in the woods ever so mournful; and I heard an owl, away off, who-whooing about somebody that was dead, and a whippowill and a dog crying about somebody that was going to die; and the wind was trying to whisper something to me and I couldn't make out what it was, and so it made the cold shivers run over me. Then away out in the woods I heard that kind of a sound that a ghost makes when it wants to tell about something that's on its mind and can't make itself understood, and so can't rest easy in its grave and has to go about that way every night grieving. I got so down-hearted and scared, I did wish I had some company. Pretty soon a spider went crawling up my shoulder, and I flipped it off and it lit in the candle; and before I could budge it was all shriveled up. I didn't need anybody to tell me that that was an awful bad sign and would fetch me some bad luck, so I was scared and most shook the clothes off of me. I got up and turned around in my tracks three times and crossed my breast every time; and then I tied up a little lock of my hair with a thread to keep witches away. But I hadn't no confidence. You do that when you've lost a horse-shoe that you've found, instead of nailing it up over the door, but I hadn't ever heard anybody say it was any way to keep off bad luck when you'd killed a spider.

Huck, like any American, does not feel free unless he is alone, and yet solitude makes him fear that he is no part of the creation, however the world happened or came about. His extraordinary pathos results from his ambivalence towards a freedom he necessarily cannot evade for very long at a time.

II

V.S. Pritchett found in *Adventures of Huckleberry Finn* evidence of an American limitation, when compared to the more civilized modes of European literature:

> It is not a book which grows spiritually, if we compare it to *Quixote*, *Dead Souls* or even *Pickwick*; and it is lacking in that civilised quality which you are bound to lose when you throw over civilisation—the quality of pity. One is left with the cruelty of American humor.

Pritchett perhaps forgot that throwing over civilization and its discontents is not so easily accomplished, Huck's discomfort with culture is acute, but he is hardly "a natural anarchist and bum" to whom ideas and ideals are "repugnant," as Pritchett thought. Nor is he "the servant of the river-god," which was Lionel Trilling's trope, a mythologization that derived Huck's supposedly "very intense moral life" from his "perpetual adoration of the Mississippi's power and charm." That is to compound Huck with T.S. Eliot, for whom "the Boy is also the spirit of the River." Huck indeed is now part of the American mythology, but hardly because he is the spirit of the river, which is not a god for Twain, whatever it was to be for Trilling and for Eliot. Twain tells us that the Mississippi is well worth reading about, is remarkable, and manifests many eccentricities. Huck too is well worth reading about, is quite remarkable, and is a wonderfully eccentric boy. Critics are fond of finding a moral in him, or at least want to see him as a kind of Sancho Panza to Tom Sawyer's Don Quixote. Tom Sawyer, alas, is something of a bore and not very quixotic, and Huck has little in common with the shrewd and pragmatic Sancho. There is however a touch of the quixotic in Huck, who is a great storyteller, a boy who lies merely to keep in practice.

Huck's fictions are lies *against* time, against an impossible father, against society and history; but not against reason and nature. They are not lies *for* anything; Huck does not seek benefits from them. Like the strong poets, Huck always has the desire to be different, the desire to be elsewhere. Change and travel are necessary for Huck; without them he cannot be independent. But we would do him wrong if we judged him as seeking freedom above everything else. Except for Joyce's Poldy Bloom, Huck Finn must be the most good-natured and tolerant representation of a human being in the fiction of the English language. The freedom he must have, because he is that freedom, is a freedom that he wants for everyone else. It is the freedom of the storyteller, Twain's own freedom.

That freedom, by common consent, has something to do with postponing death, with deferring the fear of dying. Divination, the sidestepping of dangers to the magic, occult, ontological self, is a fundamental component of the urge to tell stories. Huck of course is never going to be an adult, and so never will have to die. Yet that sounds wrong, because Huck rejects a maturation that is merely the death drive. The superego haunts Huck, yet cannot dominate him, because Huck will not surrender his gift for lying. "You don't know about me," Huck begins by saying, and he ends with the insistence that he will be out there ahead of the rest of us:

> But I reckon I got to light out for the Territory ahead of the rest, because Aunt Sally she's going to adopt me and sivilize me and I can't stand it. I been there before.

Huck's discomfort with civilization stems from his wholehearted rejection of guilt, sin, and solipsism, all of them Eliotic attributes, or should one say virtues? We can call Huck's attributes his virtues, because Huck, like his creator, is essentially an enlightened rationalist, though retaining considerable zest for the romance of superstitions. Unlike Eliot, Huck is not a Christian, and his prayer is not, "And let my cry come unto Thee," but something more naturalistic and buoyant:

> Sometimes we'd have that whole river all to ourselves for the longest time. Yonder was the banks and the islands, across the water; and maybe a spark—which was a candle in a cabin window—and sometimes on the water you could see a spark or two—on a raft or a scow, you know; and maybe you could hear a fiddle or a song coming over from one of them crafts. It's lovely to live on a raft. We had the sky, up there, all speckled with stars, and we used to lay on our backs and look up at them, and discuss about whether they was made, or only just happened. Jim he allowed they was made, but I allowed they happened; I judged it would have took too long to *make* so many. Jim said the moon could a *laid* them; well, that looked kind of reasonable, so I didn't say nothing against it, because I've seen a frog lay most as many, so of course it could be done. We used to watch the stars that fell, too, and see them streak

down. Jim allowed they'd got spoiled and was hove out of the nest.

This delightful compromise upon a myth of creation is "kind of reasonable," and wholly characteristic of Huck's cheerful skepticism. Even more characteristic is the joy of being that opens chapter 19 with what must be the most beautiful prose paragraph yet written by any American:

Two or three days and nights went by; I reckon I might say they swum by, they slid along so quiet and smooth and lovely. Here is the way we put in the time. It was a monstrous big river down there—sometimes a mile and a half wide; we run nights, and laid up and hid day-times; soon as night was most gone, we stopped navigating and tied up—nearly always in the dead water under a tow-head; and then cut young cottonwoods and willows and hid the raft with them. Then we set out the lines. Next we slid into the river and had a swim, so as to freshen up and cool off; then we set down on the sandy bottom where the water was about knee, deep, and watched the daylight come. Not a sound, anywheres—perfectly still—just like the whole world was asleep, only sometimes the bull-frogs a-cluttering, maybe. The first thing to see, looking away over the water, was a kind of dull line—that was the woods on t'other side—you couldn't make nothing else out; then a pale place in the sky; then more paleness, spreading around; then the river softened up, away off, and warn't black any more, but gray; you could see little dark spots drifting along, ever so far away—trading scows, and such things; and long black streaks—rafts; sometimes you could hear a sweep screaking; or jumbled up voices, it was so still, and sounds come so far; and by-and-by you could see a streak on the water which you know by the look of the streak that there's a snag there in a swift current which breaks on it and makes that streak look that way; and you see the mist curl up off of the water, and the east reddens up, and the river, and you make out a log cabin in the edge of the woods, away on the bank on t'other side of the river, being a wood-yard, likely, and piled by them cheats so you can throw a dog through it anywheres; then the nice breeze springs up, and comes fanning you from over there, so cool and fresh, and sweet to smell, on account of the woods and the flowers; but sometimes not that way, because they've left dead fish laying around, gars, and such, and they do get pretty rank; and next you've got the full day, and everything smiling in the sun, and the song-birds just going it!

This is a cosmos that was not made, but "only just happened." It is no part of romance or legend, not myth, but a representation of a natural reality seen in its best aspect, where the days and nights swim and slide by. We hesitate to call this a fiction, since it lacks any residual Platonism. Even Freud had his last touch of Platonism, the transcendentalism that he called the "reality principle." Twain and Huck tell us a story about reality, but without reference to any principle.

III

Eminent critics have disagreed vigorously over the way in which Twain chose to end his masterpiece. That something is seriously wrong with the conclusion is palpable, but what is wrong may only be that in this book no conclusion is possible anyway. T.S. Eliot and Lionel Trilling both argued the formal adequacy of the long episode at the Phelps place, in which Tom Sawyer arrives again to organize the "rescue" of Jim, the runaway slave who in some clear sense has become Huck's true family. But the critical decision here certainly goes to Leo Marx, who sees the novel's end as its self-defeat:

> Should Clemens have made Huck a tragic hero? Both Mr. Eliot and Mr. Trilling argue that that would have been a mistake, and they are very probably correct. But between the ending as we have it and tragedy in the fullest sense, there was vast room for invention. Clemens might have contrived an action which left Jim's fate as much in doubt as Huck's. Such an ending would have allowed us to assume that the principals were defeated but alive, and the quest unsuccessful but not abandoned. This, after all, would have been consonant with the symbols, the characters, and the theme as Clemens had created them—and with history.

Marx is aware that he asks for too much, but that is the lasting power of the book that Twain wrote until he reached the Phelps place episode. We are so transported by *Huckleberry Finn* that we cannot surrender our hopes, and of these the largest is a refusal to abandon the desire for a permanent image of freedom. Twain could not extend that image into a finality, but the image endures nevertheless, as a permanent token of something evermore about to be.

BERNARD DeVOTO

Introduction to The Portable Mark Twain

T he first truly American literature grew out of the tidewater culture of the early republic. It was the culture of a people who, whatever their diversity, were more homogeneous in feeling and belief than Americans as a people have ever been since them. We have come to think of the literature whose greatest names are Emerson and Poe, Thoreau and Melville, Hawthorne and Whitman, as our classic period, and in a very real sense the republic that shaped their mind was classical. It felt a strong affinity for the Roman Republic, it believed that Roman virtues and ideas had been expressed in the Constitution, it gave us a great architectural style because it identified its own emotions in the classic style. When Horatio Greenough let a toga fall from Washington's naked shoulders he was not out of tune with contemporary taste: Washington seemed a kind of consul, so did Jefferson, and in the portraits of them which our stamps and coins preserve they have a Roman look. This classical republican culture was at its most vigorous when our classic writers were growing up. But there is an element of anachronism in all literature, and while these men were themselves in full vigor American culture entered a new phase.

The culture of the early republic crossed the Alleghenies in two streams, one Southern, the other mainly New England; but they were more like each other than either was like the one which their mingling presently

---

From *The Portable Mark Twain* © 1946, renewed 1974 by The Viking Press.

helped to produce. For beyond the mountains people found different landscapes, different river courses, different relationships of sky and wind and water, different conceptions of space and distance, different soils and climates—different conditions of life. Beyond still farther mountains lay Oregon and California—and they were implicit in the expanding nation as soon as the treaty that gave us Louisiana was signed—but first the United States had to incorporate the vast expanse between the eastern and the western heights of land. That area is the American heartland. Its greatest son was to call it the Egypt of the West because nature had organized it round a central river and it touched no ocean, but it came into the American consciousness as the Great Valley. When the tidewater culture came to the Great Valley it necessarily broke down: new conditions demanded adaptations, innovations, new combinations and amplifications. The new way of life that began to develop there had a different organization of feeling, a different metabolism of thought. It was no more native, no more "American," than that of the first republic, but it was different and it began to react on it.

The heartland was midcontinental and its energies were oriented toward the river at its center—and were therefore turned away from Europe, which had been a frontier of the early republic. And life in the heartland, with its mingling of stocks, its constant shifting of population, and its tremendous distances, led people in always increasing numbers to think continentally. Both facts were fundamental in the thought and feeling of the new culture.

The American littoral came only slowly, with greater slowness than the fact demanded, to realize that the nation's center of gravity was shifting westward. It tragically failed to understand one consequence of that shift, thirty years of contention between the Northeast and the South to dominate the Great Valley or at least achieve a preferential linkage with it. The failure to understand was in great part a failure to think continentally—as was made clear at last when the Civil War demonstrated that no peaceful way of resolving the contention had been found. Even now too many Americans fail to understand that the war, the resolution by force, only made explicit the organization of our national life that is implicit in the geography which the Great Valley binds together. Abraham Lincoln understood our continental unity; he argued it persistently down to the outbreak of the war and from then on. And Lincoln was a distillation of the heartland culture.

Lincoln's feeling for the continentalism of the American nation was so intense that it almost transcended the transcendent facts. It was a deposit in the very cells of his bones from the soil of the Great Valley. He was, Herndon rightly says, one of the limestone men, the tall, gaunt, powerful, sallow, saturnine men who appear in quantity enough to constitute a type when the wilderness on both sides of the Ohio comes under the plow. His radical democracy was wrought from the experience of the Great Valley. In his ideas and beliefs as in the shadowed depths of his personality there is apparent a new articulation of American life. His very lineaments show it. When you turn from the Jefferson nickel to the Lincoln penny as when you turn from Jefferson's first inaugural address to any of Lincoln's state papers, in the flash of a total and immediate response you understand that you have turned from one era to a later one. You have turned from the tidewater republic to the continental empire.

Lincoln expressed a culture and brought a type to climax. Similarly, when that culture found major literary expression it did so from a rich and various, if humble, literary tradition. As always, the literary expression was the later one; the economic, social, and political impact was felt much earlier. The lag, however, was not so great as Walt Whitman thought. Whitman was sixty when in 1879 he traveled across the Great Valley to its western limit, where the Front Range walls it off. He traversed it with a steadily growing conviction that here in the flesh were the people whose society he had envisioned in so many rhapsodies, Americans who had been fused, annealed, compacted (those are his words) into a new identity. He felt that literature had not yet spoken to these prairie people, "this continental inland West," that it had not yet spoken for them, that it had not made images for their spirit.

The poet supposed that he was speaking of things still to come but he was already wrong by a full ten years. The thing had happened. And the first notification that it had happened can be dated with an exactness not often possible in the history of literature. That notification came in 1869 with the appearance of a book of humorous travel sketches by Samuel Langhorne Clemens, who, faithful to the established tradition, signed it with a pen name, Mark Twain.

Innocents Abroad was greeted with an enthusiasm that made Mark Twain a celebrity overnight, and with too much misunderstanding of a kind that was to persist throughout his career. It was a funny book and a cardinal part of its fun was its disdain of European culture. This disdain, the mere fact of making humor of such disdain, and its frequent exaggeration into burlesque all produced an effect of shock—in most ways a delightful shock but in some ways an uneasy one. Yet the point was not the provinciality of such humor, though it was frequently provincial, and not its uncouthness, though it was sometimes uncouth, but the kind of consciousness it implied. Again it is absurd to speak of this as the first American literature that was independent of European influences, for our literature had obediently divorced itself from Europe as soon as Emerson ordered it to. The humorous core of *Innocents Abroad* was not independence of Europe, but indifference to it. Thoreau and Emerson and Poe were detached from Europe but completely aware of being heirs to it, but here was a literature which had grown up in disregard of Europe—which had looked inward toward the Mississippi and not outward beyond the Atlantic. Failure to appreciate the implications of this difference was one reason, no doubt the weightiest one, why for two full generations literary critics thought of Mark Twain as no more than a clown. But the same identity, the same organization of personality, that made Lincoln the artificer of our continental unity was what made Mark Twain a great writer.

There are striking affinities between Lincoln and Mark Twain. Both spent their boyhoods in a society that was still essentially frontier; both were rivermen. Both absorbed the midcontinental heritage: fiercely equalitarian democracy, hatred of injustice and oppression, the man-to-man individualism of an expanding society. Both were deeply acquainted with melancholy and despair; both were fatalists. On the other hand, both were instinct with the humor of the common life and from their earliest years made fables of it. As humorists, both felt the basic gravity of humor; with both it was an adaptation of the mind, a reflex of the struggle to be sane; both knew, and Mark Twain said, that there is no humor in heaven. It was of such resemblances that William Dean Howells was thinking when he called Mark Twain "the Lincoln of our literature."

II

Samuel Clemens was born at Florida, Monroe County, Missouri, on November 30, 1835, a few months after his parents reached the village from Tennessee. His father was a Virginian, his mother a Kentuckian, and as a family they had made three moves before this one. Florida was a handful of log cabins only two hundred miles east of the Indian Country and in the earliest stage of frontier economy. Though he could have only a generalized memory of it, Sam's earliest years were thus spent in the "Sweet Betsy from Pike" society which has contributed a color and a flavor of its own to American legendry. More: the town was located at the forks of that Salt Creek which figures in the folk proverbs. He could retain little conscious memory of the chinked-log, open-fireplace hamlet with its woods-runners and movers; mostly it would mean the immediacy of nature, the infinity of the forest, the ease of escape into solitude and an all-encompassing freedom.

He was still short of four when the Clemenses made their last move, this time eastward. They seem to have been movers by force of circumstance, not instinct; it was always the pressure of poverty and the hope of betterment that impelled them on. But they bequeathed restlessness to their son.

The final move brought them to Hannibal, an older settlement than Florida and perhaps four times as large but still short of five hundred inhabitants. Hannibal is the most important single fact in the life of Samuel Clemens the person and Mark Twain the writer. It too was lapped round by forest; it maintained the romantic mystery, the subliminal dread, and the intimacy with nature that he had been born to; but it had passed the pioneering stage. It must be seen as a later stage that characterized all our frontiers east of the great plains, after the actual frontier of settlement had pushed westward, after the farms had been brought in and functional communities had been established, but while the frontier crafts and values and ways of thinking lingered on, a little mannered perhaps, a little nostalgic, but still vital. The frontier thugs had passed to other fields or degenerated to village loafers and bullies. There were a few Indians near by and sizable numbers not too far away but they were a spectacle, not a threat. A few hunters and trappers ranged the woods but they were relics, brush folk, not of the great race. There were as many frame houses as log cabins; if the schoolhouse had a puncheon floor, the squire's wife had a silk dress from St. Louis. Caste lines were almost nonexistent. Hannibal was a farmers' market village. More than half of its inhabitants were Southerners, but Southerners modified by the Great Valley. Its slaves were servants, not gang laborers.

But also Hannibal was on the Mississippi. Here enters the thread of cosmopolitanism that is so paradoxically interwoven with the extreme provincialism of this society. Steamboats bore the travelers and commerce of half a continent past the town wharf. Great rafts of logs and lumber—it was the latter kind that Huck and Jim traveled on—came down from Wisconsin. A population of freighters, movers, and mere drifters in shanty boats, keelboats, broadhorns, mackinaws, and scows added pageantry. Other types and other costumery came down from the lakes and northern rivers: voyageurs, trappers, winterers, Indians of the wilderness tribes always seen in ceremonial garments on their way to make treaties or collect annuities. All these belonged to the rapidly widening movement of the expanding nation. Moreover, Hannibal was within the aura of St. Louis, eighty miles away, and St. Louis was the port through which the energies of a truly imperial expansion were moving toward Santa Fe, Oregon, and California. Perhaps dimly but quite permanently any river town so near St. Louis would give even the most local mind an awareness of the continental divide, the

Columbia, the Pacific, the Southwest. A town that may have never heard of
Zebulon Pike or John Ledyard or Jonathan Carver nevertheless felt the
national will that had turned them westward. The year of Mark's birth, 1835,
may properly be taken as the year when the final phase of our continental
expansion began. And the fruitfulness of Hannibal for Mark's imagination
may reasonably be said to have stopped with his tenth year, just before that
final phase raised up the irrepressible conflict.

For two things remain to be said of the society that shaped Sam
Clemens's mind and feelings: that its post-pioneer, frontier stage stops short
of the industrial revolution, and that the sectional conflict which produced
the Civil War has not yet shown itself. The life which is always most
desirable in Mark's thinking is the pre-industrial society of a little river town;
it is a specific identification of Hannibal. Whereas the evils of life are the
eternal cruelties, hypocrisies, and stupidities of mankind which have nothing
to do with time or place but result from Our Heavenly Father's haste in
experimenting when He grew dissatisfied with the monkey.

As the St. Petersburg of *Tom Sawyer*, Hannibal is one of the superb
idyls of American literature, perhaps the supreme one. A town of sun, forest
shade, drowsy peace, limpid emotions, simple humanity—and eternity going
by on the majestic river. Even here, however, a mood of melancholy is
seldom far away: a melancholy of the river itself, of our westering people who
had always known solitude, and of a child's feeling, which was to grow
through the years, that he was a stranger and a mysterious one under the
stars. And below the melancholy there is a deeper stratum, a terror or disgust
that may break through in a graveyard at midnight or at the sound of
unidentified voices whispering above the water. This is in part fantasy, but in
part also it is the weary knowledge of evil that paints Hannibal in far different
colors in *Pudd'nhead Wilson* or *Huckleberry Finn*.

Almost as soon as he begins to write, Mark Twain is a citizen of the
world, but he is always a citizen of Hannibal too. He frequently
misunderstood himself, but he knew that quite clearly. In a postscript to the
fragment of a letter "to an unidentified person," printed on page 773
(omitted in the text because Mark himself crossed it out), he says:

> And yet I can't go away from the boyhood period & write
> novels because capital [that is, personal experience] is not
> sufficient by itself & I lack the other essential: interest in
> handling the men & experiences of later times.

While still a boy, he was apprenticed to a printer and so got the education that served more nineteenth-century American writers than any other. (It was a surprisingly extensive education. By twenty he knew the English classics thoroughly, was an inveterate reader of history, and had begun to cultivate his linguistic bent.) The trade eventually led him to newspaper reporting but first it took him on a series of *Wanderjahre* toward which heredity may have impelled him. At eighteen he went to St. Louis and on to New York. Philadelphia followed, Muscatine, St. Louis again, Keokuk (where he began to write humorous newspaper sketches), and Cincinnati, always setting type on a newspaper or in a job shop. He was twenty-two years old (and, if his memory can be trusted, ripe with a characteristic fantasy of South American adventure) when the American spectacle caught him up. In 1857 he began his apprenticeship to a Mississippi pilot.

Little need be said about his piloting in a book that includes "Old Times on the Mississippi," a study in pure ecstasy. The book is of course stamped from his memory, which was always nostalgic, and from the romancing half of his twinned talent. It records a supreme experience about whose delight there can be no doubt whatever, and it testifies to Mark's admiration of all skills and his mastery of one of the most difficult. But piloting gave him more than ever got into "Old Times" or its enlargement, *Life on the Mississippi*. "Flush Times" would have done as well as "Old Times" to describe the climactic years of the prewar Mississippi Valley with the rush and fever of the expanding nation. Those years vastly widened Mark's knowledge of America and fed his insatiable enjoyment of men, his absorbed observation of man's depravity, and his delight in spectacle.

The Civil War put an end to piloting. Mark has described his experience and that of many others in that war, in all wars, in a sketch which is one of the best things he ever wrote. "The Private History of a Campaign That Failed" could not be spared from the mosaic of our national catastrophe; it is one of the contexts in which Mark Twain has perfectly refracted a national experience through a personal one. When his military career petered out in absurdity, he joined the great national movement which even civil war could not halt. His older brother, the gentle zany Orion, was made Secretary of the Territory of Nevada and, paying the Secretary's passage west, Mark went along. In Nevada he found another national retort, another mixed and violent society, another speculative flush times. He became a drunkard of speculation, a prospector, a hunter of phantasmal mines, a silver miner, a laborer in a stamp mill, and at last a newspaperman. He went to work for that fabulous paper *The Territorial Enterprise* of Virginia City as an "editor," that is to say a reporter. And it was here that he took his immortal *nom de plume*, a phrase from the pilot's mystery. "Mark Twain" was signed to a species of humor in which Sam Clemens had been immersed ever since his apprenticeship, the newspaper humor of the Great Valley, which was in turn a development of the pungent oral humor he had heard from childhood on. Far from establishing a literary tradition, Mark Twain brought one to culmination.

After less than two years on the *Enterprise* he went to California, in 1864. He had met Artemus Ward in Nevada; now he joined the transient, bright Bohemia of the Golden Gate: Bret Harte, Prentice Mulford, Charles Warren Stoddard, Charles H. Webb, Ada Clare, Ina Coolbrith, still slighter and more forgotten names. He got a new kind of companionship and his first experience of literary sophistication. After a short time as a reporter he began to write humor for the Coast's literary papers, the *Californian* and the *Golden Era*. Promptly his work developed a strain of political and ethical satire which it never lost: the humorist was seldom separable from the satirist from this year on. That is to say, the individual humor of Mark Twain with its overtones of extravaganza and its undercurrent of misanthropy was, however crude and elliptical, fully formed by the end of 1864. He had not yet revealed the novelist's power to endow character with life, but it—together with a memorable talent for the vernacular—was made clear to anyone with eyes on December 16, 1865, when the New York *Saturday Press* published "Jim Smiley and His Jumping Frog."

The immortal story derived from still another Western experience, one which had made Mark, however lackadaisically, a pocket miner. He had sent it east at Artemus Ward's suggestion, but only an accident got it into type. It was a momentary smash hit, and so Mark was not altogether an unknown when he went to New York in 1867. Before he went there, however, he had reached the farthest limit of the expansionist dream, having gone to the Sandwich Islands as a newspaper correspondent. That voyage in turn had initiated his career as a lecturer. He had a marked histrionic talent; for years he barnstormed or made occasional appearances as a public "reader" and story-teller; all his life was making the after-dinner appearances of that vanished age, which pleased his vanity and gratified the longings of an actor *manqué*. But he went to New York as a correspondent: he had arranged to travel to Europe and the Holy Land with a conducted tour. In 1867 he published his first book, a collection of sketches called *The Celebrated Jumping Frog of Calaveras County* after the best of them, but the year is more notable for the travel letters he wrote for the *Alta California* and the New York *Tribune*. He made a book of them after his return, meanwhile writing free-lance humor and Washington correspondence. The book, *Innocents Abroad*, was published in 1869.

All this has been detailed to show how deep and various an experience of American life Mark Twain had had when he began to write. The rest of his biography is also strikingly typical of nineteenth-century America, but the seed-time has now been accounted for. It is not too much to say that he had seen more of the United States, met more kinds and castes and conditions of Americans, observed the American in more occupations and moods and tempers—in a word had intimately shared a greater variety of the characteristic experiences of his countrymen—than any other major American writer. The selections printed in this book have been chosen to show, as well as may be, the richness of that variety. Mark Twain's work is almost as diverse as his experience, and no selection can justly represent it in a single volume. The decision has been to sacrifice first of all the funny man, the professional joker working at his trade from day to day. Not the humorist, for Mark's humor is as much style as joke and is more personality. than style, and he could not write about even death or man's depravity without infusing them with the humor that kept him sane. The fabulist of *Tom Sawyer* is also unrepresented: the reader must accept that greater fable, *Adventures of Huckleberry Finn*, and for the idyl of St. Petersburg is referred to John Quarles's farm. The most serious distortion is that our selections hardly even suggest the extent of Mark's *ad hoc* satire. It would have been obligatory, if it had been possible, to include much from his forty years of tireless castigation of American society, government, morals, and manners, and more than appears here of his quarrel with France, the German language, and literary sentimentality. The decision has been to hold to the more general and more profound satire, which becomes misanthropic in his last fifteen years and, after transformation, reaches a climax in *The Mysterious Stranger*. The hope is that enough else has been exhibited to lead anyone who needs leading to the rich remainder.

III

Mark Twain was a man of moods, of the extreme of moods. He had a buoyancy which, twinned as it was with gentleness and intuition and wit, gave him a personal magnetism which his friends did not hesitate to call enchantment. Yet it alternated with an anger that readily became fury and was rooted in a revulsion between disgust and despair. The alternation suggests a basic split; it is clearly marked in his personality and equally evident in his books. The splendor his friends felt, his kindness to the unfortunate and the lowly and the oppressed, his generosity, his sensitiveness unite in a singular luminosity of spirit. Yet he was capable of savage vindictiveness, he exaggerated small or imaginary grievances out of all reason, and on little or no provocation he repeatedly believed himself misrepresented or betrayed. One doubts if any other American writer was ever so publicly beloved or privately adored; one is certain that no other was involved in so many lawsuits. "I am full of malice, saturated with malignity," he wrote eight months before his death. His malice and malignity of that moment were for the damned human race, but he could feel them in his private life whenever he thought he had been wronged. When *A Connecticut Yankee* was finished he wrote Howells that if he could write it over again "there wouldn't be so many things left out. They burn in me and they keep multiplying and multiplying, but now they can't even be said. And besides they would require a library—and a pen warmed up in hell." With a pen warmed up in hell he did fill a library and an extraordinary bulk of letters too. If it was sometimes avenging personal, usually imaginary wrongs, that private activity was only a reflex of the public function. For what burned in him was hatred of cruelty and injustice, a deep sense of human evil, and a recurrent accusation of himself. Like Swift he found himself despising man while loving Tom, Dick, and Harry so warmly that he had no proper defense against the anguish of human relationships. The trouble was that in terms of either earth or heaven he was never sure what to make of Samuel L. Clemens and so is recorded on both sides.

He is usually to be found on both sides of any question he argues. His intelligence was intuitive, not analytical. He reasoned fluently, with an avidity that touched most of the surface flow of his time, but superficially and with habitual contradictions. He had little capacity for sustained thought and to get to the heart of a question had to abandon analysis and rely on feeling. The philosophy which he spent years refining and supposed he had perfected is a sophomoric determinism. Even so, it is less a philosophy than a symbol or a rationalization; the perceptions it stood for are expressed at the level of genius in his fiction—not as idea but in terms of human life. Most of the nineteenth century's optimisms were his also. He fiercely championed the democratic axioms; they are the ether of his fiction and the fulcrum of his satire. He thought too that the nineteenth century, especially as Progress, and more especially as Progress in the United States, was the happiest estate of man; he believed that it was bringing on a future of greater freedom and greater happiness. This was basic and spontaneous in his mind, but at the same time he felt something profoundly wrong. There seemed to be some limitation to freedom, some frustration of happiness. He never really came to grips with the conflict. Only in the last fifteen years of his life did he ascribe any part of what might be wrong to any but superficial injustices in

American life or any but slight dislocations in our system. By the time he became aware of serious threats to freedom they did not seem to matter much: he was so absorbed in the natural depravity of man that the collapse or frustration of democracy, which he was by then taking for granted, seemed only an unimportant detail. Ideally, his last years would have been spent in more rigorous analysis—if not of the objective data, then of his intuitive awareness of them. They were not and so his judgments remained confused—and his principal importance in our literature belongs to his middle years, the period when his mind and feelings are in healthy equilibrium. It is an importance of his perceptions, not his thinking, and it exists primarily in his fiction, most purely in *Huckleberry Finn*. The best of Mark Twain's fiction is, historically, the first mature realization in our literature of a conflict between the assumptions of democracy and the limitations on democracy. Between the ideal of freedom and the nature of man.

Not less important is the fact that there is a reconciliation, even an affirmation. Detachment could be no greater but it is still somehow compassionate; condemnation could be no more complete, but it is somehow magnanimous. The damned human race is displayed with derision and abhorrence, yet this is on the ground that it has fallen short of its own decencies. Moreover at least *Huckleberry Finn* has a hero, the only heroic character (apart from Joan of Arc, a debauch of gyneolatry) he ever drew, and it is the essence of what Mark Twain had to say that the hero is a Negro slave. It has also a vindication not only of freedom, but of loyalty and decency, kindness and courage; and it is the essence of Mark Twain that this vindication is made by means of a boy who is a spokesman of the folk mind and whom experience has taught wariness and skepticism. Like all great novels *Huckleberry Finn* moves on many levels of significance, but it describes a flight and a struggle for freedom, and the question it turns on is a moral question.

Mark found zest and gusto—nouns that do not describe very much American literature of the first rank—in whatsoever was alive. He liked few novels except those of his intimate friends. What he praised in the ones he did like was reality of behavior, speech, or motive; his notebooks are sulphurous with comments on merely literary, that is false, characters. His taste was for biography, autobiography, history—life direct, men revealing themselves. No doubt the race was damned but it was fascinating. And that was proper for if his fiction is the best of his work, his most salient talent as a novelist is the life giving power. It is a careless and prodigal fecundity, but nevertheless remarkably concentrated. Old Man Finn, for instance, is greatly imagined and he seems to fill the first half of the book, yet he appears in only a few pages. Mrs. Judith Loftus lives completely in a single chapter. A mere passer-by, a casual of the river or a thug heard talking in a frowzy town, may reveal a whole personality in a few paragraphs. Nor is this fecundity confined to Mark's fiction, for the framework of all his books is anecdotal and all the people in them are dramatized. The whole population of his principal books, nine-tenths of the population of all his books, has the same vividness. Boys, villagers, the rivermen, the Negroes, Colonel Sellers, the two great vagabonds—there is nothing quite like the Mark Twain gallery elsewhere in American literature.

But there is a striking limitation: nowhere in that gallery are there women of marriageable age. No white women, that is, for the slave Roxana in *Pudd'nhead Wilson* lives as vividly as Old Man Finn himself. It must be significant that the only credible woman of an age that might sanction desire is withdrawn from desire behind the barrier of race. None of Mark Twain's nubile girls, young women, or young matrons are believable; they are all bisque, saccharine, or tears. He will do girl children in the romantic convention of boys' books and he is magnificent with the sisterhood of worn frontier wives whom Aunt Polly climaxes, but something like a taboo drains reality from any woman who might trouble the heart or the flesh. There is no love story in Mark Twain, there is no love at all beyond an occasional admission, for purposes of plot only, that someone is married or is going to be. Women seldom have husbands and men seldom have wives unless they are beyond middle age. Mark's endless absorption in human motives did not, for literary purposes at least, extend to sexual motives. Sex seems to be forbidden unless it can be treated mawkishly, and this writer of great prose who habitually flouted the genteel proprieties of language was more prudish than the most tremulous of his friends in regard to language that might suggest either desire or its gratification. So there is a sizable gap in the world he created. That gap has never been accounted for. Certainly there was nothing bloodless about Mark Twain; and his marriage, one of the happiest of literary marriages, was clearly passionate. Yet he did not marry till he was thirty-five (1870), and there may have been something permissive—to a man whose characters have usually lost a father if not both parents—in the fact that he married an invalid.

Few Americans have written as much as Mark Twain. His published works are not much greater in bulk than his unpublished manuscripts, the books he finished fewer than the ones he broke off and abandoned. He wrote on impulse and enthusiasm and while they lasted he wrote easily, but he wrote as needs must, for he had little faculty of self-criticism and but small ability to sustain or elaborate an idea. He was best at the short haul. Not only his fiction but the personalized narrative that is the vehicle of *Innocents Abroad*, *A Tramp Abroad*, *Life on the Mississippi*, and much else is episodic. When what he was writing was in circuit with his deepest perceptions he was superb. The breaking of the circuit always threw him into extemporization, which meant that fiction fell away into extravaganza and satire into burlesque. At such times he did not know that he was flatting; the serious artist could become a vaudeville monologuist in a single page without being aware that the tone had changed. That such a well-imagined novel as *Pudd'nhead Wilson* was written round the grotesque joke called "Those Extraordinary Twins" would be incredible if the same tone-deafness were not plentifully evident elsewhere. He thought the mawkish *Joan of Arc* and the second-rate *The Prince and the Pauper* his best work. He interrupted his masterpiece before it was half-finished, liking it so little that he threatened to burn it, and ignored it for six years during which, though he wrote constantly, he wrote nothing of importance. Then he finished it almost as casually as he had begun it. There is no greater book in American literature, but critics agree that the last quarter of it is impaired by the extravaganza that begins when Huck gets to Uncle Silas's farm. It is typical of Mark Twain that he felt no difference in kind or key between this admittedly superb extravaganza and the searching of American society and human experience that precedes it. In fact, the delivery of Jim from the dungeon was one of Mark's favorite platform readings.

Furthermore, he lacked the attribute of the artist—whatever it may be that enables him to think a novel through till its content has found its own inherent form. Of his novels only *Joan of Arc*, *The Prince and the Pauper*, and *Tom Sawyer* have structures that have developed from within; significantly, all are simple and only one is first-rate. Mark lived with his material for a long time, sometimes for many years, but not consciously, not with critical or searching dissatisfaction. A book must come of its own momentum from the unconscious impulse, be it as a whole, as a fragment, or as something that hardly got started before it broke off. This is to say that he had no conscious esthetic. He stood at the opposite pole from Henry James, with the other great contemporary of both, Howells, in between but nearer to James. Yet he had as large a share as either of them in creating the modern American novel.

The explanation for his lack of self-criticism and for his innocence of esthetics is not to be found in the supposed naïveté of the society that bore him. In the first place, that society was far from naïve; in the second place, not only did the fine artist Howells come from it, but Mark himself raised its native tale-telling to a fine art, which surely establishes a discipline. He had, besides, two other disciplines: that of the daily job, which he observed as faithfully as any writer who ever lived, and the taskmastership of a great style. Nor can Mark's own explanation, which he pleads so earnestly in the letter to Andrew Lang, be supported: that he wrote for the belly and members only. *Huckleberry Finn* is no more written for the belly and members only than *War and Peace* is or *Recherche du Temps Perdu*. But it is written at the behest of an instinctive drive, and explanation need go no farther if it could, for this time at least Mark's whole personality was behind it. In short, he wrote trivially or splendidly or magnificently as what appears to have been little more than chance might determine: he was not a fully self-conscious artist. But when he wrote greatly he was writing from an inner harmony of desire and will. Or call it a harmony of his deepest self and his inheritance from the Great Valley. Only that harmony, seen in relation to time and history, can explain him. For no man ever became a great writer more inadvertently than Mark Twain. He first became famous as a superior Artemus Ward, and that corresponded to his idea of himself. A long time passed before he had any desire to be more. He exploited a joke-maker's talent as systematically as a production manager could have done it for him, delighted by the discovery that he could raise his status, prestige, and income beyond Tom Sawyer's dreams. Nevertheless there is the paradox that almost from the beginning the attack of the funny man had been supported by that of a serious artist. Already in "The Jumping Frog" mastery of fictional character is clearly presaged, and the prophecy is fulfilled as early as *The Gilded Age* (1874). By *The Gilded Age* also a satirist is dealing maturely with a wide expanse of American life. From this composite the funny man cannot be separated out for a long time, and during that time there are only sporadic indications that Mark saw either the novelist or the satirist as more than instrumentalities of the humorist. The paradox resists criticism. One can only repeat that Mark Twain's greatness developed because the time and the continent had shaped him at their core.

This representative centrality goes on undiminished after the establishment of his fame. Following his marriage he was briefly a newspaper owner in Buffalo but abandoned that career to move to a provincial New England city, Hartford, and set up as a professional writer. His periodic restlessness continued; he never spent the full year in Hartford, he made at least twelve trips abroad, and he once expatriated himself for nine years. The Hartford period, 1874–1891, covered his greatest happiness and the beginning of his catastrophe. His was an unusually happy family life, and he was the center of an always widening circle. Howells and the Rev. Joseph Twichell were his closest friends; Cable, Aldrich, most of the leading writers of his generation were of the circle, and it widened to include the rich, the famous, the powerful, and the great. Mark ruled it by divine right: there have always been conflicting opinions about his books, but only one has ever been possible about his dominion over men's affections. He seemed alien to mortality. A fantasy of his childhood is frequently set down in notes and fragments of manuscript: the child had identified himself with a romantic stranger in Hannibal, a mysterious, perhaps supernatural visitor from Elsewhere. As the one-gallus village boy came to be a world figure, that fantasy seemed on the way to being confirmed. There was further confirmation as the author of *The Gilded Age* entered with a blithe and innocent heart on another career as a speculator, and the stamp-mill operator and tramp printer, who sincerely believed all his life that he was a member of the laboring class, undertook with the same innocence to be an industrial promoter.

Always convinced that his publishers were defrauding him, Mark had established his own firm to publish his books. The expansion it underwent in order to handle the bestseller of the generation, *Personal Memoirs of U.S. Grant*, could not be sustained. The firm sank into insolvency and finally went bankrupt. It could probably have been saved except that the most fantastic of Mark's promotions failed at the same time and left him bankrupt. For years he had been pouring his earnings and his wife's fortune into a mechanical typesetter which would indeed have made him a multimillionaire if it had succeeded. Its failure and that of the publishing firm were only the beginning of a series of disasters on the same scale as his fantastic rise. He paid off his indebtedness by a heroic lecture tour that took him round the world but his health broke. The oldest of his three daughters, the one who seemed most like him in temperament and talent, died during his absence. An agonizing personality change in his youngest daughter was finally diagnosed as epilepsy. Mrs. Clemens declined into permanent invalidism and in 1904 died.

This prolonged catastrophe brought Mark's misanthropy out of equilibrium; it dominated the rest of his life. The disasters were, of course, personal and yet it is hardly straining the facts to find him here also representative of the nineteenth-century America that had already found so much expression in him. As the century neared its end there was a good deal of pessimism and disenchantment in the United States. A wave of doubt and questioning swept many minds. The people who began an imperialistic adventure in the Pacific with the same naïve enthusiasm that had taken Mark Twain into the industrial life were widely, at the very time they stepped out on the world stage, beginning to be troubled about themselves. The nineteenth century, looking back on its course, found cause to be dismayed. Was the democratic dream being served as well as the nation had assumed?

Had the United States gone wrong somewhere during the avalanche of expansion? Were there, then, limits to what democracy could do, or flaws or contradictions in its theses, or impassable barriers in its path? Was the good time ending, were the vigorous years running out under a gathering shadow?

However deep or shallow this *fin de siècle* weariness may have been in the United States at large, Mark Twain's last fifteen years must be seen as related to it, if only distantly. During this period he wrote as much as in any similar length of time in his life, perhaps more, but most of it is fragmentary, unfinished.[1] Almost all of it deals with the nature of man, man's fate, and man's conceptions of honor and morality. There are fables, dialogues, diatribes—sometimes cold, sometimes passionate, derisive, withering, savage. Mark sees the American republic perishing, like republics before it, through the ineradicable cowardice, corruption, and mere baseness of mankind. He elaborates theories, which he embodies in imaginary histories of the world (and sometimes of extra-mundane societies) to support his prophecy, and yet he cannot be much troubled by the going-down of this western land, for year by year he is writing a general apocalypse. The Old Testament fables had always served him for humorous derision of man's gullibility, but now he uses them as missiles in a ferocious attack on human stupidity and cruelty. Man is compact of malignity, cowardice, weakness, and absurdity, a diseased organism, a parasite on nature, a foolish but murderous animal much lower than the swine.

Yet *What Is Man?* (published anonymously in 1906 but written before the turn of the century), the fullest of many developments of these themes, cannot be seen solely as a document in anthropophobia. It is also in complex ways a justification, even a self-justification. Its fixed universe, with an endless chain of cause and effect from the beginning of time, permits Mark to compose many variations on the theme of human pettiness, but also it serves to free man of blame—and thus satisfies a need deeply buried in Mark's personal remorse. To this period also belongs *Mark Twain's Autobiography*, which serves him as an escape into the security of the boyhood idyl he had made immortal in *Tom Sawyer*. The need to escape is significant, but the release is even more so, for it breaks the obsession signified by *What Is Man?* But a much truer release and a fulfillment as well came, as always, when Mark turned from reasoning to the instinctual portions of his mind. The highest reach of his last period is *The Mysterious Stranger*. It is an almost perfect book—perfect in expression of his final drive, in imaginative projection of himself, in tone and tune, in final judgment on the nature of man and the experience of Mark Twain. It is on a humbler level than his great books. More than any of them it is Mark Twain somewhat in disregard of

America. It is not, finally, a major work; but in its small way it is a masterpiece. Those who know and love Mark Twain will always find it as revealing as *Huckleberry Finn*.

IV

Mark Twain died in 1910 with, as he had foretold, the return of the mysterious visitor from beyond the solar system under whose sign he had been born, Halley's comet. His last years had been as full of honors as his middle years had been of fame. Even so, in 1910 it was hardly possible to define his importance in American literature as clearly as we can after another generation.

No doubt his first importance in that literature is the democratizing effect of his work. It is a concretely liberating effect, and therefore different in kind from Whitman's vision of democracy, which can hardly be said to have been understood by or to have found a response among any considerable number of Americans. Mark Twain was the first great American writer who was also a popular writer, and that in itself is important. Much more important is the implicit and explicit democracy of his books. They are the first American literature of the highest rank which portrays the ordinary bulk of Americans, expresses them, accepts their values, and delineates their hopes, fears, decencies, and indecencies as from within. The area proper to serious literature in the United States was enormously widened by them, in fact widened to the boundaries it still observes today. There have been no acknowledged priorities of caste in American writing since Mark Twain. Moreover, in his native equalitarian point of view, in his assertion of the basic democratic axioms, in his onslaught on privilege, injustice, vested power, political pretense, and economic exploitation (much of it admittedly superficial or confused, though much else is the most vigorous satire we have), in his transmutation of the town-meeting or country-store sharpness of judgment into a fine art—he is mid-nineteenth-century American democracy finding its first major voice in literature, ultimately its strongest voice. In him the literature of democracy becomes more robust than it had been before, such part of that literature, at least, as may be said to contain multitudes and speak to them. And this, to return to our starting point, embodies the transforming experience of the American people as they occupied the Great Valley and pushed beyond it, on the way forging the continental mind.

The nature of his writing is hardly less important. Mark Twain wrote one of the great styles of American literature, he helped develop the modern

American style, he was the first writer who ever used the American vernacular at the level of art. There has been some failure to understand this achievement. Shortly before this Introduction was written, the most pontifical American critic guessed that Mark must have turned to the vernacular of *Huckleberry Finn* because he lacked education, was unacquainted with literary traditions, and therefore wrote thin or awkward prose. That absurdity disregards Mark's life and his books as well. The reader may determine herein whether the style of *The Mysterious Stranger* lacks strength or subtlety, lacks any quality whatever for the effects required of it, or if that represents too late a period, may turn to "Old Times on the Mississippi," which was written before *Huckleberry Finn*, or "The Private History of a Campaign That Failed," which was written while *Huck* was still half finished. Mark Twain wrote English of a remarkable simplicity and clarity, and of singular sensitiveness, flexibility, and beauty as well. Its simplicity might deceive a patronizing reader for the sentence structure is not involved, usually consisting of short elements in natural sequence, and in order to understand without analysis how much art has gone into it one must have an ear for the tones and accents of speech as well as some feeling for the vigor of words. It is so lucid that it seems effortless—but just what is style?

Now, it is important that Mark made the American vernacular the medium of a great novel. Even before that he had used local, class, and racial dialects with immeasurably greater skill than anyone before him in our literature. "The Jumping Frog" raised such dialects above the merely humorous use which was the only one they had previously had and gave them a function in the writing of fiction. And the first two chapters of *The Gilded Age* bring to American literature genuine Negro speech and a rural dialect that are both genuine and an instrument of art—literally for the first time. In the rendition of Negro speech he may have had one equal, though there are those who will not grant that Harris is an equal; but it is doubtful if anyone has used the dialects of the middle South, or for that matter any other American dialect, as well as he. This on the basis of *The Gilded Age* and its immediate successors: the achievement of *Huckleberry Finn* is greater still. Huck's style, which is the spoken language of the untutored American of his place and time, differentiates the most subtle meanings and emphases and proves capable of the most difficult psychological effects. In a single step it made a literary medium of the American language; the liberating effect on American writing could hardly be overstated. Since *Huckleberry Finn* the well of American undefiled has flowed confidently.

Nevertheless, Mark's principal service to the American language was not Huck's vernacular: it lay within the recognized limits of literary prose.

Within those limits he was a radical innovator, a prime mover who changed the medium by incorporating in it the syntax, the idioms, and especially the vocabulary of the common life. The vigor of his prose comes directly from the speech of the Great Valley and the Far West. A superlative may be ventured: that Mark Twain had a greater effect than any other writer on the evolution of American prose.

His place in that evolution cannot be analyzed or even illustrated here. He is in the direct succession and he powerfully accelerates the movement. The evolution is of course older than our independence, even older than our nationality—which it helped to produce. Only an American could have said, "We must all hang together, or assuredly we shall all hang separately" in the traditional context. Only an American could have written, "It is not necessary that a man should earn his living by the sweat of his brow unless he sweats easier than I do." Only an American could have written, "the calm confidence of a Christian with four aces." The sequence is Franklin, Thoreau, Mark Twain; and the point here made lightly can be made with as profound a search into the fusion of thought, expression, and nationality as anyone may care to undertake. But before Mark Twain no American, no one writing in English, could have launched a novel into the movement of fiction with such a passage as:

> At the end of an hour we saw a far-away town sleeping in a valley
> by a winding river, and beyond it on a hill, a vast gray fortress
> with towers and turrets, the first I had ever seen out of a picture.
>   "Bridgeport?" said I, pointing.
>   "Camelot," said he.

Such questions as these, however, interest the historian of literature more than the general reader. The general reader who, it may be worth reminding you, continues to read Mark Twain, here and in Europe, more often by far than any other of our great dead. It is not difficult to say why.

The Americanism just mentioned is part of it. Any unidentified quotation from Mark Twain will be recognized at sight as American. It is, furthermore, a national Americanism; his great books are set along the Mississippi, but no one can think of them as local or regional. But there is also a kind of centripetal Americanism, so that he seems frequently to speak for the nation. The character of national spokesman is in his work as early as *Innocents Abroad*; by *Huckleberry Finn* it is self-evident. Fifteen years before he died it was generally acknowledged—so that if the nation's mood changed or its honor came in peril, the newspapers could hardly be put to bed till Mark Twain had spoken.

But there is something more basic. What the millions who have gone on reading Mark Twain since 1869 have chiefly wanted and received from him is precisely those images which, three years after *Tom Sawyer* and four years after "Old Times on the Mississippi" had been published, Walt Whitman was still hoping someone would forge from the new national life.

So long as anyone may be interested in our past there will be readers for the books in which Mark embodied his plentiful share of it. These are chiefly *Life on the Mississippi*, *Roughing It*, and the *Autobiography*. But he is so persistently an autobiographer that the same lens repeatedly refracts something deeply American and casual contexts suddenly rise to the level of his better books. It may be a lynching in Marion County, a reminiscence of General Grant, a pocket-miner's tomcat, Harriet Beecher Stowe in her dotage fetching a warwhoop behind someone's ear—but it is more likely to be a page or two of dialogue which make a society transparent and register a true perception forever. This more than the verbal humor is likely to preserve some of the lesser books, perhaps even *Following the Equator*, though the always painful burlesque that is now intolerable predominates in others. The humor that was the essential Mark Twain remains; it is interstitial, it is the breathing of his mind. Whether it be exuberance, an individual way of letting light in, the passion of a man hardly able to contain his wrath, or the deadlier laughter in suspension that means a tortured mind's adaptation to reality, it is the fundamental attribute of Mark Twain. The critic who for a moment forgets that Mark was a humorist is betrayed.

In the end, however, Mark's fiction is the best part of him. *The Prince and the Pauper* and *Joan of Arc* have already lost their luster, though the first still charms children as it once charmed Victorian adults. A middle group which lost their audience for a while have begun to regain it, books with great qualities in them but marred by the improvisation or the failure of artistic intelligence that have been described above. *Pudd'nhead Wilson*, the most courageous of Mark's books, has a fine verve, a theme he never dared to face outside it, the magnificent Roxana, and a certain historical importance as one of the few serious treatments in American fiction of any aspect of slavery. It is a matter of some regret that Mark began writing fiction with *The Gilded Age*, for he was still inexpert at narrative and in fact hardly in earnest as a novelist, and the exceedingly serious book suffers in consequence. It is also too bad that he wrote it with a collaborator, for Mark would have contributed enough mistakes by himself, whereas Charles Dudley Warner quadruples them, adding the melodrama of the wronged girl for good measure. Nevertheless *The Gilded Age* named an era for all American thinking since it and remains one of the very few contemporary attacks on that venal period. Finally, it has Colonel Sellers in it and so is immortal.

Shorter pieces range from the fathomlessly mawkish "Horse's Tale" and "Dog's Tale" (a similar and worse one of the same kind remains unpublished) to "The Man Who Corrupted Hadleyburg" and "Captain Stormfield's Visit to Heaven," which are part of the Mark Twain canon and contain essential portions of his quarrel with mankind. The best of his shorter pieces, however, is "Tom Sawyer Abroad." Presumably because the setting (a navigable balloon) makes it look like burlesque, most critics have ignored it. It is a deliberate exploration of the provincial mind and its prejudices, ignorances, assumptions, wisdoms, cunning. It memorably differentiates three stages of that mind, by way of the familiar Tom, Huck, and Nigger Jim. It is among the very best of Mark's work, frequently on a level with *Huckleberry Finn* itself, and must eventually be recognized as what it is.

A Connecticut Yankee in King Arthur's Court is the most tragically marred of Mark's books. It might have been a masterpiece, it repeatedly flashes to greatness, some of its satire is Mark Twain at his most serene or most savage; but nothing is sustained, tinny extravaganza or burlesque sooner or later spoils every clearly sounded note, and in short the book is at war with itself. Within a single set of covers Mark repeated every error of judgment that can be found in the *Collected Works*. Probably it will always be read for its fine moments but no one will ever name it among his great books.

Those are *The Adventures of Tom Sawyer* and *Adventures of Huckleberry Finn*. Here the images Walt Whitman desired of and for the new society are actually forged. They are the America of their time speaking with many voices—and the sharp difference between them corresponds not only to the dichotomy in Mark's mind but to one that is basic in our thinking about ourselves. Between them the idyllic *Tom* and the corrosive *Huck* express most of the American consciousness. Forgetting that he himself had made several plays of it, Mark once refused to let an applicant dramatize *Tom Sawyer* because you cannot make a hymn into a play. It is a hymn: to boyhood, to the fantasies of boyhood, to the richness and security of the child's world, to a phase of American society now vanished altogether, to the loveliness of woods and prairies that were the Great Valley, to the river, to many other things in which millions of readers have recognized themselves and their inheritance. It is wrought out of beauty and nostalgia. Yet Mark is nowhere truer to us, to himself, or to childhood than in the dread which holds this idyl inclosed. The book so superbly brings the reader within its enchantment that some reflection is required before be can realize of what ghastly stuff it is made murder and starvation, grave-robbery and revenge, terror and panic, some of the darkest emotions of men, some of the most terrible fears of children, and the ghosts and demons and death portents of the slaves. The book could have been written nowhere but in America and by no American but Mark Twain, but it has passed out of our keeping. It is the fantasy of boyhood in world literature.

Huckleberry Finn also has become a universal possession. It is a much deeper book than *Tom Sawyer*—deeper as of Mark Twain, of America, and of humanity. When after some stumbling it finds its purpose, it becomes an exploration of an entire society, the middle South along the river. In accomplishing this purpose it maintains at the level of genius Mark's judgment in full on the human race. It is well to remember that no one had spoken so witheringly to Americans about themselves before Huck raised his voice. But the book is not only the judgment on the damned human race which the much later *What Is Man?* only tried to be, it is also incomparably rich with the swarming life that so absorbed Mark Twain—and contains a forthright assertion of the inalienable dignity of man. It is the most complete expression of Mark Twain.

Like *Tom* and in much greater measure it has a mythic quality. This is in part the river itself, the Mississippi which had dominion over Mark's imagination and here becomes a truly great symbol. It is in part the symbol of the downriver journey—made the more momentous by a boy's bewilderment and a slave's flight for freedom. But in greater part it is the developing pageantry which becomes ecstatic when two vagabonds join Jim and Huck, and the Duke of Bilgewater and the "pore disappeared Dauphin, Looy the Seventeen," take their place in a small company of literature's immortals.

Thus realism, fantasy, satire, mythology, and the tragic knowledge of man, all of them a good many layers deep, united in Mark Twain's masterpiece. It is the book he was meant to write. A book of itself alone, unlike any other, unique, essentially Mark Twain, essentially America, it also has transcended our national literature. Every new generation of readers discovers that it belongs to mankind.

NOTE

1. This period of Mark Twain's work has been studied only once and in part. See "The Symbols of Despair," in Bernard DeVoto, *Mark Twain at Work*, 1942. Note that even

Mark Twain's Autobiography was not finished; in fact it was not meant to be. *What Is Man?* consists of a series of dialogues selected from a much larger number more or less loosely related. The chapter here referred to discusses various states of *The Mysterious Stranger*.

T.S. ELIOT

Introduction to
The Adventures of Huckleberry Finn

*T*he *Adventures of Huckleberry Finn* is the only one of Mark Twain's various books which can be called a masterpiece. I do not suggest that it is his only book of permanent interest; but it is the only one in which his genius is completely realized, and the only one which creates its own category. There are pages in *Tom Sawyer* and in *Life on the Mississippi* which are, within their limits, as good as anything with which one can compare them in *Huckleberry Finn*; and in other books there are drolleries just as good of their kind. But when we find one book by a prolific author which is very much superior to all the rest, we look for the peculiar accident or concourse of accidents which made that book possible. In the writing of *Huckleberry Finn* Mark Twain had two elements which, when treated with his sensibility and his experience, formed a great book: these two are the Boy and the River.

Huckleberry Finn is, no doubt, a book which boys enjoy. I cannot speak from memory: I suspect that a fear on the part of my parents lest I should acquire a premature taste for tobacco, and perhaps other habits of the hero of the story, kept the book out of my way. But *Huckleberry Finn* does not fall into the category of juvenile fiction. The opinion of my parents that it was a book unsuitable for boys left me, for most of my life, under the impression that it was a book suitable only for boys. Therefore it was only a few years ago that I read for the first time, and in that order, *Tom Sawyer* and *Huckleberry Finn*.

From *The Adventures of Huckleberry Finn*. © 1950 by The Cresset Press.

Tom Sawyer did not prepare me for what I was to find its sequel to be. *Tom Sawyer* seems to me to be a boys' book, and a very good one. The River and *the* Boy make their appearance in it; the narrative is good; and there is also a very good picture of society in a small mid-Western river town (for St. Petersburg is more Western than Southern) a hundred years ago. But the point of view of the narrator is that of an adult observing a boy. And Tom is the ordinary boy, though of quicker wits, and livelier imagination, than most. Tom is, I suppose, very much the boy that Mark Twain had been: he is remembered and described as he seemed to his elders, rather than created. Huck Finn, on the other hand, is the boy that Mark Twain still was, at the time of writing his adventures. We look at Tom as the smiling adult does: Huck we do not look at—we see the world through his eyes. The two boys are not merely different types; they were brought into existence by different processes. Hence in the second book their roles are altered. In the first book Huck is merely the humble friend—almost a variant of the traditional valet of comedy; and we see him as he is seen by the conventional respectable society to which Tom belongs, and of which, we feel sure, Tom will one day become an eminently respectable and conventional member. In the second book their nominal relationship remains the same; but here it is Tom who has the secondary role. The author was probably not conscious of this, when he wrote the first two chapters: *Huckleberry Finn* is not the kind of story in which the author knows, from the beginning, what is going to happen. Tom then disappears from our view; and when he returns, he has only two functions. The first is to provide a foil for Huck. Huck's persisting admiration for Tom only exhibits more clearly to our eyes the unique qualities of the former and the commonplaceness of the latter. Tom has the imagination of a lively boy who has read a good deal of romantic fiction: he might, of course, become a writer—he might become Mark Twain. Or rather, he might become the more commonplace aspect of Mark Twain. Huck has not imagination, in the sense in which Tom has it: he has, instead, vision. He sees the real world; and he does not judge it—he allows it to judge itself.

Tom Sawyer is an orphan. But he has his aunt; he has, as we learn later, other relatives; and he has the environment into which he fits. He is wholly a social being. When there is a secret band to be formed, it is Tom who organizes it and prescribes the rules. Huck Finn is alone: there is no more solitary character in fiction. The fact that he has a father only emphasizes his loneliness; and he views his father with a terrifying detachment. So we come to see Huck himself in the end as one of the permanent symbolic figures of fiction; not unworthy to take a place with Ulysses, Faust, Don

Quixote, Don Juan, Hamlet and other great discoveries that man has made about himself.

It would seem that Mark Twain was a man who—perhaps like most of us—never became in all respects mature. We might even say that the adult side of him was boyish, and that only the boy in him, that was Huck Finn, was adult. As Tom Sawyer grew up, he wanted success and applause (Tom himself always needs an audience). He wanted prosperity, a happy domestic life of a conventional kind, universal approval, and fame. All of these things he obtained. As Huck Finn he was indifferent to all these things; and being composite of the two, Mark Twain both strove for them, and resented their violation of his integrity. Hence he became the humorist and even clown: with his gifts, a certain way to success, for everyone could enjoy his writings without the slightest feeling of discomfort, self-consciousness or self-criticism. And hence, on the other hand, his pessimism and misanthropy. To be a misanthrope is to be in some way divided; or it is a sign of an uneasy conscience. The pessimism which Mark Twain discharged into *The Man That Corrupted Hadleyburg* and *What is Man?* springs less from observation of society, than from his hatred of himself for allowing society to tempt and corrupt him and give him what he wanted. There is no wisdom in it. But all this personal problem has been diligently examined by Mr. Van Wyck Brooks; and it is not Mark Twain, but *Huckleberry Finn*, that is the subject of this introduction.

You cannot say that Huck himself is either a humorist or a misanthrope. He is the impassive observer: he does not interfere, and, as I have said, he does not judge. Many of the episodes that occur on the voyage down the river, after he is joined by the Duke and the King (whose fancies about themselves are akin to the kind of fancy that Tom Sawyer enjoys) are in themselves farcical; and if it were not for the presence of Huck as the reporter of them, they would be no more than farce. But, seen through the eyes of Huck, there is a deep human pathos in these scoundrels. On the other hand, the story of the feud between the Grangerfords and the Shepherdsons is a masterpiece in itself: yet Mark Twain could not have written it so, with that economy and restraint, with just the right details and no more, and leaving to the reader to make his own moral reflections, unless he had been writing in the person of Huck. And the *style* of the book, which is the style of Huck, is what makes it a far more convincing indictment of slavery than the sensationalist propaganda of *Uncle Tom's Cabin*. Huck is passive and impassive, apparently always the victim of events; and yet, in his acceptance of his world and of what it does to him and others, he is more powerful than his world, because he is more *aware* than any other person in it.

Repeated readings of the book only confirm and deepen one's admiration of the consistency and perfect adaptation of the writing. This is a style which at the period, whether in America or in England, was an innovation, a new discovery in the English language. Other authors had achieved natural speech in relation to particular characters—Scott with characters talking Lowland Scots, Dickens with cockneys: but no one else had kept it up through the whole of a book. Thackeray's Yellowplush, impressive as he is, is an obvious artifice in comparison. In *Huckleberry Finn* there is no exaggeration of grammar or spelling or speech, there is no sentence or phrase to destroy the illusion that these are Huck's own words. It is not only in the way in which he tells his story, but in the details he remembers, that Huck is true to himself. There is, for instance, the description of the Grangerford interior as Huck sees it on his arrival; there is the list of the objects which Huck and Jim salvaged from the derelict house:

> We got an old tin lantern, and a butcher-knife without any handle, and a bran-new Barlow knife worth two bits in any store, and a lot of tallow candles, and a tin candlestick, and a gourd, and a tin cup, and a ratty old bedquilt off the bed, and a reticule with needles and pins and beeswax and buttons and thread and all such truck in it, and a hatchet and some nails, and a fish-line as thick as my little finger, with some monstrous hooks on it, and a roll of buckskin, and a leather dog-collar, and a horseshoe, and some vials of medicine that didn't have no label on them; and just as we was leaving I found a tolerable good curry-comb, and Jim he found a ratty old fiddle-bow, and a wooden leg. The straps was broke off of it, but barring that, it was a good enough leg, though it was too long for me and not long enough for Jim, and we couldn't find the other one, though we hunted around.
> And so, take it all round, we made a good haul.

This is the sort of list that a boy reader should pore over with delight; but the paragraph performs other functions of which the boy reader would be unaware. It provides the right counterpoise to the horror of the wrecked house and the corpse; it has a grim precision which tells the reader all he needs to know about the way of life of the human derelicts who had used the house; and (especially the wooden leg, and the fruitless search for its mate) reminds us at the right moment of the kinship of mind and the sympathy between the boy outcast from society and the negro fugitive from the injustice of society.

Huck in fact would be incomplete without Jim, who is almost as notable a creation as Huck himself. Huck is the passive observer of men and events, Jim the submissive sufferer from them; and they are equal in dignity. There is no passage in which their relationship is brought out more clearly than the conclusion of the chapter in which, after the two have become separated in the fog, Huck in the canoe and Jim on the raft, Huck, in his impulse of boyish mischief, persuades Jim for a time that the latter had dreamt the whole episode.

> '... my heart wuz mos' broke bekase you wuz los', en I didn' k'yer no mo' what become er me en de raf'. En when I wake up 'en fine you back agin', all safe en soun', de tears come en I could a got down on my knees en kiss' yo' foot, I's so thankful. En all you wuz thinkin' 'bout wuz how you could make a fool uv ole Jim wid a lie. Dat truck dah is *trash*; en trash is what people is dat puts dirt on de head er dey fren's en makes 'em ashamed.' ...
>
> It was fifteen minutes before I could work myself up to go and humble myself to a nigger—but I done it, and I warn't ever sorry for it afterwards, neither.

This passage has been quoted before; and if I quote it again, it is because I wish to elicit from it one meaning that is, I think, usually overlooked. What is obvious in it is the pathos and dignity of Jim, and this is moving enough; but what I find still more disturbing, and still more unusual in literature, is the pathos and dignity of the boy, when reminded so humbly and humiliatingly, that his position in the world is not that of other boys, entitled from time to time to a practical joke; but that he must bear, and bear alone, the responsibility of a man.

It is Huck who gives the book style. The River gives the book its form. But for the River, the book might be only a sequence of adventures with a happy ending. A river, a very big and powerful river, is the only natural force that can wholly determine the course of human peregrination. At sea, the wanderer may sail or be carried by winds and currents in one direction or another; a change of wind or tide may determine fortune. In the prairie, the direction of movement is more or less at the choice of the caravan; among mountains there will often be an alternative, a guess at the most likely pass. But the river with its strong, swift current is the dictator to the raft or to the steamboat. It is a treacherous and capricious dictator. At one season, it may move sluggishly in a channel so narrow that, encountering it for the first time at that point, one can hardly believe that it has travelled already for hundreds of miles, and has yet many hundreds of miles to go; at another season, it may obliterate the low Illinois shore to a horizon of water, while in its bed it runs with a speed such that no man or beast can survive in it. At such times, it carries down human bodies, cattle and houses. At least twice, at St. Louis, the western and the eastern shores have been separated by the fall of bridges, until the designer of the great Eads Bridge devised a structure which could resist the floods. In my own childhood, it was not unusual for the spring freshet to interrupt railway travel; and then the traveller to the East had to take steamboat from the levee up to Alton, at a higher level on the Illinois shore, before he could begin his rail journey. The river is never wholly chartable; it changes its pace, it shifts its channel, unaccountably; it may suddenly efface a sandbar, and throw up another bar where before was navigable water.

It is the River that controls the voyage of Huck and Jim; that will not let them land at Cairo, where Jim could have reached freedom; it is the River that separates them and deposits Huck for a time in the Grangerford household; the River that re-unites them, and then compels upon them the unwelcome company of the King and the Duke. Recurrently we are reminded of its presence and its power.

> When I woke up, I didn't know where I was for a minute. I set up and looked around, a little scared. Then I remembered. The river looked miles and miles across. The moon was so bright I could a counted the drift-logs that went a-slipping along, black and still, hundreds of yards out from shore. Everything was dead quiet, and it looked late, and *smelt* late. You know what I mean— I don't know the words to put it in.
>
> It was kind of solemn, drifting down the big still river, laying on our backs looking up at the stars, and we didn't ever feel like talking loud, and it warn't often that we laughed, only a little kind of a low chuckle. We had mighty good weather as a general thing, and nothing ever happened to us at all, that night, nor the next, nor the next.
>
> Every night we passed towns, some of them away up on black hillsides, nothing but just a shiny bed of lights, not a house could you see. The fifth night we passed St. Louis, and it was like the whole world lit up. In St. Petersburg they used to say there was twenty or thirty thousand people in St. Louis, but I never believed it till I see that wonderful spread of lights at two o'clock that still night. There warn't a sound there; everybody was asleep.

We come to understand the River by seeing it through the eyes of the Boy; but the Boy is also the spirit of the River. *Huckleberry Finn*, like other great works of imagination, can give to every reader whatever he is capable of taking from it. On the most superficial level of observation, Huck is convincing as a boy. On the same level, the picture of social life on the shores of the Mississippi a hundred years ago is, I feel sure, accurate. On any level, Mark Twain makes you see the River, as it is and was and always will be, more clearly than the author of any other description of a river known to me. But you do not merely see the River, you do not merely become acquainted with it through the senses: you experience the River. Mark Twain, in his later years of success and fame, referred to his early life as a steamboat pilot as the happiest he had known. With all allowance for the illusions of age, we can agree that those years were the years in which he was most fully alive. Certainly, but for his having practised that calling, earned his living by that profession, he would never have gained the understanding which his genius for expression communicates in this book. In the pilot's daily struggle with the River, in the satisfaction of activity, in the constant attention to the River's unpredictable vagaries, his consciousness was fully occupied, and he absorbed knowledge of which, as an artist, he later made use. There are, perhaps, only two ways in which a writer can acquire the understanding of environment which he can later turn to account: by having spent his childhood in that environment—that is, living in it at a period of life in which one experiences much more than one is aware of; and by having had to struggle for a livelihood in that environment—a livelihood bearing no direct relation to any intention of writing about it, of *using* it as literary material. Most of Joseph Conrad's understanding came to him in the latter way. Mark Twain knew the Mississippi in both ways: he had spent his childhood on its banks; and he had earned his living matching his wits against its currents. Thus the River makes the book a great book. As with Conrad, we are continually reminded of the power and terror, of Nature, and the isolation and feebleness of Man. Conrad remains always the European observer of the tropics, the white man's eye contemplating the Congo and its black gods. But Mark Twain is a native, and the River God is his God. It is as a native that he accepts the River God, and it is the subjection of Man that gives to Man his dignity. For without some kind of God, Man is not even very interesting.

Readers sometimes deplore the fact that the story descends to the level of *Tom Sawyer* from the moment that Tom himself re-appears. Such readers protest that the escapades invented by Tom, in the attempted "rescue" of Jim, are only a tedious development of themes with which we were already too familiar—even while admitting that the escapades themselves are very amusing, and some of the incidental observations memorable.[1] But it is right that the mood of the end of the book should bring us back to that of the beginning. Or, if this was not the right ending for the book, what ending would have been right?

In *Huckleberry Finn* Mark Twain wrote a much greater book than he could have known he was writing. Perhaps all great works of art mean much more than the author could have been aware of meaning: certainly, *Huckleberry Finn* is the one book of Mark Twain's which, as a whole, has this unconsciousness. So what seems to be the rightness, of reverting at the end of the book to the mood of *Tom Sawyer*, was perhaps unconscious art. For Huckleberry Finn, neither a tragic nor a happy ending would be suitable. No worldly success or social satisfaction, no domestic consummation would be worthy of him; a tragic end also would reduce him to the level of those whom we pity. Huck Finn must come from nowhere and be bound for nowhere. His is not the independence of the typical or symbolic "American Pioneer, but the independence of the vagabond. His existence questions the values of America as much as the values of Europe; he is as much an affront to the "pioneer spirit" as he is to "business enterprise"; he is in a state of nature as detached as the state of the saint. In a busy world, he represents the loafer; in an acquisitive and competitive world, he insists on living from hand to mouth. He could not be exhibited in any amorous encounters or engagements, in any of the juvenile affections which are appropriate to Tom Sawyer. He belongs neither to the Sunday School nor to the Reformatory. He has no beginning and no end. Hence, he can only disappear; and his disappearance can only be accomplished by bringing forward another performer to obscure the disappearance in a cloud of whimsicalities.

Like Huckleberry Finn, the River itself has no beginning or end. In its beginning, it is not yet the River; in its end, it is no longer the River. What we call its headwaters is only a selection from among the innumerable sources which flow together to compose it. At what point in its course does the Mississippi become what the Mississippi *means*? It is both one and many; it is the Mississippi of this book only after its union with the Big Muddy— the Missouri; it derives some of its character from the Ohio, the Tennessee and other confluents. And at the end it merely disappears among its deltas: it is no longer there, but it is still where it was, hundreds of miles to the North. The River cannot tolerate any design, to a story which is its story, that might interfere with its dominance. Things must merely happen, here and there, to the people who live along its shores or who commit themselves to its current. And it is as impossible for Huck as for the River to have a beginning or end—

a *career*. So the book has the right, the only possible concluding sentence. I do not think that any book ever written ends more certainly with the right words;

> But I reckon I got to light out for the Territory ahead of the rest, because Aunt Sally she's going to adopt me and civilize me, and I can't, stand it. I been there before.

NOTE

1. *e.g.* "Jim don't know anybody in China."

F.R. LEAVIS

Introduction to Pudd'nhead Wilson

*P*udd'nhead Wilson is not faultless—no book of Mark Twain's is that—but it is all the same the masterly work of a great writer. Yet it is very little known. One cannot easily find anyone, English or American, who has read it (at least that is my experience), and it would seem never at any time to have had the beginnings of the recognition that is its due. Its reputation—if it may be said to have a reputation—would not encourage a strenuous search for a copy of the book, unless in an admirer of *Huckleberry Finn* who was curious to look over one of the author's ephemeral productions, one that also dealt in its way with life in Hannibal, Missouri, the village of Mark Twain's childhood.

The explanation, I think, is partly that *Pudd'nhead Wilson* is so very unlike *Huckleberry Finn*. But it is also, I think, that the nature of the greatness of *Huckleberry Finn* itself tends not to be fully recognized. There are, then, two reasons for hoping that *Pudd'nhead Wilson* may come to be appreciated as it deserves: it is a classic in its own right (if an unrecognised classic may be said to *be* one); and, further, for all the unlikeness, it bears a very close relation to *Huckleberry Finn*; a relation of such a kind that to appreciate the lesser work is to have a surer perception of the greatness of the greater.

Huckleberry Finn, by general agreement Mark Twain's greatest work, is supremely the American classic, and it is one of the great books of the world. The significance of such a work doesn't admit of exhaustive recognition in a

From *Commentary* (February 1956) by permission; all rights reserved.

simple formula, or in several. Mark Twain himself was no simple being, and the complexity of his make-up was ordinarily manifested in strains, disharmonies, and tormenting failures of integration and self-knowledge. These, in his supreme masterpiece, can be seen to provide the creative drive. There is of course the aspect of return to boyhood, but the relation to complexity and strain represented by *Huckleberry Finn* is not one of escape from them—in spite of the qualities that have established the book as a classic for children (and in spite of Mark Twain's conviction, at times, that its appeal should be as such). It is true that the whole is given through Huck, the embodiment of that Western vernacular, or of the style created out of that, in which the book is written. But that style, perfectly as it renders the illiterate Huck, has been created by a highly sophisticated art to serve subtle purposes, and Huck himself is of course not merely the naïve boyish consciousness he so successfully enacts; he is, by one of those triumphant sleights or equivocations which cannot be judiciously contrived, but are proof of inspired creative possession, the voice of deeply reflective maturity—of a life's experience brooded on by an earnest spirit and a fine intelligence. If Mark Twain lacked art in Arnold Bennett's sense (as Arnold Bennett pointed out), that only shows how little art in Arnold Bennett's sense matters, in comparison with art that is the answer of creative genius to the pressure of a profoundly felt and complex experience. If *Huckleberry Finn* has its examples of the unintelligence that may accompany the absence of sustained critical consciousness in an artist, even a great one, nevertheless the essential intelligence that prevails, and from the poetic depths informs the work, compels our recognition—the intelligence of the whole engaged psyche; the intelligence that represents the integrity of this, and brings to bear the wholeness.

For in his supreme creation the complex and troubled Mark Twain did achieve a wholeness; it is manifested in the nature of the creative triumph. The charged significance of *Huckleberry Finn* brings together a strength of naïveté and a strength of mature reflective wisdom. Let me quote, with immediate relevance, Mr Bernard DeVoto, most penetrating of the commentators on Mark Twain I am acquainted with:

> "fundamentally Huck is an expression—a magnificent expression, a unique expression—of the folk mind. The folk mind, that is, in mid-America in the period of the frontier and immediately following, the folk mind shaped for use by the tremendous realities of conquering a hostile wilderness and yet shadowed by the unseen world. He is one of the highest reaches of American fiction.

"But if Huck expresses the folk mind, he is also Mark Twain's surrogate, he is charged with transmitting what that dark, sensitive, and complex consciousness felt about America and the human race.... Mark Twain was not a systematic thinker. Customarily, like the creature of fable who was his brother Orion, he held in succession all possible opinions about every subject he tried to analyse, held none of them long, and was able to drive none very deep beneath the surface. Especially as a metaphysician he was as feeble a novice as ever ventured into that stormy sea. But in what he perceived, in what he felt, in the nerve-ends of emotion, in the mysterious ferments of art which transform experience, he was a great mind—there has been no greater in American literature. Be it said once more and ever so wearily: insufficiencies and mental defects prevented him from ever completely implementing the artist throughout the whole course of a book. That does not matter—in *Huckleberry Finn* we get the finest expression of a great artist, the fullest report on what life meant to him."[1]

When Mr DeVoto speaks of the "folk mind" in *Huckleberry Finn* he is making a plainly valid observation; an observation duly offset, as the quoted passage shows, by the recognition of quite other aspects of the book. But insistence on the "folk" element sometimes goes with an attempt to make *Huckleberry Finn* American in a sense that would make it an immeasurably lesser thing than the great work it is. Mr Van Wyck Brooks writes: "He was the frontier story-teller, the great folk writer of the American West, and raised to a pitch unparalleled before him the art of oral story-telling and then succeeded in transferring its effects to paper."[2] Such an account (and there is a formidable representative intention behind it) serves as a licence for insisting on the force of the reply—the obvious and unanswerable reply: Mark Twain was something very much more than a folk—writer, and the art of *Huckleberry Finn* is no mere matter of managing effects—suspense, surprise, climax, and so on. One cannot intelligently discuss the art without discussing the complex and reverse of naïve outlook it conveys. Mr Brooks, recognising, as any reader must, an insistent moral preoccupation in the theme, quotes Paine, Mark Twain's biographer: "the author makes Huck's struggle a psychological one between conscience and the law on one side, and sympathy on the other." But there is more to the moral theme of *Huckleberry Finn* than that suggests. What the book conveys is the drama in a mind in which conscience finds that it is not single, and that the "law" doesn't speak with one voice, and that what Paine calls "sympathy" itself engages a moral imperative. In fact, as I have noted elsewhere,[3] *Huckleberry Finn* has as a central theme the complexity of ethical valuation in a society with a complex tradition—a description that applies (for instance) to any "Christian" society.

The book is a profound study of civilised man. And about its attitude towards civilisation as represented by the society depicted in it there is nothing simple or simplifying, either in a "frontier" spirit or in a spirit of reductive pessimism. It is not to the point to adduce such private utterances of Mark Twain's as: "We have no real morals, but only artificial ones—morals created and preserved by the forced suppression of natural and healthy instinct." "Never trust the artist; trust the tale": Lawrence's dictum might have been addressed to Mark Twain's case. *Huckleberry Finn*, the tale, gives us a wholeness of attitude that transcends anything ordinarily attainable by the author. The liberation effected by the memories of youth and the Mississippi was, for the creative genius at his greatest, not into irresponsibility but the reverse. The imaginatively recovered vitality of youth ministered, in sum, no more to the spirit of *Pudd'nhead Wilson's Calendar* than to nostalgia or daydream, but to the attainment of a sure and profound moral maturity. That is, to call *Huckleberry Finn* a great work is not an exaggeration.

I insist in this way because of a tendency in America (and Transatlantic fashions regarding American literature tend to be taken over uncritically here) to suggest that the beginnings of the truly American in literary tradition come from the frontier and the West. According to this view Mark Twain is a more truly American writer than Hawthorne or Henry James. It is a view that, in offering to exalt him, actually denies his greatness, for it makes the attributed advantage in Americanness a matter of his being alienated from English and European tradition as Hawthorne and James are not. Such an alienation could only be an impoverishment: no serious attempt has been made to show that any sequel to disinheritance could replace the heritage lost. Mark Twain is indeed "frontier" and Western, but in being greatly American he bears as close and essential a relation to England and Europe as that which we recognise in Hawthorne or in James (in some ways he strikes an English reader as being less foreign, less positively un-English, than either of them). The Americanness of alienation may be represented by Dreiser, Scott Fitzgerald and Hemingway: the author of *Huckleberry Finn*, when we think of those writers, seems to belong to another world. Nor as we read the book are we prompted to reflect that he is a fellow-countryman of Walt Whitman.

It is not my business here to enforce these observations in a detailed analysis of *Huckleberry Finn*, but, with them in view, to suggest how that book is related to *Pudd'nhead Wilson*, which, different as it is (it makes no show of frontier naïveté, but belongs frankly to sophisticated literary tradition), is nevertheless unmistakably by the same hand, develops the same preoccupations and expresses the same moral outlook. With the oral tradition of story-telling, the potent element of recovered boyhood that has so recommended *Huckleberry Finn* is absent too. But the Mississippi is there in *Pudd'nhead Wilson*, and its evoked presence occasions a significant expansion:

"The hamlet's front was washed by the clear waters of the great river; its body stretched itself rearward up a gentle incline; its most rearward border fringed itself out and scattered its houses about the base-line of the hills; the hills rose high, inclosing the town in a half-moon curve, clothed with forests from foot to summit.

"Steamboats passed up and down every hour or so. Those belonging to the little Cairo line and the little Memphis line always stopped; the big Orleans liners stopped for hails only, or to land passengers or freight; and this was the case also with the great flotilla of 'transients'. These latter came out of a dozen rivers—the Illinois, the Missouri, the Upper Mississippi, the Ohio, the Monongahela, the Tennessee, the Red River, the White River, and so on; and were bound every whither and stocked with every imaginable comfort or necessity which the Mississippi's communities could want, from the frosty Falls of St Anthony down through nine climates to torrid New Orleans."

Here, quite plainly, speaks a proud imaginative delight in the memory of the great river; the great river as Mark Twain had known it in boyhood and in his piloting days; and in the memory, or vision, we feel the sense of freedom, beauty and majesty that informs *Huckleberry Finn*; but there is something further too: the passage unmistakably conveys the sense, sanguine and exalted, of an expanding and ripening civilisation.

Mark Twain, we are told, was brought up in a frontier society. "Think," it has been written, "of the squalor of those villages, their moral and material squalor, their dim and bounded horizon, their petty taboos: repression at one extreme, eruption at the other, and shiftlessness for a golden mean." But what *Pudd'nhead Wilson* should make us recognise is that "frontier" is an insidious term. It suggests cultural deprivation and loss—a dropping of the heritage in the battle with pioneer hardship. And no doubt it could be argued that the account just quoted fairly describes Dawson's Landing; or that so we should have agreed if we had had to live there. But as a matter of fact this is not the tone, this is not how the stress falls, in *Pudd'nhead Wilson*. After the evocation of the river we read:

> "The town was sleepy and comfortable and contented. It was fifty years old, and was growing slowly—very slowly, in fact, but still it was growing."

It may have been sleepy, but what Mark Twain conveys with great power is an effect quite other than one of rawness and squalor:

> "In 1830 it was a snug little collection of modest one- and two-storey frame dwellings whose white-washed exteriors were almost concealed from sight by climbing tangles of rose-vines, honeysuckles, and morning-glories. Each of these pretty homes had a garden in front, fenced with white palings and opulently stocked with hollyhocks, marigolds, touch-me-nots, prince's feathers and other old-fashioned flowers; while on the window-sills of the houses stood wooden boxes containing moss-rose plants and terra-cotta pots in which grew a breed of geraniums whose spread of intensely red blossoms accented the prevailing pink tint of the rose-clad house-front like an explosion of flame. When there was room on the ledge outside of the pots and boxes for a cat, the cat was there—in sunny weather—stretched at full length, asleep and blissful, with her furry belly to the sun and a paw curved over her nose. Then that house was complete, and its contentment and peace were made manifest to the world by this symbol, whose testimony is infallible. A home without a cat—and a well-fed, well-petted, and properly revered cat—may be a perfect home, perhaps, but how can it prove title?
>
> "All along the streets, on both sides, at the outer edge of the brick sidewalks, stood locust-trees with trunks protected by wooden boxing, and these furnished shade for summer and a sweet fragrance in spring when the clusters of buds came forth."

The comfort, well-being and amenity evoked here have more than a material significance; they are the outward signs of an inward grace. Provincial as Dawson's Landing may be, it represents a society that has kept its full heritage of civilisation. True, it is provincial, and Wilson's fate—the

"Pudd'nhead" and the long failure to make way against that estimate—figures for us its attitude towards originality of mind. Moreover an English reader gets what are for him (the human world presented being so essentially unforeign) startling glimpses of mob lawlessness as an accepted social institution. Yet the effect of the opening description of Dawson's Landing remains: this is a civilised community—one qualified to have exacted a very much more favourable report than any brought back by Martin Chuzzlewit.

And further, it is not unaware of its provinciality, and is far from having lost the desire to keep in touch with the remoter centres of its civilisation and with its past. This comes out notably in its reception of the twins, the presentment of which illustrates the complex poise of Mark Twain's attitude. The comedy of the reception is not satiric. Dawson's Landing displays, not merely its crudenesses and limitations, but also a touching positive humility, a will to pay homage to something other than provinciality and philistinism and the standards of everyday life. The exhibition of democratic *moeurs* at Aunt Patsy's is finely and subtly done, and quite clear in its significance. These democrats, without being in the least inclined to go back on their democracy, respond imaginatively to their traditional memories and to the sense of ideal values belonging to a richer life that is now remote from them. It is an utterly different thing from snobbery, and, as Mark Twain presents it, something that the social crudity of the occasion sets off as the reverse of trivial or crude:

> "None of these visitors was at ease, but, being honest people, they didn't pretend to be. None of them had ever seen a person bearing a title of nobility before, and none had been expecting to see one now, consequently the title came upon them as a kind of pile-driving surprise and caught them unprepared. A few tried to rise to the emergency, and got out an awkward 'My lord', or 'Your lordship', or something of that sort, but the great majority were overwhelmed by the unaccustomed word and its dim and awful associations with gilded courts and stately ceremony and anointed kingship, so they only fumbled through the handshake and passed on speechless."

Then, significantly, this homage to a glimpsed ideal superiority is followed by the homage to art:

> "Here a prodigious slam-banging broke out below, and everybody rushed down to see. It was the twins knocking out a

classic four-handed piece on the piano in great style. Rowena was satisfied—satisfied down to the bottom of her heart.

"The young strangers were kept long at the piano. The villagers were astonished and enchanted with the magnificence of their performance, and could not bear to have them stop. All the music that they had ever heard before seemed spiritless prentice-work and barren of grace or charm when compared with these intoxicating floods of melodious sound. They realised that for once in their lives they were hearing masters."

The poise is beautifully maintained; those first two sentences serve only to enforce the serious and profound significance of the last, the closing one of the chapter.

In its whole attitude towards distinction that appeals to standards other than the "democratic", Dawson's Landing represents a subtler civilisation than accounts of "the pioneer community" might suggest. Consider, for instance, the special licence accorded judge Driscoll in an environment that doesn't encourage moral independence or free play of mind. "Judge Driscoll", says Mark Twain, "could be a freethinker and still hold his place in society because he was the person of most consequence in the community, and therefore could go his own way and follow out his own notions." But York Leicester Driscoll isn't represented as having achieved his leading place by preeminence in the qualities that one would have expected to tell most among pioneering democrats. We are told of him:

"He was very proud of his old Virginian ancestry, and in his hospitalities and his rather formal and stately manners he kept up the tradition. He was fine and just and generous. To be a gentleman—a gentleman without stain or blemish—was his only religion, and to it he was always faithful. He was respected, esteemed, and beloved by all the community."

It is quite unequivocal: he is "respected, esteemed and beloved" (a set of terms that defines something quite different from the attitudes towards the smart and therefore successful man) because he is a "gentleman", representing as such an ideal that doesn't belong to the realm of material "success" and is above the attainment of the ordinary member of the community. And we come here to that complexity of ethical background which I have spoken of as providing a central preoccupation of Mark Twain's, in *Pudd'nhead Wilson* as in *Huckleberry Finn*. I am not thinking merely of the persistence of an aristocratic tradition in a democratic society. That society has also its Christian allegiance, and, while the judge is "just and generous", the total concept of "gentleman" is decidedly not Christian. When we come to Pembroke Howard, for whom to be a gentleman is *not* his only religion, the situation, with its irony, is focussed in the one actor:

> "He was a fine, brave, majestic creature, a gentleman according to the nicest requirements of the Virginian rule, a devoted Presbyterian, an authority on the 'code', and a man always courteously ready to stand up before you in the field if any act or word of his had seemed doubtful or suspicious to you, and explain it with any weapons you might prefer from bradawls to artillery. He was very popular with the people, and was the judge's dearest friend."

For the gentleman, "honour stood first": the laws of honour "required certain things of him which his religion might forbid him: then his religion must yield—the laws could not be relaxed to accommodate religion or anything else." And the Christian and democratic community, with a complete and exalted conviction, gave its approval.

> "The people took more pride in the duel than in all the other events put together, perhaps. It was a glory to the town to have such a thing happen there. In their eyes, the principals had reached the summit of human honour."

There is nothing remarkable about the ability to observe such facts. What is remarkable is the subtlety of the appraising attitude that Mark Twain, in terms of impersonal art, defines towards them—as towards the whole inclusive situation presented in the book. Astringent as is the irony of *Pudd'nhead Wilson*, the attitude here has nothing of the satiric in it (the distinctively satiric plays no great part in the work as a whole). Mark Twain unmistakably admires judge Driscoll and Pembroke Howard. And it is important to note that, if they are "fine", the "fineness" is not a mere matter of their being "just and generous". The total attitude where they are concerned is not altogether easy to describe, not because it is equivocal, but because it is not a simple one, and has called for some subtlety of dramatic means to convey it. The two most sympathetic characters in the drama give the "code" itself their active endorsement. It is not for instance suggested that Wilson, in acting as second in the duel, does so with any self-dissociating reservations or reluctance, and he rebukes Tom for not telling his uncle about the kicking and "letting him have a gentleman's chance": "if I had known the circumstances," he says, "I would have kept the case out of court until I got word to him and let him have a gentleman's chance."

> "'You would?' exclaimed Tom, with lively surprise. 'And it your first case! And you know perfectly well there would never have *been* any case if he had got that chance, don't you? And you'd have finished your days a pauper nobody, instead of being an actually launched and recognised lawyer to-day. And you would really have done that, would you?'
>
> "'Certainly.'
>
> "Tom looked at him a moment or two, then shook his head sorrowfully and said:
>
> "'I believe you—upon my word I do. I don't know why I do, but I do. Pudd'nhead Wilson, I think you're the biggest fool I ever saw.'"

This reminder of the circumstances of the rebuke will serve to enforce the point that Wilson, the poised and preeminently civilised moral centre of the drama, whom we take to be very close in point of view to Mark Twain is not, all the same, to be identified with him. Wilson is an actor in a dramatic whole that conveys its significances dramatically. The upshot of the drama is to set a high value on the human qualities fostered by the aristocratic code: to endorse the code even as far as Wilson does would be quite a different matter, and no reader of the book can suppose it to be doing that. Against the pride and the allegiance to an ideal of conduct that make personal safety a matter of comparative indifference, we see the ignominy and ugliness of Tom's complete self-centredness, which is as unchecked by pride or concern for any ideal as by imaginative sympathy. Hearing that the judge, fighting in his cause, has survived the duel, he reflects immediately, with an exasperation untouched by shame, how blessedly all problems would have been solved had the judge been killed: the duel has been wasted.

The exposure of human nature in Tom Driscoll has an essential part in the total astringency of the book. But it will not do to suggest that human nature, as the book presents it, reduces to Tom. If the Wilson of *Pudd'nhead Wilson's Calendar* is not the Wilson of the drama, neither does he represent the imagination and the sensibility that inform this as a conceived and realised whole. Such utterances of Mark Twain's as this marginal note from a book, characteristic as they are, mustn't be credited with a kind of conclusive authority they certainly haven't:

> "What a man sees in the human race is merely himself in the deep and honest privacy of his own heart. Byron despised the race, because he despised himself. I feel as Byron did and for the same reason."

The exhibition of Tom's viciousness has its convincing force, no doubt, because *we* recognise in ourselves the potentiality, as Mark Twain did in *him*self. But it would be misleading to say that we despise Tom; that would be to suggest an animus that we do *not* feel when we place him, unequivocally, as contemptible: we are not engaged and involved in that way. The irony of the work as a whole means a very secure poise, and the poise is secure because the author has achieved a mature, balanced and impersonal view of humanity. He himself is not involved in the personal way that involves animus in condemning.

The attitude of *Pudd'nhead Wilson* is remote from cynicism or pessimism. The book conveys neither contempt for human nature nor a rejection of civilisation. It is concerned with the complexities of both human nature and civilisation as represented in a historical community—for Dawson's Landing, it may reasonably be said, is one that, at a given time in actual American history, Mark Twain had intimately known.

We are not, by way of dismissing the suggestion of any general contempt, confined to adducing Wilson himself and the "fine, brave, majestic creatures" who uphold the code of the F.F.V. Most impressively, there is Roxy. It is true that her heroic maternal devotion plays against the extremity of mean heartless egotism given us in Tom. But her significance is not exhausted in that irony. We feel her dominating the book as a triumphant vindication of life. Without being in the least sentimentalised, or anything but dramatically right, she plainly bodies forth the qualities that Mark Twain, in his whole being, most values—qualities that, as Roxy bears witness, he profoundly believes in as observable in humanity, having known them in experience. Although born a slave, she is herself a "fine, brave, majestic creature", whose vitality expresses itself in pride, high-spiritedness and masterful generosity. Her reckless presence at the duel defines Mark Twain's attitude towards the "code" more decisively than Wilson's participation does. When she proudly tells Tom that he is descended from the best blood of Virginia the effect, for all the irony, is not satiric. And her confident and justified reliance on the loyal comradeship, not only of her fellow-niggers, but also of the officers of the *Grand Mogul*, has its part in the appraisal of human nature conveyed by the book as a whole.

Mr DeVoto makes the point that she represents a frank and unembarrassed recognition of the actuality of sex, with its place and power in human affairs, such as cannot be found elsewhere in Mark Twain. That seems to me true and important. It is an aspect of the general fact, that she is the presence in the book of a free and generous vitality, in which the warmly and physically human manifests itself also as intelligence and spiritual strength. It is this far-reaching associative way in which, so dominating a presence, she stands for—she *is*—triumphant life that gives the book, for all its astringency and for all the chilling irony of the close, its genial quality (to be both genial and astringent is its extraordinary distinction).

How far from satiric the spirit of *Pudd'nhead Wilson* is may be seen in the presentment of the subtleties of conscience and ethical sensibility in Roxy. Consider the episode of the stolen money and the threat to sell the negro servants down the river. We are no doubt very close to the satiric note in the irony with which the chapter ends—in Percy Driscoll's self-gratulation on his magnanimity: "that night he set the incident down in his diary, so that his son might read it in after years and be thereby moved to deeds of gentleness and humanity himself." But we are emote from satire here:

> "The truth was, all were guilty but Roxana; she suspected that the others were guilty, but she did not know them to be so. She was horrified to think how near she had come to being guilty herself; she had been saved in the nick of time by a revival in the coloured Methodist Church, a fortnight before, at which time and place she had 'got religion'. The very next day after that gracious experience, while her change of style was fresh upon her and she was vain of her purified condition, her master left a couple of dollars lying unprotected on his desk, and she happened upon that temptation when she was polishing around with a dust-rag. She looked at the money awhile with a steadily rising resentment, and then she burst out with "'Dad blame dat revival, I wisht it had 'a be'n put off till to-morrow!'
>
> "Then she covered the tempter with a book, and another member of the kitchen cabinet got it. She made this sacrifice as a matter of religious etiquette; as a thing necessary just now, but by no means to be wrested into a precedent; no, a week or two would limber up her piety, then she would be rational again, and the

next two dollars that got left out in the cold would find a comforter—and she could name the comforter.

"Was she bad? Was she worse than the general run of her race? No. They had an unfair show in the battle of life...."

In spite of that last phrase, we know that what we have been contemplating is not just, an exhibition of negro traits: "her race" is the human race. These naïve and subtle changes and adjustments of conscience and the moral sense we can parallel from our own inner experience. But there is nothing cynically reductive in Mark Twain's study of the moral nature of man; he shows the clairvoyance of a mind that is sane and poised, and the irony that attends the illustration of subtleties and complexities throws no doubt on the reality or the dignity or the effectiveness in human affairs of ethical sensibility.

I have not yet touched on the central irony of the book, the sustained and complex irony inherent in the plot. *Pudd'nhead Wilson* should be recognised as a classic of the use of popular modes—of the sensational and the melodramatic—for the purposes of significant art. The book, I have said, is not faultless, and an obvious criticism lies against the unfulfilled promise represented by the twins—the non-significant play made with them, their history and the sinister oriental dagger. Mark Twain, we can see, had intended to work out some interplay of the two parallel sets of complications: twins and interchanged babies. He abandoned the idea, but didn't trouble to eliminate that insistent focussing of expectation upon the twins. The fault is in a sense a large one, and yet it is not, after all, a very serious one: it doesn't affect the masterly handling of the possibilities actually developed.

The ironic subtleties that Mark Twain gets from the interchange of the babies in their cradles seem, as one ponders them, almost inexhaustible. There is the terrible difference, no more questioned by Roxy than by her master, between the nigger and the white. The conventionality of the distinction is figured by the actual whiteness of Roxy, whose one-sixteenth of negro blood tells only in her speech (with which, indeed, it has no essential relation, as is illustrated later by the inability of "Valet de Chambers", now revealed as the pure-white heir, to shed the nigger-speech he learnt in childhood). So awful, ultimate and unchangeable is the distinction that Roxy, as, in order to save her child from the fate hanging over the slave (to be "sold down the river"), she changes the babies in their cradles, justifies herself by the example of God. The rendering is an irresistible manifestation of genius, utterly convincing, and done with a delicate subtlety of ironic significance:

"She flung herself on her bed and began to think and toss, toss and think. By-and-by she sat suddenly upright, for a comforting thought had flown through her worried mind:

"'Tain't no sin—*white* folks has done it! It ain't no sin, glory to goodness it ain't no sin! *Dey's* done it—yes, en dey was de biggest quality in de whole bilin', too—*kings!*'"

She began to muse; she was trying to gather out of her memory the dim particulars of some tale she had heard some time or other. At last she said:

"'Now I's got it; now I 'member. It was dat ole nigger preacher dat tole it, de time he come over here fum Illinois en preached in de nigger church. He said dey ain't nobody kin save his own self—can't do it by faith, can't do it by works, can't do it no way at all. Free grace is de *on'y* way, en dat don't come fum nobody but jis' de Lord; en *he* kin give it to anybody he please, saint or sinner—*he* don't kyer. He do jis' as he's a mineter. He s'lect out anybody dat suit him, en put another one in his place, en make de fust one happy for ever en leave t'other one to burn wid Satan.'"

There is of course a glance here at the Calvinism of Mark Twain's youth. And it is to be noted that Roxy, while usurping the prerogative of the predestinating Deity, has shown a wholly human compassion, and has invoked a compassionate God in doing so:

"'I's sorry for you, honey; I's sorry, God knows I is—but what *kin* I do, what *could* I do? Yo' pappy would sell him to somebody, some time, en den he'd go down de river, sho', and I couldn't, couldn't, *couldn't* stan' it.'"

In saving the child from the consequences of the awful distinction that she assumes to be in the nature of things she demonstrates its lack of any ground but convention; she demonstrates the wholly common humanity of the nigger and the white. The father himself cannot detect the fraud: he cannot tell his own child from the other. And—one of the many ironies—it is his cruel, but confidently righteous, severity that imposes the full abjectness of slave mentality upon his own child, who becomes the defence less and rightless servant of the slave's child. On the other hand, Roxy's success in saving Valet de Chambers (the name her proud tribute to an ideal "white" lordliness) from the fate of the slave erects a dreadful barrier between child and mother. Treated as "young Marse Tom", not only does he become that different order of being, the "master"; in Roxy herself the slave attitudes that she necessarily observes towards him find themselves before long attended by the appropriate awe. When at last, outraged by the humiliating and cruel rebuffs that meet her appeal for a little kindness (she is in need) to the old "nigger-mammy", she forgets habit and the ties of motherhood, and pants for revenge, she has to recognise that she has placed him in an impregnable position: no one will believe her tale. A further irony is that, if he has turned out bad, a portent of egocentric heartlessness, that is at least partly due to his spoiling as heir and young master, the lordly superior being.

It is a mark of the poised humanity characterising the treatment of the themes of *Pudd'nhead Wilson* that, worthless and vicious as "Tom" is, we feel, when he has to face the sudden revelation that he is a nigger, some compassion for him; we don't just applaud an irony of poetic justice when he is cornered into reflecting, with an echo of his mother's self-justifying recall of the Calvinistic God:

> "'Why were niggers and whites made? What crime did the untreated first nigger commit that the curse of birth was decreed for him? And why is this awful difference made between black and white?'"

Compassion, of course, soon vanishes as the dialectic of utter selfishness unfolds in him. The developments of his incapacity for compassion are done with a convincingness that the creator of Tito Melema would have envied. When Roxy offers to be sold back into slavery in order to save "Tom" from being disinherited, and he, with dreadfully credible treachery, sells her "down the river", the opposite extremes of human nature are brought together in an effect that belongs wholly to the mode of *Pudd'nhead Wilson*, and is equally removed from melodrama and from cynicism. It can hardly be said, when we close the book, that the worst in human nature has not been confronted; yet the upshot of the whole is neither to judge mankind to be contemptible nor to condemn civilisation. And it is remarkable how utterly free from animus that astringency, is which takes on so intense a concentration in the close:

> "Everybody granted that if 'Tom' were white and free it would be unquestionably right to punish him—it would be no loss to anybody; but to shut up a valuable slave for life—that was quite another matter.

"As soon as the Governor understood the case, he pardoned
Tom at once, and the creditors sold him down the river."

It is an irony of the tale that this, the fate to secure him against which
Roxana had committed her crime, is, as an ultimate consequence of that
crime, the fate he suffers.

NOTES

1. Bernard DeVoto, *Mark Twain at Work*, p. 99.
2. *The Times of Melville and Whitman*. Mr Brooks says much the same in *The Ordeal of Mark Twain*.
3. In the Introduction to Marius Bewley's *The Complex Fate*.

Mark Twain

Everybody knows that a profound incoherence marked the life of Samuel Clemens, whose very existence was one long double take and who lived with a double that he had summoned into existence in order, himself, to exist at all. His feelings on any subject, but especially on the subject of himself, were violently divided; his humor was the cry of despair of a man incapable of feeling himself worthy of love. In his last coma, out of the old obsession and a self-knowledge that had never, however; proved deep enough to be redemptive, he spoke of a dual personality and of Dr. Jekyll and Mr. Hyde.

We know, too, that there was an especially bitter division of feeling in relation to the backward region of Clemens' birth and the great world of thriving modernity that he went out so successfully into, and between the past and the present—or rather, the future. When the little band of Confederate irregulars to which Sam Clemens belonged dissolved without firing even one shot in anger, Sam simply cut himself off from his Southern heritage, his father's ill-grounded pride in high Virginia lineage, and the aura of glory about the mahogany sideboard brought from Kentucky. He resigned, in a sense, from history, which he indifferently left in the hands of Confederate or Yankee heroes, and headed West, where the future was all. Later he was to regard Sir Walter Scott as the source of the Southern disease whose contagion he had thus fled and was, in *A Connecticut Yankee at King*

From *Southern Review* 8, no. 3 (Summer 1972). © 1972 by Robert Penn Warren.

Arthur's Court, to equate chivalry with the barbarous irrationality that the rational Yankee tries to redeem. But though the young Sam did repudiate the historical past, he did not, or could not, repudiate the personal past and for his *doppelgänger* Mark Twain, the story of that past became the chief stock-in-trade.

What is equally significant is the complex of feelings that went into the telling of that tale. Twain knew the hard facts of his world. He knew that Hannibal, Missouri, had its full quota of degradation and despair. He knew that the glittering majesty of the steamboat was not much more than a cross between a floating brothel richly afflicted with venereal disease and a gambling hell full of stacked decks and loaded dice. Indeed, in cold print both Hannibal and the South were to get their realistic due, and in 1876, writing to one of the erstwhile boys of Hannibal, Twain chides his old companion's nostalgic yearnings:

> As for the past, there is but one good thing about it, ... that it is past.... I can see by your manner of speech, that for more than twenty years you have stood dead still in the midst of the dreaminess, the romance, the heroics, of sweet but happy sixteen. Man, do you know that this is simply mental and moral masturbation? It belongs eminently to the period usually devoted to physical masturbation, and should be left there and outgrown.

In the wilderness of paradox and ambivalence in which he lived, Twain, during the first days of his happy marriage, enjoying a mansion and a solid bank account, could yet write to another companion:

> The old life has swept before me like a panorama; the old days have trooped by in their glory again; the old faces have looked out of the mists of the past; old footsteps have sounded in my listening ears; old hands have clasped mine; and the songs I loved ages and ages ago have come wailing down the centuries.

In all the new splendor and bliss of mutual love, Twain discovered the poetry of the old life and, in fact, certain restrictions of the new that, before many years had passed, would make him look back on the time when he had been a demigod in the pilothouse watching the stars reflected in the mysterious river and declare nostalgically that the pilot was "the only unfettered and entirely independent human being that liked upon the earth." And make him, in a letter to the widow of another boyhood companion, declare: "I should greatly like to relive my youth ... and be as we were, and make holiday until fifteen, then all drown together."

But Sam Clemens did not drown. He went out into the world and became Mark Twain, with his head chock-full of memories of Hannibal, his ears ringing with the language of that village, and his heart torn in a tumult of conflicting feelings.

In spite of such doublenesses and incoherences in life, there is an extraordinary coherence in the work of the *doppelgänger* of Sam Clemens, the most obvious example being the use of the personal incoherence to provide the dramatic tension of creation. This internal coherence of motivation suggests also a coherence of relation among the individual works, a dynamic of growth by which everything, good and bad, could be absorbed into the master works and by which all subsequent works appear as exfoliations and refinements. In turn, the internal coherence is suggested by the key image of Twain's work, that of the journey. For if Twain were a wanderer who, with no address ever definitely fixed, founded our "national literature," the key image we refer to here is not a record of his surroundings back and forth over two continents but of the journey into the darkest of all continents—the self. In *A Connecticut Yankee*, the explorer gets as close to the heart of darkness as he ever could—or dared—get, and all subsequent works represent merely additional notes and elaborations of detail of that shocking experience.

It may be useful to remind ourselves what discoveries in earlier works led to the creation of the big fulfilling books, *Adventures of Huckleberry Finn* and *A Connecticut Yankee*.

In *Innocents Abroad* (1869) Twain discovered what kind of book he could write. First, he came upon the image of the journey, obviously a simple objective journey but not quite so obviously a journey in which the main character is ruefully or outrageously puzzled by the lunacies of the world through which he travels. Second, the book represents a double vision—in this early. instance rather simple and schematic, a travel book that is at the same time a parody of travel books. Third, Mark Twain-actor playing the role of Mark Twain on the lecture platform's here transformed into Mark Twain-author writing a book in which Mark Twain is the main character. Fourth, the book represents Twain's discovery of the rich new middle class of the Gilded Age in America, the class into which he was to marry, by whose standards he would live, whose tyrannies he would fret against, and whose values he would loathe, here for the first time experiencing an ambivalence that was to become more bitter and significant. Fifth, Twain here struck upon a method that was to stand him in good stead. He learned how to make the method of the lecture platform into a book. He once said that his characteristic lecture (derived from the oral anecdote of frontier humor, full of turns and booby-traps) was like a plank with a line of square holes into which he could put plugs appropriate for a particular moment or a particular audience, and this structure persisted, for better and worse, through later work though, with increasing sophistication, often played against the developmental structure of fictional action and theme.

Mark Twain's second book, *Roughing It* (1872), also took a journey for its "plank," but where the narrator of *Innocents Abroad* had been static, simply the "lecturer" transferred from platform to book, now the narrator is in motion, is undergoing step by step the "education of the West," is being forced to submit his romantic illusions to the shock of reality. When the book ends he is a new man, and Twain has discovered his version of the great American theme of initiation that is to be central for his finest work. But there is another important development. On board the *Quaker City* the narrator had merely faced, in his traveling comparisons, individual examples of a world, selected more or less at random, but now in *Roughing It* he must create a world. This movement toward fiction is more importantly marked, however, in the fact that the narrator himself is more of a creation, and we have now observed the first step in the process by which the author will find fictional identification with Huck or Hank.

In his first novel, *The Gilded Age* (1874), which was to give the epoch its name, Twain again, though less explicitly, used both the image of a journey and the plank-and-plug technique. Both the image and the technique were, however, of a sort to compound rather than correct the hazards of a collaboration—and this was, of course, a collaboration—with Charles Dudley Warner who, as one of the breed of novelists battening on the new middle class, was supposed to provide the fictional know-how for the inexperienced Twain. Though scarcely more than a huddle of improvisation *The Gilded Age* did its own part in preparing the way for Twain's greatness. Here, for the first time, he created a fully rounded fictional character. Colonel Beriah Sellers—"*the* new American character," as William Dean Howells called him—was a gaudy combination of promoter and bunkum artist, dreamer and con man, idealist and cynic, ballyhoo expert, and vote-broker; and, in the Reconstruction world, an expert in bribery, the old Confederate learning the way of new Yankeedom and collaborating with a good Unionist to get rich at the public expense while ostensibly trying to elevate the black freedman: "Yes, sir, make his soul immortal but don't touch the nigger as he is."

Beyond Colonel Sellers, however, and perhaps of more significance,

Twain here pictured for the first time the little towns and lost villages of backcountry America. Now they are done with grim realism; but in the same novel, for the first time in print, Twain was also exploring the world of luxury, greed, self-deception, pharisaism, and cold hypocrisy, the contempt for which was to force him to take refuge in the dream version of rural America that was to find its image in mythical Hannibal. The ambivalence about both the world of rich modernity and that of the old backcountry had already (though not in literature) been emerging, for instance, as we have seen, in the very first days of his happy marriage into the world of wealth.

With "Old Times on the Mississippi," which he undertook for the *Atlantic* in 1874, Twain developed the poetry of old America—the Edenic dream, the vision of a redemptive simplicity that haunts the tenderfoot going West, the apprentice pilot on the texas deck, and Huck on his raft, a poetry antithetical to the grim realism that had begun with *The Gilded Age* and was to continue as one pole of later work. Specifically, with "Old Times" we enter the world of Hannibal and the river in which Tom Sawyer and Huck Finn were to come to immortal life. But at a thematic level, both "Old Times on the Mississippi" and *Life on the Mississippi* are more deeply prophetic of *The Adventures of Tom Sawyer* and *Adventures of Huckleberry Finn*. As the tenderfoot in *Roughing It* learns the West, so the landlubber learns the river, and here, as before, the story of initiation concerns the correction of illusion by the confrontation of reality. Here the illusion is explicit only in its aesthetic dimension: to the uninitiated observer the river is a beautiful spectacle, but to the old pilot it is a "wonderful book." Though a "dead language to the uneducated passenger [who] ... saw nothing but all manner of pretty pictures," the same objects "to the trained eye were not pictures at all but the grimmest and most dead-earnest of reading matter." In other words, Twain is dealing with an image (and a narrative) of innocence and experience, a theme that was to prove deeply central in both *Tom Sawyer* and *Huckleberry Finn*, considered either individually or in contrast to each other. For with *Tom Sawyer* (1876) we have, as Twain declared, "simply a hymn, put into prose to give it a worldly air"—that is, we have the Edenic dream of innocence which the mystic journey of Huck will put to various tests.

In the complexity of his inspiration, *Tom Sawyer* goes back, as we have suggested, to the first days of Twain's marriage when an early draft of what was later to be Tom's courtship of Becky Thatcher, known as the "Boy's Manuscript," was (as a matter of fact) composed. And in its early form, something of the same impulse carried over into *Huckleberry Finn*, which was begun while Twain was reading proofs on *Tom Sawyer* and which he then regarded as a companion volume. But this new book did not get beyond the ramming of the raft by the steamboat before he laid it aside. Over the years he added to it, but it was not until the stimulus of writing *Life on the Mississippi* (1883) that he was able to push it through. The book was published in 1885, after an overwhelming advertising campaign and a series of lecture-readings by the author himself. The results of the advertising campaign were gratifying even to the avarice of Mark Twain, although reviewers were inclined to find the book crude, irreverent, and even vicious.

Let us rehearse the simple facts of the story. With the treasure that he now shares with Tom as a result of earlier adventures, Huck has been adopted into the respectable world of St. Petersburg under the tutelage of Widow Douglas and Miss Watson. He misses his old freedom, but begins to accept the new regime of spelling, soap, and prayers. His father reappears to claim Huck, but when in a drunken rage the old man threatens his life, Huck escapes to the island after making it seem that he has been murdered by a robber. Here he is joined by Nigger Jim, the slave of Miss Watson who, in spite of her piety, is being tempted to sell him downriver. Huck, disguised as a girl, makes a scouting expedition to shore and finds that the island is not safe from slave-catchers, and he and Jim take to the river. Huck is troubled by his conscience at thus depriving Miss Watson of her property, but follows his natural instinct. The plan to escape to freedom in a Northern state fails when they miss Cairo, Illinois, in a fog. Then the raft is sunk by a steamboat and the two, barely escaping with their lives, are separated.

Huck is taken in by the Grangerford family, aristocratic planters, and enjoys their hospitality until a slaughterous outbreak of their bloody feud with the Shepherdsons puts him on his own again. He manages to rejoin Jim, and the growth of his human understanding of the slave constitutes the psychological action, which concludes when Huck decides that if saving Jim may get him damned, he'll just have to go to hell.

Meanwhile, the pair pass through various adventures that exhibit the irrationalities of society and the cruelties possible to human nature. The life on the river comes to an end when the vagabond "King" and "Duke," the rogues whom they have befriended, betray Jim for a share in a presumptive reward and Jim is held captive on the downriver plantation of the Phelps family, kin of Tom Sawyer. When Huck goes to the plantation with the idea of rescuing Jim, he is taken for Tom who is expected on a visit. To save Jim, he accepts the role and when the real Tom appears, Tom accepts the role of Sid, another boy in the family connection. Tom institutes one of his elaborate adventures to rescue Jim, with Huck participating in the nonsense to placate Tom. After Jim's rescue, during which Tom gets shot in the leg, Jim stays with him and is recaptured; but all comes out happily, for as is now explained, Miss Watson on her deathbed had long since freed Jim, and Tom had withheld this information merely to enjoy a romantic adventure. Huck is now taken in by the Phelps family to be civilized, but he is thinking of escape to the Indian country.

The story, or rather Twain's treatment of the story, has provoked a vast body of criticism and various interpretations. The most simple view is to regard *Huckleberry Finn* as merely a companion piece to Tom Sawyer—more of the same tale of what it was like to be a boy in mythical Hannibal. As far as it goes, this view is valid. But it does not accommodate certain features of the book that are undeniably there.

The book is, indeed, a series of boyish adventures, but these adventures take place in an adult world, and the journey on the raft is, as the critic Bernard DeVoto has put it, a "faring forth with inexhaustible delight through the variety of America." The "faring forth" gives, "objectively and inwardly, a panorama of American life, comic and serious, or with the comic and serious intertwined, all levels, all types of that life."

We must remember, however, that here we refer to the objective world of the novel and to the "inwardness" of that world. But what of the "inwardness" of the observers of that adult world? With this question we engage the central issue of the novel, for whenever the boyish world of Huck and Jim touches the adult world—the "shore" world—something significantly impinges upon the "river" idyll. If the basic fact of the novel is that it is a journey, we must think not only of the things seen on the journey but also of who sees them and the effect of the seeing. The journey, in fact, has begun with inward motives of great urgency; both Huck and Jim are more than footloose wanderers—they are escaping from their respective forms of bondage, forms imposed by society. To flee they give themselves to the river; and it is not illogical to agree with the poet T.S. Eliot and the critic Lionel Trilling that the river may be taken to have a central role. As Eliot implies when he says that the river has no clear point of beginning and fades out into its delta toward the sea, the river seems to be an image of a timeless force different from the fixed order of the dry land, an image of freedom and regeneration; or as Trilling puts it, the river is a god to which Huck can turn for renewal.

In any case, the river provides not only a principle of structural continuity but also a principle of thematic continuity. The experience on the river, with its special tone of being, is set against that on land. Huck says: "It was kind of solemn, drifting down the big, still river—looking up at the stars, and we didn't ever feel like talking loud, and it warn't often we laughed." Not only does the river teach a feeling of awe before the universe, but also a kind of human relationship at odds with the vanity, selfishness, competitiveness, and hypocrisy of society: "What you want, above all things, on a raft is for everybody to be satisfied, and feel right and kind toward the others."

But society—in which people are not "satisfied"—pursues the fugitives even on the river; the steamboat runs down the raft. When Huck and Jim escape by diving deep into the bosom of the river beneath the murderous paddle-wheel, this event—like the dive that Frederick Henry, in *A Farewell to Arms*, takes into the Tagliamento River to escape the Italian battle-police and the insanity of the world of institutions—is a baptism that frees them, now fully, into the new life.

If we are to understand the significance of Huck's baptism we must understand Huck himself, for Huck is the carrier of the meaning of the novel. The focal significance of Huck is emphasized by the fact that as early as 1875, Twain in considering a sequel to *Tom Sawyer*, said to Howells (who had urged him to make Tom grow up in another book) that Tom "would not be a good character for it." He was, he said, considering a novel that would take a boy of twelve "through life," and added that the tale would have to be told "autobiographically—like *Gil Blas*." If the wanderings of the new picaroon are to be "through life," we expect the wanderer to learn something about life, and if, as Twain declared, the tale must be told as autobiography (it would be "fatal" otherwise, he said to Howells), the reason must be that the personality of the learner is crucially important.

In other words, Twain needed a hero who would be sensitive enough to ask the right questions of his adventures in growing up, and intelligent enough to demand the right answers. Furthermore, if Twain was to make the process of learning dramatically central to the tale, he could not well trust it to a third-person narrator, as in *Tom Sawyer*. The hero would have to tell his own tale with all its inwardness, and in his own telling, in the language itself, exhibit both his own nature and the meaning of his experience.

In Huck's language—"a magnificent expression," as DeVoto puts it, "of the folk mind"—Twain found a miraculous solution. It is no less miraculous for springing from a well-defined tradition, or rather, from two traditions. The first, of course, was that of the frontier humorists from Augustus Baldwin Longstreet, Davy Crockett, and the anonymous writers of the Crockett almanacs on to George Washington Harris and his *Sut Lovingood*, a tradition that had fed the humor of lecturers and journalists like Artemus Ward and the early Mark Twain. The second was that of the early writers of the local color school, such as James Russell Lowell, Harriet Beecher Stowe, and Bret Harte. But the use of dialect by writers had become more and more cumbersome and mechanical; it set up a screen between the language and the meaning. Furthermore, the dialect itself was a mark of condescension. The writer and the reader, proud of superior literacy, looked down on the dialect and the speaker.

What Twain needed was a language based on colloquial usage and carrying that flavor, but flexible and natural, with none of the mechanical burden literacy, dialect writing. At the same time, even if the speaker were of inferior literacy, his language had to be expressive enough to report subtleties oil feeling and thought. In achieving this, Twain established a new relation between American experiences as *content* and language as a direct *expression*— not merely a *medium of expression*—of that experience. The language, furthermore, implied a certain kind of fiction, a fiction that claimed certain relation to the experience it treated. That Mark Twain was aware of this situation is indicated at the very beginning of the novel: "You didn't know about me without you have read a book by the name of *The Adventures of Tom Sawyer*; but that ain't no matter. The book was made by Mr. Mark Twain, and he told the truth, mainly." Here Huck asserts himself as the literal subject about which Mr. Mark Twain had written in *Tom Sawyer*; but now he himself is to tell his own tale.

He is, then, freestanding in his natural habitat outside of both "Mr. Mark Twain's" book and his own, insisting on a special veracity about experience. Actually, Huck Finn is only another fictional dramatization, but a dramatization validated by the language that springs directly from the world treated. The invention of this language, with all its implications, gave a new dimension to our literature. As Hemingway says in *The Green Hills of Africa* (a book which directly descends from Mark Twain's travel books), "All modern American literature comes from one book by Mark Twain called *Huckleberry Finn*."

Huck's language itself is a dramatization of Huck. On one hand, it reaches back into the origins of Huck as the son of the whiskey-sodden Pap sleeping it off with the hogs; it was a language Pap could speak. It is indicative of the world of common, or even debased, life from which Huck moves to his awakening; but as we have said, it is a language capable of poetry, as in this famous description of dawn on the river:

> Not a sound anywhere—perfectly still—just like the whole world was asleep, only sometimes the bull-frogs a-cluttering, maybe. The first thing to see, looking away over the water, was a kind of dull line—that was the woods on t'other side—you couldn't make nothing else out; then a pale place in the sky; then

more paleness, spreading around; then the river softened up, away off, and warn't black any more, but gray; you could see little dark spots drifting along, ever so far away—trading scows and such things; and long black streaks—rafts; sometimes you could hear a sweep screaking; or jumbled up voices, it was so still, and sounds come so far; and by-and-by you could see a streak on the water which you know by the look of the streak that there's a snag there in a swift current which breaks on it and makes that streak look that way; and you see the mist curl up off of the water, and the east reddens up, and the river, and you make out a log cabin in the edge of the woods, away on the bank on t'other side of the river, being a wood-yard, likely, and piled up by them cheats so you can throw a dog through it anywheres; then the nice breeze springs up, and comes fanning you from over there, so cool and fresh, and sweet to smell, on account of the woods and the flowers; but sometimes not that way, because they've left dead fish laying around, gars, and such, and they do get pretty rank; and next you've got the full day, and everything smiling in the sun, and the song-birds just going it!

The first thing we notice here is what Leo Marx has called a "powerful pastoral impulse." But Huck's poetry represents more than that. It is a dramatic poetry, a poetry concerned with the human condition, and this is presumably what Howells meant when he said, in 1901, that the book was "more poetic than picaresque, and of a deeper psychology." It is the interfusion of the style with the "deeper psychology" that makes *Huck Finn* truly revolutionary and that made the discovery of Huck's personal style the base, subsequently, of Twain's own style and of the style of many writers to come. Howells called Twain the Lincoln of our literature, and we may interpret this by saying that as Lincoln freed the slave, Twain freed the writer.

In the light of the general implications of Huck's style, let us return to what it signifies about him. When we find a language capable of poetic force, we must remember that it is spoken by a speaker, and a speaker capable of poetic thought and feeling. The language derives from Pap's world, but it indicates a most un-Paplike sensibility, and this sensibility, even in its simplest poetic utterances, prepares us for Huck's moral awakening as, bit by bit, he becomes aware of the way the world really wags. The language of Huck is, then, an index to the nature of his personal story—his growing up.

Tom Sawyer, it is true, is also the story of growing up, but there is a crucial difference between the two versions. Huck's growing up is by the process of a radical criticism of society, while Tom's is by a process of achieving acceptance in society. Tom's career is really a triumph of conventionality, and though Tom is shown as the "bad" boy, we know that he is not "really bad." He is simply a good healthy boy making the normal experiments with life, and we know, from our height of indulgent condescension, that in the end all will be well.

And all is well. Tom is accepted into the world of civilized and rational St. Petersburg. Even Huck, as an adjunct to Tom, is accepted as worth to be "civilized," and this, in the light of his deplorable beginnings and generally unwashed condition, is a good American success story, cheering to parents and comforting to patriots.

Huckleberry Finn is a companion piece to *Tom Sawyer*, but a companion piece in reverse a mirror image; it is the American *un-success* story, the story that had been embodied in Leatherstocking, proclaimed by Thoreau, and was again to be embodied in Ike McCaslin of Faulkner's *The Bear*, the drama of the innocent outside of society. Tom's story ends once he has been reclaimed by society, but Huck's real story does not even begin until he has successfully penetrated the world of respectability and, in the well-meaning clutches of the Widow and Miss Watson, begins to chafe under their ministrations. Here Mark Twain indicates the thematic complexity of Huck's rebellion by two additional facts. It is not the mere tyranny of prayers, spelling, manners, and soap that drives Huck forth; Tom and Pap also play significant roles in this story.

Tom, in a sense, dominates not only his gang but Huck, too. He is an organizer and has a flair for leadership, but the secret of his power is his imagination: medieval chivalry, brigandage, piracy, treasure hunts, glorious rescues, and wild adventures drawn from his reading fill his head and must be enacted—with Tom, of course, in the major role. Against this world of fantasy and exaggeration, for which he has the name of "stretchers" or plain lies, Huck brings the criticism of fact, and when he can't keep his mouth shut. Tom calls him a "numbskull." Huck rejects this "dream" escape from civilization:

> So then I judged that all that stuff was only just one of Tom Sawyer's lies. I reckoned he believed in the A-rabs and the elephants, but as for me, I think different. It had all the marks of a Sunday-school.

In repudiating romantic adventure and criticizing the romantic view of life, Huck is simply doing what Mark Twain had done in *Roughing It* and was to do in *Life on the Mississippi*, with its criticism of his own nostalgic memories and the Southern legend, and more specifically (and more lethally) in *A Connecticut Yankee*. It is not merely that the romantic lies offend Huck's realistic sense. They offend his moral sense, too; for it is behind the façade of such lies, rationalized and justified by them, that society operates, and we notice that he concludes the remark on Tom's fantasy by saying, "It had all the marks of a Sunday-school"—Sunday school, and religion in general, being the most effective façade behind which society may carry on its secular operations. The equating of Tom's romantic lies with the lies of Sunday school tells us that Tom, in his romantic fantasies, is merely using his "stretchers" to escape from society's "stretchers"—lies as a cure for lies. And the repudiation of Tom's lies prepares us for the bitter unmasking of society's lies that is to occur on the journey downriver.

We have said that Huck has sensitivity and a poetic sense; so we must ask how this squares with his repudiation of Tom's imagination. Tom's brand of imagination is basically self-indulgent—even self-aggrandizing—in its social dimension; for instance, it makes Tom the leader, and more broadly considered, it justifies the injustices of society. But Huck's imagination, as we learn on the journey, has two distinct differences from this brand. First, it is a way of dealing with natural fact, of relating to fact, as in the night scene on the raft or the description of dawn; the poetry here derives from a scrupulously *accurate* rendering of natural fact. Second, it is a way of discovering and dealing with moral fact, a poetry that, as we have said, is concerned with the human condition and as such is the root of his growth; and this distinction comes clear in the end when Tom, on the Phelps plantation, is willing to put Jim through the rigmarole of the rescue just to satisfy his romantic imagination, when he could easily free him by reporting the facts of Miss Watson's deathbed manumission.[1] To sum up, the repudiation of Tom's imagination is of deeper significance than the flight from the Widow's soap and Miss Watson's "pecking."

Pap's role in preparing for Huck's flight is more complex than Tom's. When he reappears, he seems at first a means of escape from civilization—from prayers, spelling, manners, and soap into the freedom of nature. Certainly Pap has little contact with civilization at this level, and for one moment he does seem to be the free "outsider." But he is an "outsider" only insofar as he is *rejected*; he is the offal of civilization, a superfluous and peculiarly filthy part and parcel of civilization. His outsideness means no regeneration, for in his own filthiness he carries all the filth of civilization, as is clearly illustrated by his railing against the free Negro and his talk about the government and his vote. Pap is an outsider only by vice and misfortune—in contrast to the outsider by philosophy, which is what Huck is in the process of becoming. Pap, Tom, and the Widow, that apparently ill-assorted crew, all represent aspects of bondage and aspects of civilization from which Huck flees.

Huck, moreover, is fleeing from Pap to save his quite literal life, for whether or not Pap is the "natural" man, he is a most unnatural father bent on carving up his son with a clasp knife. This literal fact symbolically underscores the significance of the journey. The escape from Pap is symbolically, as Kenneth Lynn puts it in *Mark Twain and Southwestern Humor*, a murder. Literally, Huck has had a gun on Pap all night, clearly prepared to pull the trigger if he goes on another rampage; and later, when to fool Pap about his flight he kills a pig and sprinkles the blood about the shack, the pig is a surrogate for Pap, who sleeps with the pigs—who is, therefore, a pig. But the blood is to indicate that Huck himself has been murdered, and so we have, symbolically, not only a murder but a suicide; Huck "murders" the piglike past and himself "dies" into a new life—a theme restated by the later baptism in the river.

This episode has, in fact, an additional dimension; to grow up implies the effort of seeking individuation from society and from the father—that is, from the bond of the group and from the bond of blood. So Huck, now free from both society and his father, goes forth to find the terms on which his own life may be possible. We have here a journey undertaken, at the conscious level, as a flight, but signifying, at the unconscious level, a quest; and this doubleness is precisely what we find in the psychological pattern of adolescence.

To speak of the journey as a quest, as the stages in the movement toward freedom, we refer to the fact that Huck, episode by episode, is divesting himself of illusions. Illusion, in other words, means bondage: Tom's lies, the lies of Sunday school, all the lies that society tells to justify its values and extenuate its conduct, are the bonds. For Huck the discovery of reality, as opposed to illusion, will mean freedom. And here we may note that the pattern of the movement from illusion to reality follows that of *Roughing It* and of *Life on the Mississippi*. The main action of *Huckleberry Finn*, in fact, may be taken as the movement toward reality after the Edenic illusion of *Tom Sawyer*—i.e., Mark Twain's revision of his own idyllic dream of boyhood and Hannibal after his return to that world preparatory to writing *Life on the Mississippi*. And the contrast between illusion and reality is, of course, central to Twain's work in its most serious manifestations; it is at the root of his humor, as well.

To return to the theme of the quest, Huck's voyage toward spiritual freedom is counterpointed structurally by Jim's search for quite literal freedom. This contrapuntal relationship is complex, but the most obvious element is that many of the lies of society have to do with the enslavement of Jim. Miss Watson, though a praying woman, will sell him downriver. The woman who receives Huck in his disguise as Sarah Mary Williams will be kind to him and protect him, but when it comes to catching Jim for the reward, she innocently asks, "Does three hundred dollars lay round every day for people to pick up?" And in Pap's drunken tirade about the "free nigger" with his fine clothes and gold watch and chain, we see a deeper motivation than greed, the need of even the lowest to feel superior to someone.

Not that all of the evils of society have to do directly with Jim. There are the men on the river who would let a raft with a dying man drift on because they are afraid of smallpox. There are the Grangerfords with their bloody code of honor, and Colonel Sherburn's cold-blooded gunning down of Boggs. There is the mob that under the guise of administering justice would gratify its sadism and envy by lynching Sherburn, but will turn coward before him and then, right afterwards, go to the circus; and the mob that, justly, takes care of the rascally King and Duke, but in doing so becomes, for Huck, the image of human cruelty. Even so, all the lies, as we have observed, are forms of bondage, and the dynamic image for this theme is the slave; and this dominant image implies the idea that all lies ar one lie, that all evil springs from the same secret root.

This idea of the fusion of evil with evil leads to a fundamental lesson that Huck learns in his continuing scrutiny of society: as one evil may fuse with another, so good may fuse with evil, and neither good nor evil commonly appears in an isolable form. Society is a mixture and the human being is, too. The woman who would catch Jim for three hundred dollars is a kind woman. The men on the river (chasing runaway slaves, in fact) who are afraid of smallpox do have a human conscience, at least enough of one to make them pay two twenty-dollar gold pieces as conscience money. The Grangerfords, even with their blood-drenched honor, are kind, hospitable, dignified, totally courageous, and even chivalric in their admiration of the courage of the Shepherdsons. Sherburn, too, is a man of intelligence and courage.[2]

The discovery of the interfusion of evil with good marks a step toward Huck's growing up, but he has reached another stage when he learns that the locus of the problem of evil is his own soul. And here the relationship with Jim is crucial; for it is this relationship that provides a specific focus for the general questions raised by the scrutiny of society. Coming down the river,

Huck has more and more freed himself from the definition of Jim that society would prescribe: an inferior creature justly regarded as property. Huck even comes to "humble" himself before a "nigger" and apologize to him. The climax of this process comes in the famous Chapter XXXI when Huck's "conscience" dictates that he write to Miss Watson and turn Jim over to her. Having written the letter, he feels cleansed, "reformed," saved from the danger of hellfire. But the human reality of Jim on the raft, of Jim's affection for him, undoes all Huck's good intentions, and in a moment of magnificently unconscious irony, he bursts out, "All right, then, I'll go to hell," and tears up the letter.

Here, of course, Twain is concerned with the inherited doctrine of conscience as "revelation," in contrast with the notion of conscience as merely the voice of the particular society in which a person has been born. For him conscience was, as he put it in his *Notebook*, "a mere machine, like my heart—but moral, not physical ... merely a *thing*; the creature of *training*; it is whatever one's mother and Bible and comrades and laws and system of government and habitat and heredities have made it." In such a question, Twain, constantly and pathologically tormented by guilt and conscience, might well find the dynamic emotional center of his work. One escape from his suffering was in the idea of determinism; if he could regard man as "merely a machine, moved wholly by outside influences," then he was guiltless; and if conscience could be regarded (as a corollary) as "a mere machine ... merely a thing," then its anguishing remarks were meaningless.

In Huck, then, Twain is exploring another possibility of alleviating his torments of conscience, a way which would also relieve him from the grip of an iron determinism. Against the conscience of revelation Huck would set, not the relief of determinism, but the idea of what we may call a "free consciousness" forged by the unillusioned scrutiny of experience. Huck wants to look at the world directly, with his own eyes, and this desire and talent is the reward for being outside society, having no stake in it. When on the Phelps plantation, in the plot with Tom to rescue Jim, Huck objects to some of Tom's romantic irrelevancies, Tom says: "Huck, you don't ever seem to want to do anything regular; you want to be starting something fresh all the time." Huck is, in short, a moral pragmatist; he wants to derive his values "fresh," to quarry them out of experience, to create his own moral consciousness.

In his creation of Huck, Twain, in a revolutionary and literally radical way, is undercutting impartially both conventional society and religion, and the tradition of antinomianism in America. Twain was simply against all notions of revelation and to him the "higher law," the idea that one with God is a majority, and an encyclical all looked alike; any quarrels among Mrs. Grundy, Henry David Thoreau, Theodore Parker, the Pope of Rome, and a certified case of paranoia were, according to Twain's theory, strictly intramural.

Huck is an antinomian, to be sure, but his antinomianism is of a root-and-branch variety, and one mark of it is in emotional attitude: he is as much against the arrogance of an antinomian who would take his conscience as absolute as against that of any established order. Huck's free consciousness comes, not from any version of revelation, but from a long and humble scrutiny of experience; humility is the mark of Huck's mind. Furthermore, if Twain recognizes that conscience is conditioned, is a historical accident, he would recognize the corollary that more things than society may do the conditioning and that the appeal to "conscience," the "higher law," or to revelation from on high may simply be an expression of the antinomian's deep psychic needs, not necessarily wholesome or holy.

Huck is, in short, an antinomian of an educable "consciousness," not of the absolute "conscience." As an antinomian, he is much closer to the naturalist William James than to the idealist Emerson; he would recognize, even in the moment when he violates "conscience" and follows the dictates of "consciousness," putting his soul in jeopardy of hellfire, that a crucial decision is always a gamble (the awareness that there is no absolute standard by which a choice is to be judged). Furthermore, if the consciousness has been educated to the freedom of choice, the process has also been an education in humility—not only humility but charity—and this aspect of Huck's development comes into focus (there are many other aspects of it) when he learns to recognize and accept the love of a creature for whom he had had only the white man's contempt, however amiable, and whose company he had originally accepted only because of an animal loneliness. And here we may recall that if Jim comes to Huck originally in the moment of loneliness, it is significant that when Huck goes to seek Jim after his reported capture, the description of the Phelps plantation is centered on the impression of loneliness: "... then I knowed for certain I wished I was dead—for that the distant wail and hum of a spinning wheel is the lonesomest sound in the whole world."

The forging of Huck's free consciousness has, indeed, many aspects. With the flight from society, with the symbolic patricide, the symbolic suicide, and the symbolic baptism, Huck has lost his old self. He must seek a new self; and so we see emerging the psychological pattern in which, with every new venture back to shore—that is, to society—Huck takes on a new role, has a new personal history to tell, a new "self" to try on for size. In every instance, there is, of course, a good practical reason for this role-playing, but beyond such reasons the act represents a seeking for identity; such an identity will, presumably, allow him to achieve freedom in contact with society (and role-playing is, we should remind ourselves, characteristic of the process of growing up). Huck is not, in other words, seeking to exist outside society—to be merely an outcast, like Pap; for we must remind ourselves that at the beginning of the journey and at the Phelps farm he can suffer loneliness. What Huck is seeking, then, is simply a new kind of society, a kind prefigured by the harmony and mutual respect necessary on a raft. But Huck is also seeking a new kind of father, and here is where Jim assumes another dimension of significance; Jim is the "father" who can give love, even when the son, Huck, is undeserving and ungrateful. The role of Jim finds its clearest definition and confirmation in Chapter XXXI when Huck thinks back upon the relationship, but it has a subsidiary confirmation in the fact that Jim on the raft is the father deprived of his blood children (whom he intends to buy once he has his own freedom) who now needs to find a "son" to spend his love on.

To sum up: Though on the negative side the novel recounts the discovery of the "lies" in society and even in the "conscience," it recounts, on the positive side, the discovery of a redemptive vision for *both society and the individual*. It is a vision of freedom to be achieved by fidelity to experience, humility, love, charity, and pity for suffering, even for the suffering of those who, like the King and the Duke, are justly punished. This is not to say that such a vision is explicitly stated. It is implied, bit by bit, as Huck drifts down the river; it is, we might say, the great lesson inculcated by the symbolic river—the lesson that men can never learn on shore.

But what is the relation between this vision and the world of reality on shore?

In the last section of the novel, Huck does come back to shore, and the crucial nature of the return is signaled by the question that Mrs. Phelps asks him when he tells his lie about the blowing up of a cylinder head on the steamboat that never existed:

> "Good gracious! anybody hurt?"
> "No'm. Killed a nigger."

So with his answer Huck has fallen back into society and society's view that a "nigger" is not human, is not "anybody"—this in the very moment when he has come ashore to rescue Jim.

This moment signals, too, the issue that has provoked the most searching critical debate about the novel. According to one side of the debate, the last section undercuts all the meaning developed in the main body of the novel, and the working out of the end is, as Hemingway puts it, "just cheating."

Here we see the repetition of the old situation in which Huck had been reared, the "good" people, now Silas Phelps and Aunt Sally, holding Jim for a reward; but this fact, which earlier, on the raft, would have been recognized as one of the "lies" of society, is now quite casually accepted. Even the rescuing of Jim is presented to the reader not in terms of Huck's values as earned on the river—even though he is still the narrator—but in terms of Tom's, as a comic game. Huck's role now is simply to underscore the comic point of this game, by giving the same realistic criticisms of Tom's romantic fancies that we have known from long back.

These "land-changes" that the novel undergoes imply other, more important ones. Huck is no longer the central character, the focus of action and meaning, but now merely the narrator; and indeed he has regressed to the stage of limited awareness exhibited in *Tom Sawyer*. Associated with this regression is a change in the role of Jim: Huck no longer recognizes him as the surrogate father (whose love had been the crucial factor in his own redemptive awakening), and now simply regards him as a thing (a chattel slave is, legally, a "thing"); and so the reader is presumed to accept him as that, a counter to be manipulated in the plot and a minstrel show comic.

All of the changes that we have listen are associated with a basic change of tone. We are back in the world of *Tom Sawyer*, with a condescending and amused interest in the pranks and fancies of boyhood; and even the rescue of Jim becomes merely a lark, a charade, not to be taken seriously, for at the end we learn that Jim was free all the time, and presumably we are to accept as a charming stunt the fact that Tom has withheld this information in order to have his "adventure."

The third section simply does not hang together, and our first impulse is to ask what brought Twain to this pass. Clearly, during the process of writing the book, he was feeling his way into it, "discovering" it, and when he got to the end of the second section, he did not know where to go. Henry Nash Smith, in "Sound Heart and a Deformed Conscience" (a chapter in his *Mark Twain: the Development of a Writer*), holds that Twain finally took refuge in the tradition of backwoods humor. It is true that the novel has been, from the start, a "hybrid"—"a comic story in which the protagonists have acquired something like a tragic depth"—and so there was a certain logic in choosing the comic resolution, which would, by returning to the tone of the beginning, a structural symmetry and which would solve the main plot problem by getting Jim legally freed. In one sense, the trouble was that Twain, in the river journey, had wrought better than he knew and differently from his original intention, and the "tragic depths" he had opened up were not now to be easily papered over. Twain was, apparently, aware that he hadn't been quite able to paper things over, and so at the end does try to fuse the serious elements of the novel with the comic. First, he gives a flicker of the old role of Jim in having him stay with the wounded Tom, in that act reconverting him, from "thing" to man and echoing Jim's old role in relation to Huck. Second, Twain tacks on the last few sentences—to which we must return.

From the foregoing account, it would seem that the last section is, indeed, "cheating." But, on the other side of the debate, we find, for example, the critic Lionel Trilling and the poet T.S. Eliot. Trilling follows much the same line of thought as Smith in commenting on the "formal aptness" that returns us at the end to the world of Tom Sawyer, but finds this grounding of the arch much more satisfying than does Smith, seeming to feel that the problem of the "tragic depths" is thus exorcised. T.S. Eliot goes further, and in addition to recognizing a formal aptness in that the "mood of the end should bring us back to that of the beginning," argues that since the river, with its symbolic function of a life force, has "no beginning and no end," it is "impossible for Huck as for the River to have a beginning or end—a *career*." The novel, that is, can have no form more significant than the mere closure in tonal repetition. If this is not the right end, what, Eliot asks, "would have been right?" And he adds that no book ever written "ends more certainly with the right words"—the statement of Huck that he can't stand to be adopted and "sivilized" as Aunt Sally now threatens to do: "I been there before." He is about ready to cut out for the "territory."

Let us, however, explore what might be involved in a "right" ending for the novel. Clearly, such an ending would have to take into account the main impulse of meaning through the second section; it would, in other words, have to accommodate the new Huck. This does not imply that the story should have a happy ending—i.e., Huck in a society embodying the values of the vision on the river. Such an ideal society never existed, nor is ever likely to exist; as Bertrand Russell has remarked, the essence of an ideal is that it is *not* real. But there are different degrees in which a society may vary from the ideal; there are more acceptable and less acceptable compromises, and the new vision gained by Huck would certainly preclude the easy acceptance of the old values exemplified on the Phelps plantation and by the whole action of the third section. The compromise here simply isn't good enough. We want *both* the "formal satisfaction" of returning the arch of narrative to the firm grounding in the original world of Tom Sawyer (that is, in the "real" world) and a "thematic satisfaction."

Here we must emphasize that the novel is not, ultimately, about a literal Huck (though he is literal enough, God knows) and the possibility of a final perfection in the literal world. Imagine, for example, an ending in which land-society, like that on the raft, would become a utopia, with all tensions resolved between man and man, man and society, and man and nature. Such an ending would be totally irrelevant to the novel we now have. What the present novel is about is, rather, the eternal dialectic between the real and the ideal. It is, more specifically, about the never-ending effort in life to define the values of self-perfection in freedom. But if the distinction made earlier between "conscience" and "consciousness" be followed to its logical conclusion, the freedom would be one in which man, even in repudiating the "lies" of society, would not deny the necessity of the human community and would assume that the "dream" of such a "freedom" would somehow mitigate the "slavery" of the real world.

Or should the novel be taken to deny the necessity of community? Does it suggest that the human community is not only beyond redemption in the ideal, but beyond hope in the slow, grinding amelioration perhaps possible in the real process of history, and that, therefore, the only integrity to be found is in the absolute antinomianism of "flight"—literal or symbolic—to the "territory"? But even if Huck must take flight from society, is the flight negative or positive in its motivation? Does Huck—or will Huck—flee merely in protest against the real world, or in the expectation that in the "territory" he will find the ideal community? The original flight from Pap and Miss Watson was, of course, negative—simply "flight from." What about the possibility now envisaged in the end? Even if one professes to be uncertain about Huck's expectations, there can be no uncertainty about Twain's. He knew all too well what Huck, however far West he went, would find—a land soon to be swept by buffalo-skinners, railroad builders, blue-coated cavalry, Robber Barons, cold deck artists, miners, whores, schoolteachers, cowhands, bankers, sheep raisers, "bar-critters," and a million blood brothers of Old Pap and a million blood sisters of Miss Watson. Or, to treat the flight West as symbolic rather than literal, Twain knew that there is no escaping the real world—not even by dreaming of Hannibal or the Mississippi in moonlight, viewed from the texas deck.

Considering all this, we might take Huck as the embodiment of the incorrigible idealism of man's nature, pathetic in its hopeful self-deception and admirable in its eternal gallantry, forever young, a kind of Peter Pan in patched britches with a corncob pipe stuck in the side of his mouth, with a penchant for philosophical speculation, a streak of poetry in his nature, and with no capacity for growing up.

But thus far we have been scanting one very important element that bears on interpretation—the function of Jim. His reduction, in the third section, from the role of father seems to be more than what we have been taking it to be—merely one of the sad aspects of the land-world. To go back, we remember that he had assumed that role after the symbolic patricide performed by Huck, and that the role was central to the development of Huck on the journey downriver. But once he and Huck are ashore, the relationship ends; Huck loses the symbolic father. But—and we must emphasize this fact—he also loses the literal father, for now Jim tells him that Old Pap is, literally, dead. So, to translate, Huck is "grown up." He has entered the world, he must face life without a father, symbolic or literal, the "good" father of the dream on the river or the "bad" father of the reality on shore.

In this perspective of meaning *Huckleberry Finn* is, in addition to whatever else it may be, a story of growing up, of initiation—very similar, for instance, to Hawthorne's "My Kinsman, Major Molineux" and Katherine Anne Porter's "Old Mortality." Jim's report of the death of Pap clinches the fact that Huck must now go it alone and, in doing so, face the grim necessity of re-living and re-learning, over and over, all the old lessons. The world has not changed, there will be no utopia, after all. Perhaps, however, Huck has changed enough to deal, in the end, with the world—and with himself. Or has he changed enough? If he lights out for the territory will that mean that he has grown up? Or that he has not? Is the deep meaning of the famous last sentence so clear, after all? It often seems clear—but—

And here we may recall that the two great stories by Hawthorne and Katherine Anne Porter are open-ended—are stories of the dialectic of life.

There are, indeed, incoherences in *Huckleberry Finn*. But the book survives everything. It survives not merely because it is a seminal invention of a language for American fiction, nor because Huck's search for a freedom of "consciousness" dramatizes the new philosophical spirit which was to find formulation with William James; nor because it is a veracious and compelling picture of life in a time and place, or because Huck is vividly alive as of that time and place; nor because, in the shadow of the Civil War and the bitter aftermath, it embodies a deep skepticism about the millennial dream of America, or because it hymns youthful hope and gallantry in the face of the old desperate odds of the world. All these things, and more, are there, but the book survives ultimately because all is absorbed into a powerful, mythic image.

That mythic image, like all great myths, is full of internal tensions and paradoxes, and it involves various dimensions—the relation of the real and the ideal, the nature of maturity, the fate, of the lone individual in society. In its fullness, the myth is not absorbed formally into the novel. It bursts out of the novel, stands behind the novel, overshadows the novel, undercuts the novel. Perhaps what coherence we can expect is not to be sought in the novel itself, in formal structure, plot, theme, and so on. Perhaps it resides in the attitude of the author who, as novelist facing the myth he has evoked, finally throws up his hands and takes refuge; cynically if you will, in the tradition of backwoods humor, repudiating all sophisticated demands and norms. He throws up his hands, however, not merely because he cannot solve a novelistic problem (which is true?), but because the nature of the "truth" in the myth cannot be confronted except by, irony—perhaps an irony bordering upon desperation—an irony that finds a desperately appropriate expression in the refuge in a reductive, primitive form that makes a kind of virtue of the inability to control the great, dark, and towering genii long since and unwittingly released from the bottle.

And so we may find in the ending of *Huckleberry Finn* a strange parallel to Twain's manner on the lecture platform, as described by an early reviewer. According to that report, he would gaze out of his "immovable" face, over "the convulsed faces of his audience, as much as to say, 'Why are you laughing?'" Now, at the end of *Huckleberry Finn*, having released the dark genii from the bottle, he turns his "immovable" face on us, his audience, and pretends there is no genii towering above us and that he has simply been getting on with his avowed business of being the "funny man."

But with this very act, he has taken another step toward the dire time when he will "never be quite sane at night."

In *The Prince and the Pauper*, a children's book laid in Tudor England, Mark Twain had, in 1881, taken his first excursion into historical fiction. This work, which interrupted the composition of *Huckleberry Finn*, was nothing more than a piece of sentimental junk cynically devised to captivate his own children, clergymen of literary inclinations, nervous parents, and genteel reviewers, but it broke ground for *A Connecticut Yankee*. That work, however, was on the direct line of Mark Twain's inspiration; it was connected with the grinding issues of his nature, and it drew deeply on earlier work. Laid in the sixth century, in Arthurian England, it put the new American mind in contrast with feudal Europe, the remains of which the "Innocents" of the *Quaker City*, and their chronicler, had had to face on their tour. But *A Connecticut Yankee* also harks back to the contrast between the "feudal" South and the "modern" North that looms so large in *Life on the Mississippi*; it embodies not only the spirit of social criticism found in *Huckleberry Finn*, but something of Huck's pragmatic mind that always wanted to start things "fresh"; and in a paradoxical way, after it celebrates the new Yankee order of industry, big business, and finance capitalism, it also returns to the Edenic vision of Hannibal and the river found in *Tom Sawyer* and *Huckleberry Finn*.

Most deeply, however, *A Connecticut Yankee* draws on the social and personal contexts of the moment in which it was composed. At this time Mark Twain was totally bemused by one James W. Paige, the inventor of a typesetting machine which Twain was trying to organize a company to manufacture, and by which he dreamed of becoming a financial titan. Behind Hank Morgan the Yankee stands Paige. And, we may add, stands Twain himself, for if Hank—a superintendent in the Colt Arms Company—is an inventor, he claims that he can invent, contrive, create anything; he quickly becomes the "Boss," a titan of business such as Twain dreamed of becoming.

The medieval values that Hank confronts were not confined to Arthurian Britain. For one thing, there was also present-day England, for whatever remnants had remained of an Anglophilia once cherished by Twain were now totally demolished by Matthew Arnold, who, after a visit to America, had declared, in "Civilization in the United States," that the idea of "distinction" in this country could not survive the "glorification of 'the average man' and the addiction to the 'funny man.'" In his outraged patriotism and outraged *amour propre*, Twain, a "funny man," tended to merge the England of Arthur with that of Victoria.

In addition, the Romantic movement had discovered—or created—the Middle Ages, and made them current in nineteenth-century thought and art. Tennyson's *Idylls of the King* ranked in the esteem of the pious only a little lower than the New Testament, and James Russell Lowell's "The Vision of Sir Launfall" was a close contender for the popularity prize with the Book of Common Prayer. The poetry of William Morris and the painting of the Pre-Raphaelites, with Ruskin's Gothic aestheticism and the related social theories that pitted medieval spirituality and happy craftsmanship against the age of the machine, had great vogue in the United States, a vogue that found its finest bloom in Henry Adams and Charles Eliot Norton, who wistfully pointed out to his students at Harvard that there were in America no French cathedrals.

This cult of medievalism had a strongly marked class element; usually it was cultivated by persons of aristocratic background or pretensions, often with an overlay of sentimental Catholicism. It was also associated with wealth, but with inherited wealth as contrasted with that, usually greater, of the new kind of capitalist; for inherited wealth, untainted by immediate contact with the crude world of business, was "genteel." It was only natural, then, that a poem like Sidney Lanier's "Symphony" and the early novels attacking business should use the aristocratic feudal virtues as the thongs with which to scourge the business man. So when Hank guns down Malory's knights in armor with his six-shooters, he is also gunning down Tennyson, Ruskin, Lowell, Lanier, et al. *A Connecticut Yankee* is, in fact, the first fictional glorification of the business man.

But Hank is arrayed not only against Sir Sagramour le Desirious and Alfred Lord Tennyson and their ilk, but also against the spectral legions of Lee, abetted by the ghost of Sir Walter Scott. It was highly appropriate that Twain should have given a first public reading of *A Connecticut Yankee* (an early version) to an audience in which sat General William Tecumseh Sherman, for if anybody was equipped to understand Hank's kind of warfare, it was the gentleman who, as first president of the Louisiana State University, had remarked to a Southern friend that "In all history no nation of mere agriculturalists had ever made successful war against a nation of mechanics," and who, a little later, was to lift the last gauzy film of chivalric nonsense to expose the stark nakedness of war.

If the anachronistically slaveholding society of Britain is an image of the Old South and if Hank's military masterpiece, the Battle of the Sand Belt, in which, after the explosion of Hank's mines, the air is filled with the ghastly drizzle of the atomized remains of men and horses, is an image of the Civil War (the first "modern" war), then Hank's program for Britain is a fable of the Reconstruction of the South and the pacification of that undeveloped country. Furthermore, in being a fable of that colonial project, this is also a fable of colonialism in general and of the great modern period of colonialism in particular, which was now well under way from the Ganges to the Congo; thus to Hank, Britain is simply something to develop in economic terms—with, of course, as a paternalistic benefit to the natives, the by-product of a rational modern society. In this context *A Connecticut Yankee* is to be set alongside Conrad's *Nostromo* and *The Heart of Darkness* and the works of Kipling.

There is, however, another and more inclusive context in which to regard it. More and more in our century we have seen a special variety of millennialism—the variety in which bliss (in the form of a "rational" society) is distributed at gunpoint or inculcated in concentration camps. So in this context, *A Connecticut Yankee* is to be set alongside historical accounts of

Fascist Italy, Nazi Germany, or Communist Russia. This novel was prophetic.

The germ of *A Connecticut Yankee* was, however, much more simple than may have just been suggested. An entry from 1884 in Mark Twain's notebook read:

> Dream of being a knight errant in armor in the middle ages. Have the notions and habits of thought of the present day mixed with the necessities of that. No pockets in the armor. No way to manage certain requirements of nature. Can't scratch. Cold in the head—can't blow—can't get a handkerchief, can't use iron sleeve. Iron gets red hot in the sun—leaks in the rain, gets white with frost and freezes me solid in winter. Suffer from lice and fleas. Make disagreeable clatter when I enter church. Can't dress or undress myself. Always getting struck by lightning. Fall down, can't get up. See Morte d'Arthur.

What Twain began with was burlesque, merely the torpedoing of high falutin' pretensions. But within a year after the first entry, there is a note for a battle scene "between a modern army with gatling guns (automatic) 600 shots a minute ... torpedos, balloons, 100-ton cannon, iron-clad fleet & Prince de Joinville's Middle Age Crusaders?" Thus we have what we may take as the poles of Mark Twain's inspiration for the book, on the one hand the satirical burlesque and on the other the sadistic and massive violence motivated by a mysterious hatred of the past.

The body of the work has to do with Hank's operations from the moment when he decides that he is "just another Robinson Crusoe," and has to "invent, contrive, create, reorganize things." The narrative proceeds in a two-edged fashion: there is the satirical exposure of the inhuman and stultifying life in Arthur's kingdom, with the mission for modernization and humanitarian improvement, but there is also the development of Hank's scheme for his economic and political aggrandizement, his way of becoming the "Boss." By and large, it seems that the humanitarian and selfish interests coincide; what is good for Hank is good for the people of Britain, and this would imply a simple fable of progress; with the reading that technology in a laissez faire order automatically confers the good life on all. There is no hint, certainly, that Twain is writing in a period of titanic struggle between labor and capital, a struggle consequent upon the advent of big technology. In the new order in Britain there are no labor problems. The boys whom Hank had secretly recruited and instructed in technology are completely

loyal to him, and as his Janissaries, will fight for him in the great
Armageddon to come, enraptured by their own godlike proficiency; if they
represent "labor" they have no parallel in the nineteenth-century America of
the Homestead strike and the Haymarket riot.

In the fable there are, indeed, many lags and incoherences that, upon
the slightest analysis, are visible. Twain had not systematically thought
through the issues in his world, or his own attitudes, and he did not grasp, or
did not wish to grasp, the implications of his own tale. During the course of
composition he had written—in a letter of either cyclical deception or
confusion of mind—that he had no intention of degrading any of the "great
and beautiful characters" found in Malory, and that Arthur would keep his
"sweetness and purity," but this scarcely square's with the finished product.
Again, though the narrative, once finished, shows no hint of the tensions in
the world of the new capitalism, Twain most inconsistently could, when the
socialist Dan Beard illustrated the first edition and made the fable apply to
contemporary persons and abuses,[3] enthusiastically exclaim, "What luck it
was to find you!" And though Twain, now reading Carlyle's *French Revolution*,
could proclaim himself a "Sans-culotte," he was at the same time dreaming
of his elevation to the angelic choir of Vanderbilt, Rockefeller, and other
Bosses. And most telling of all, though *A Connecticut Yankee* was rapturously
received, even by such discerning readers as Howells, as a great document of
the democratic faith, and though Twain himself, sometimes at least, took it
as such, Hank is not ethically superior to Jay Gould or Diamond Jim Brady
in many of his manipulations. What Hank turns out to be is merely the
"Boss," more of a boss than even Boss Tweed ever was, something like a cross
between a Carnegie and a commissar.

There are various other logical confusions in *A Connecticut Yankee*, but
one is fundamental. If the original idea of the book had been a celebration of
nineteenth-century technology, something happened to that happy
inspiration, and in the end progress appears a delusion, Hank's
modernization winds up in a bloody farce, and Hank himself can think of the
people whom he had undertaken to liberate as merely "human muck." In the
end Hank hates life, and all he can do is to look nostalgically back on the
beauty of pre-modern Britain as what he calls his "Lost World," and on the
love of his lost wife Sandy, just as Twain could look back on his vision of
boyhood Hannibal.

What emerges here is not only the deep tension in Twain, but that in
the period. There was in America a tension concerning the Edenic vision, a
tension between two aspects of it: some men had hoped to achieve it in a
natural world—as had Jefferson—but some had hoped to achieve it by the

conquest of nature. The tension, in its objective terms, was, then, between an agrarian and an industrial order; but in subjective terms the tension existed, too, and in a deep, complex way it conditioned the American sensibility from *Snow-Bound* through *A Connecticut Yankee* and Henry Adams' idea of the Virgin versus the dynamo, on through the poetry of T.S. Eliot and John Crowe Ransom, to the debased Rousseauism of a hippie commune.

The notion of the Edenic vision reminds us of *Huckleberry Finn*, for thematically *A Connecticut Yankee* is a development of that work—and the parallel in the very names of the heroes suggests the relation: *Huck/Hank*. Huck journeys through the barbarous South, Hank through barbarous Britain, both mythic journeys into a land where mania and brutality are masked by pretensions of chivalry, humanity, and Christianity. After each encounter with a shocking fact of the land-world, Huck returns to his private Eden on the river and in the end contemplates flight to an Edenic West. In other words, Huck belongs to the world of Jefferson's dream, in which man finds harmony with man in an overarching harmony of man in nature. Hank, however, is of sterner stuff. When he encounters a shocking fact he undertakes to change it—to conquer both nature and human nature in order to create rational society.

Both Huck and Hank come to a desperate collision with reality, Huck on the Phelps farm and Hank at the Battle of the Sand Belt; but the end of the project of regeneration through technology and know-how is more blankly horrible than life on the Phelps farm, with not even a façade of humor but only the manic glee of the victors exalted by their expertise of destruction. The "human muck" has refused the rule of reason—and the prophet of reason has done little more than provide magnificently lethal instruments by which man may vent his mania.

When the book was finished, Twain wrote to Howells: "Well, my book is written—let it go. But if it were only to write over again there wouldn't be so many things left out. They burn in me.... They would require a library—and a pen warmed up in hell." But the pen had already been warmed enough to declare that dark forces were afoot in history and in the human soul to betray all aspiration, and with this we find, at the visceral level of fable, the same view of history later to be learnedly, abstractly, and pitilessly proclaimed by Henry Adams and dramatized in (to date) two world wars.

As for Mark Twain himself, the shadows, were soon to gather. The metaphysical despair of *A Connecticut Yankee* was shortly to be compounded by personal disasters, bankruptcy (from which, with an irony worthy of his own invention, he was to be rescued by one H.H. Rogers, of the Standard Oil trust, one of the more ruthless of the Barons), the death of Livy (by which was added to grief his guilt of having robbed her of the Christian faith), the deaths of the adored Suzy and of a second daughter, Jean, the deaths of friends, and what seems to have been a struggle against madness. His fame continued; he walked up and down Fifth Avenue in his eye-catching white suit that advertised his identity; he consorted with the rich and great, and once Andrew Carnegie even addressed him in a letter as "Saint Mark"; be played billiards to the point of exhaustion; he received an honorary degree from Oxford, which mollified the Anglophobia that had been enshrined in *A Connecticut Yankee*; he railed at the degeneracy of the age and the abuses of wealth and power and at American imperialism in the Philippines and at Belgian imperialism; in the Congo, and greeted Gorky, on his visit to the United States, as an apostle of Russian democracy. But nothing really helped much, as he was never, as he put it, "quite sane at night"

Nothing helped much, that is, except writing. He kept on wielding his pen "warmed up in hell," with flashes of genius, as in *Pudd'nhead Wilson* (1894), *The Man that Corrupted Hadleyburg* (1899), and *The Mysterious Stranger* (published posthumously), in work that obsessively rehearsed, in various disguises, his own story and his own anguish. He took refuge in a massive autobiography, in which chronology is replaced by association as a principle of continuity and as a method for mastering his own experience and plumbing his own nature; he was trying to achieve truth by thus recording a voice to speak from the grave.

But perhaps there was no truth to be achieved. Perhaps there was only illusion, after all, as he put it in the unfinished story called "The Great Dark" and in a letter to Sue Crane, his sister-in-law:

> I dreamed that I was born and grew up and was a pilot on the Mississippi and a miner and a journalist in Nevada and a pilgrim in the *Quaker City*, and had a wife and children and went to live in a villa at Florence—and this dream goes on and on and sometimes seems so real that I almost believe it is real. But there is no way to tell, for if one applied tests they would be part of the dream, too, and so would simply aid the deceit. I wish I knew whether it is a dream or real.

NOTES

1. The English critic V.S. Pritchett, in an essay in the *New Statesman and Nation* (August 2, 1941), says that "Huck never imagines anything except fear," and contrasts him

with Tom, who might grow up "to build a civilization" because "he is imaginative." Huck, he continues, "is lowdown plain ornery, because of the way he was brought up with 'Pap.'" That is, he is a natural "bum." It would seem that the critic is, simply, wrong. If his view is correct, what of the series of moral criticisms that Huck brings to bear on society?

2. The treatment of Colonel Sherburn, and especially of the Grangerfords, illustrates how Twain, the artist, lifts himself above the specific views and prejudices of Clemens, the man. Clemens, shall we say, abhors Sir Walter Scott and the Scott-infected South with its chivalric pretensions, but Twain, in spite of the brutal gunning of Boggs, recognizes the basic courage in Sherburn when he stands off the mob. As for the Grangerfords, Huck is enchanted by them, even by "The Battle of Prague" played on the tinny little piano by the Grangerford girls. Here it must be remembered that Huck is the index of response for the novel, and even if a little fun is being had at Huck's innocence, we cannot basically discount his response. The Grarangerfords are indeed full of absurdity—even bloody absurdity— but they play out their drama with generosity, warmth, courage, and flair. They are, to say the least, outside the "genteel tradition" from which Huck—and Twain, the artist—are fleeing. Another aspect of the Grangerford interlude, the love passage between the Shepherdson Romeo and the Grangerford Juliet, is very important: a little later we have the absurdity of the balcony scene of Shakespeare's play presented by the King and the Duke, and this counterpoints the absurd but real—and in the end, tragic—parody of Shakespeare already given. The relation between the absurd and the serious is very complex: irony within irony. By the way, it is of some significance that Huck is drawn into the Shepherdson–Grangerford love story, and this counterpoints, with differences. the way he is drawn into the romantic charades of Tom Sawyer.

3. For instance, one illustration shows two examples of the standard allegorical female figure of justice blindfolded, one for the sixth century and one for the nineteenth, the former holding up scales in which a hammer tagged "Labor" is outweighed by a crown tagged "Title," and the latter with a scales in which a hammer is outweighed by a fat bag tagged" $1,000,000.

JAMES M. COX

Life on the Mississippi *Revisited*

I should first explain my title. It has been more than fifteen years since I wrote about *Life on the Mississippi*.[1] I then sought the formal connections in the book that would betray a coherence beneath the drifting and disparate current of narration. Failing to find enough of them to satisfy my craving for literary unity, I tended to conclude that the book, though remarkable in parts, could not really stand by itself. And so, in dealing with it in my book on Mark Twain, I treated "Old Times on the Mississippi" as a separate entity precisely because it offered sufficient focus and form to represent a complete moment in Mark Twain's progression toward and away from what I, along with most other critics, determined was his masterpiece: *Adventures of Huckleberry Finn*. My determination determined me to use Mark Twain's long account of his return to the river in *Life on the Mississippi* as little more than a preview of Huck Finn's adventures. This time I want to see the book as a book in the life of Mark Twain.

Given its title, it ought to be a book about life on the Mississippi River, yet anyone who has read it realizes that, though it is about the great river running out of and through the heart of the nation, it is just as much a book about the life of Mark Twain. No, that is not quite right. It is rather a book in which the life of Samuel Clemens is both converted and enlarged into the myth of Mark Twain. But there is more. We cannot read this book—or any

From *The Mythologizing of Mark Twain.*, Sara de Saussure Davis and Philip D. Beidler, ed. © 1984 The University of Alabama Press.

of Mark Twain's books—without helplessly participating in and even contributing to this myth, for all his works, rather than being ends in themselves, seem means toward the end of mythologizing their author. Thus I shall begin by suggesting how both we and he have collaborated in creating the myth.

No one would deny that we have mythologized Mark Twain as a native literary genius—and that "we" is not merely the popular audience but the academic or literary audience as well. The very fact that two audiences always come to mind in our thinking about Mark Twain indicates how profoundly Mark Twain (as the name implies) divided and still divides his audience. He was, after, all, a popular writer and at the same time a great writer. He was recognized as such in his own time and remains so recognized to this day. And as such he represents a division—almost a contradiction—for there is more than a little doubt on both sides of the equation whether the two identities are not mutually exclusive. We on the academic side are even more prone to see the mutual exclusiveness, it seems to me, than those who love Mark Twain as a popular writer.

This initial or "master" division is but an index to a host of divisions Mark Twain has both represented and excited. There are the embattled arguments about whether he is Western or Eastern, vernacular or genteel in identity; whether he is a journalist or an artist, a writer or performer, a confident voice of the people or an embittered misanthrope; and finally whether he is an author or a businessman. Far from being of recent vintage, these arguments, or some of them, took shape in Mark Twain's lifetime; and in the work of Paine, Mencken, Brooks, DeVoto, and Henry Smith they were developed, intensified, and refined. Their persistence until this day reminds us of how deep the divisions have always been.

Equal to the divisions, and even controlling them, is a unity of a very special kind. The reason the persistent divisions have attracted adherents is that Mark Twain always seems to occupy both sides of each division. If there was some underground rift, there was nonetheless the single public personality operating under an exposed pen name—a personality which seemed in his own time, and seems in our time too, to be larger than his writing, or at least seemed and seems not confinable to what we are pleased to call literature. It was just this larger figure that spent itself in lecturing, investing, philosophizing, advertising, and tycooning in the expansive age of finance capitalism in which he had his being. We see, and Mark Twain's contemporary audience saw, the divisions because Mark Twain in both his lecturing and writing railed at his own involvement in such "extra-literary" activity. At the same time, there was a single Mark Twain who never even tried to conceal Samuel Clemens (though Samuel Clemens on occasion recklessly tried to conceal Mark Twain) because the pen name, even as it exposed the divisions, nonetheless contained them. The containment was managed through a humor and a clarity that perpetually disarmed the anger and the contradictory complexity the divisions somehow generated.

To face Samuel Clemens' pen name is not only to see the divisions Mark Twain's audience saw but also to see the figure of the author who projected them. Much as we might wish to see this author in the businessman's or lecturer's role of betraying his "literary" career, making the writer in him subordinate to the businessman or speculator or inventor also in him, there remains a Mark Twain who emerges before us as nothing but writing. To read his notebooks is to see him turning everything at hand into writing. If he is traveling, it is never to take a vacation to get away from his "profession" but to turn every trip and every observation into a book.

Of course it is possible to say that the books aren't literature so much as padded filler to meet the subscription contracts he had entered into, as if writing were a business instead of a profession. There is no gainsaying such an evaluation; not even Mark Twain could gainsay it as he struggled to complete the books on time (and "completion" for him often meant filling out or up a number of pages even as he angrily knew his inspiration tank was dry) for the best market moment. Yet if he could not gainsay the evaluation, he nonetheless had a deeper knowledge that something about the whole realm of what had come to be called literature in the nineteenth century was confining, even suffocating, for the figure he all but helplessly knew himself to be. The literary world was a world that, in its refinements, became filled with grown-up one-horse men, whereas the world toward which he journeyed was to be occupied by boys he would imagine in a mythic form much larger than the race of men that descended from them. Moreover, this author of boyhood knew that he would always be freer and larger than the books he wrote. In other words, the books, rather than effacing him and thereby becoming representations of his authorship, or dramatizing him and thereby reducing him to a character, were made to *enlarge* him precisely because they could not contain him.

By way of touching upon this enlargement, I want to stress just how the East–West division, though it has constituted a continual critical debate about Mark Twain's identity, is actually a very reduced image of the geographical space Mark Twain mythically occupied. Such an axis—accentuated by the criticism and contention of Brooks and DeVoto—fails to take into account the North–South axis that Mark Twain also occupied. For Mark Twain touches all four points of this country's compass. Small wonder that he would finally wish to girdle the world in *Following the Equator* even as he was beginning to imagine fantasies of polar seas.

If we look at Hannibal, Missouri, where Samuel Clemens grew up, we see that it is on the Mississippi River, which was then flowing south into slavery. At the same time, it is just far enough north to be where West was South and East was North—since the Missouri Compromise of 1820 had polarized the country on a North–South axis along the line that surveyors Mason and Dixon had driven west in the eighteenth century. That political axis came to dominate the identity of his home state and village. And if the drift of the river of his youth was directly north to south, dividing east from west (as the Appalachian Mountains, running south-southwest, had previously divided them), the stretch of river he piloted was from St. Louis due south (albeit meanderingly so) to New Orleans.

If we sketched his life out of this historical and geographical configuration, we could say that Samuel Clemens fled (or deserted or escaped) the political North–South axis, once it completely volatilized, to go West where he would find a pseudonym with its origins inescapably in the river world he had left behind him, and then came into an East (which had been North) as a Westerner, there to begin reconstructing, in the age of Reconstruction, a South of Boyhood which had never existed but which he made the most real dream in our literature. That is why the language of *Huckleberry Finn*, predicated on the profound Northern sentiment of freedom, is nonetheless Southern much more than Western in its identity—which is why, by virtue of its one fatal word, it is under threat of ban to this day.

Seeing ourselves at the edge of the ban, we might be able to understand that the Concord Public Library was trying to tell us something when it banned the book upon its appearance. How wonderful that it was the Concord Library that did it, confirming just how literary the home of Emerson, Thoreau, and Hawthorne had become by 1885. I find it extremely comforting when touring Concord to remember the fact. It would never do to assault the guides with the knowledge; it is so much better to keep it in genteel restraint, at the threshold of consciousness, as one gapes at the impressive Emerson collection in the library.

But I digress. Back to the Mark Twain who at once designates the four points on the American compass and spans the time in which those four points had been confused by politics, morality, law, and finally war. If the war was the violence which clarified the morality and politics by rewriting the law, it was also the moment when Samuel Clemens found the pseudonym by means of which he reentered the Union, to which he had been a traitor, and evaded the Confederacy from which he had deserted.

He was indeed a Western outlaw in the deepest sense of the term. Of all our major writers, only Ezra Pound is a match for him in this regard. Unlike Pound, who was completing his long revolutionary poetic life when he became a traitor, Mark Twain's treason preceded his long career in prose, and, when the Civil War ended, he needed all of the humor afforded by his pseudonymous identity to disarm the moral sense of the Northeastern society he determined to enter—a society ready to judge, and even to sentence, the historic identity of Samuel Clemens.

When, after fifteen years of humorously reconstructing himself in New England society, he returned to the Mississippi in 1882 for the express purpose of writing the travel book that was to be *Life on the Mississippi*, he was at last returning in the person of Mark Twain to the river where the very term of his pen name had its origin. By the time of his return, he had made what he rightly called his *nom de guerre*, if not a household word, at least sufficiently famous that he met a steamboat of that name on the river of his youth.

He had, as we know, already returned to the river in his writing, having written seven sketches which William Dean Howells had published in the *Atlantic* (from January to August 1875) under the title "Old Times on the Mississippi," and when he came to the actual business of writing his travel book, he inserted those sketches wholesale. They constitute chapters 4 to 18 of *Life on the Mississippi* and are often referred to as the "first half" of the book, though they constitute only one-fourth of its contents. These are inevitably the chapters critics cite as the "strong part" of the book, whereas the remaining three-fourths are often dismissed as one more example of Mark Twain's unfortunate hauling and filling and padding for the subscription trade. Rarely are they incorporated into a critical vision of the book's esthetic; they are instead used by biographers to fill out the life of Samuel Clemens.

It is not my purpose in revisiting this book to show the marvelous unity that is perceptible beneath the discontinuous multiplicity of these chapters. When I wrote my book fifteen years ago, I think that was my purpose, and when I could not really see the unity, I found ways of devaluing this portion of the book. I was proceeding chronologically through the work of Mark Twain, and having devoted a chapter to "Old Times on the Mississippi," I merely used *Life on the Mississippi* as a means of beginning a discussion of *Huckleberry Finn*. Unable to reduce this travel book to the closed form literary criticism can comfortably deal with, I tended to see the book as material with which to reinforce a critical construct of Mark Twain's progress toward *Huckleberry Finn*. Lest I fall into the easy indulgence of self-criticism, I should emphasize that Mark Twain pursued exactly the same strategy in using "Old Times on the Mississippi" to build up the very book I am revisiting.

Even so, that earlier writing, "Old Times on the Mississippi," seems to have more so-called unity than the travel portion of the completed book. Being a work of memory rather than a book worked up from travel notes, and being devoted to the more univocal subject of Mark Twain's apprenticeship as a pilot, it has a more continuous narrative line than the discursive chapters that recount the actual return to the river. Yet anyone who truly detaches all seven sketches and looks at them will see that there was much discontinuity in "Old Times," particularly in the last two sketches, in which Mark Twain, departing from the Bixby-Cub vaudeville structure to detail the nature of the pilot's power and independence, thrusts in statistics of racing times and records to accompany a string of anecdotes and historical incidents connected with the great days of steamboating. And anyone who looks at the critical literature on Mark Twain will see that what has been most emphasized about "Old Times" is the humorous vision of Mark Twain learning to be a pilot who could "read" the river.[2] Indeed, the famous passage that invariably is trotted out of that book (as if it might be a "trot" for all future students) is the one in which Mark Twain sees the river as a text the pilot literally has to read in order to see the snags and reefs which, while dimpling the surface and adding beauty to the current, pose the threats and potential disasters that the experienced pilot's eye recognizes on the face of the water.

Such a passage, in addition to standing out as a wonderfully easy landmark for literary readers whose stock in trade is seeing the world in the figure of a text, has the summarizing clarity that is the very trademark of Mark Twain's prose. I certainly don't want to negate it, but it shouldn't be allowed to characterize either the book or the river.

At the same time, if we see why it is such a dominating passage we can by inference begin to see why "Old Times" is equally dominating in the later structure of *Life on the Mississippi*. The passage, in projecting the river as a text, shows the relation of piloting to writing. Similarly, in the career of Mark Twain "Old Times" represented (and here I am seeing it as the *Atlantic* sketches, not as part of *Life on the Mississippi*) that moment when Samuel Clemens, reconstructing his life under his pen name, had, in reaching the river of his youth, reached the place in his life where the name "Mark Twain" is sounded. And of course it is sounded in those sketches—once when Bixby runs the Hat Island Crossing, to the applause of an audience of experienced pilots who, having gathered to watch, have stayed to admire the feat. The call "Mark Twain" is in this instance a crisis call, not a safe-water sign. But Bixby, calm and deadpan, guides the boat through with such ease and grace that one of the onlookers says: "It was done beautiful." The second time the term is sounded, the perennially confident and complacent cub is at the wheel. By way of administering a lesson to Pride, Bixby has arranged for the leadsman to make false calls in safe water, and has also arranged for an audience to watch the fun. Hearing "Mark Twain" in what he has hitherto been confident is a bottomless crossing, the cub loses his confidence and desperately shouts to the engine room, "Oh Ben, if you love me, *back* her! ... back the immortal *soul* out of her," only to be met with a gale of humiliating laughter from the assembled onlookers. Thus, as Samuel Clemens reconstructs his life under his pen name, he sounds the name not once but *twice* (which takes us right back to the divisions with which we began): once as a mark of the crisis so close beneath the deadpan mastery of Bixby's art, and once as a false call arranged by the master to humiliate the cub. And always this sound rings out for an audience's admiration or ridicule.

From these two moments which define the art of the master and the humiliation of the apprentice, who themselves constitute the division contained in the unified humorous reconstruction of the past (written in the waning years of national reconstruction), we can, I think, begin to see the dimensions of the world Samuel Clemens was inventing under the signature of Mark Twain. It was a world where art was a guild of master and apprentice come into the industrial age of steam; it involved both experience and memory (the master artist and pilot, Bixby, had both to know the river and to remember it); and it was art as a performance before an audience—in other words, public art, or at least art performed in public.

The signature of the author, who had once been the humiliated cub and now humorously reconstructs the past, was actually a call—a sound—and thus was a *sounding* in the full meaning of the word. In its original meaning it designated shallow water that could be safe or precarious, depending on whether a steamboat was approaching shallows or leaving them. The art of piloting lay precisely in negotiating depths so slight that the dangerous bottom could all but be perceived on the surface. Moreover, the greatest demands of the art were required in going downstream. In such a situation, the pilot had force behind him in the form of the natural, powerful, treacherous, and wandering drift of a mighty current he had to cross and recross as he pursued the unmarked channel forever changing on each trip he made. The art of piloting, though it all but enslaved the pilot to the current on which he rode, paradoxically conferred upon him a privilege and power that made him independent of all social and political pressures. Majestically isolate in the pilothouse, he looked with lordly freedom upon the beauty and danger of the moving river bearing him upon its current.

The pilot and his art were, as every critic of Mark Twain sooner or later comes to realize, not only the embodiment of Mark Twain's experience on the river; they were metaphors for the figure of Mark Twain the writer.[3] The remembered independence of the pilot was thus an expression of the writer's dream of autonomy and his determination to be free of conventional form. And the pilot's necessarily skeptical eye, surveying the deceptions of current and surface, was but a promise of the very identity of the writer and his pen name. For even in discussing Mark Twain's art we cannot quite tell whether we are discussing "the art of Samuel Clemens. What we know, and all we know, is that there is a difference between them, a difference exposed in the text of every title page. Yet, for the life of us, we can't quite tell what the difference is. Neither Mark Twain nor Samuel Clemens could, I think, quite tell the difference—other than that a division was being signified even as a reconstructed unity was being discovered.

We can perhaps tell this much. The past life of Samuel Clemens was being humorously invented by virtue of, and by vice under, the authority of Mark Twain. The virtue was no doubt the art; the vice was no doubt the lie. And in "Old Times" the reconstruction had reached back across the division of the Civil War (which, if it had once divided the country, now divided the history of the country between the Old Republic and the New Union) to the river where Samuel Clemens could remember his youth even as Mark Twain could at last be sounded. To see so much ought to allow us to see that the signified division between Mark Twain and Samuel Clemens comes to us as a doubt—a doubt as deep, we want to say, as that with which Nathaniel Hawthorne invested his creative enterprise. But I want to say that it was and is as shallow as the depth the sounding "Mark Twain" designates. It is not a deep doubt but is right on the surface where we always see it but never know how to read it precisely because it is so easy to see and is humorously and pleasurably and clearly and easily right in front of us.

So much for the "Old Times" of the *Atlantic* sketches; now for *Life on the Mississippi*. Here the first point to see is that it is not Mark Twain reconstructing the life of Samuel Clemens as his own life but the record of Samuel Clemens returning to the Mississippi in the person of Mark Twain whom he cannot hide. In "Old Times" the *I* of the narrative, effacing both Samuel Clemens and Mark Twain in the comic act of apprenticeship played out by Bixby and the Cub, showed Mark Twain approaching the edge of fiction. It is hardly accidental that, at the time of writing the Atlantic sketches, he had just finished collaborating with Charles Dudley Warner on the satiric novel *The Gilded Age* (the collaboration itself signifying Mark Twain's entry into fiction, as well as his—and Samuel Clemens'—inability to write a novel by himself/themselves). But *The Gilded Age* and "Old Times" put him at the threshold of full-length fiction. As a matter of fact, even before he completed the Atlantic sketches he was at work on *Tom Sawyer*—the book he was to call a hymn written in prose to give it a worldly air.

In the figure of Tom Sawyer, he had indeed reached the poetic origins of youth lying behind the past of both Mark Twain and Samuel Clemens. More important, through the figure of Tom Sawyer, Mark Twain had discovered Huck Finn, whom he would release to begin his own narrative. But Huck's voice, released in the first centennial of the Republic (and surely one of the best things invented in that first centennial), couldn't complete its own story in that first surge. Instead, Mark Twain's inspiration tank ran dry.

This early portion of *Huckleberry Finn*, Mark Twain's raft book, stands in relation to the completed novel much as "Old Times" stands in relation to *Life on the Mississippi*, his steamboat book—and I think it of no little consequence that Mark Twain was actually in the process of completing both books as he returned to the Mississippi.[4] He had already begun the latter, publicly, in "Old Times" (though of course he had given no public inkling in the sketches that this was to be the beginning of a travel book, and there is no evidence that he thought of it at the time as a beginning). The other he had driven to the point where the raft is run over by a steamboat (a hiatus which shows, both precisely and symbolically, the two books running into each other).[5] To begin to see such a possibility is to see that it would take a trip back to the great river itself to drive the books on their parallel courses.

When he actually came to compose *Life on the Mississippi*, Mark Twain set up a casual but nonetheless definite structure, dividing the history of the river into five stages. Here is the way he asserted his structure on the fourth page of the Author's National Edition:

> Let us drop the Mississippi's physical history, and say a word about its historical history—so to speak. We can glance briefly at its slumbrous first epoch in a couple of short chapters; at its second and wider-awake epoch in a couple more; at its flushest and widest-awake epoch in a good many succeeding chapters; and then talk about its comparatively tranquil present epoch in what shall be left of the book.[6]

Using his declaration of structure as a means of finishing off the three-page first stage, the river's physical history, he proceeded to devote the slight remainder of chapter 1 and all of chapter 2 to the historical history, primarily concentrating on the river's great explorers. To the third stage, the wider-awake epoch, he devoted only one chapter, despite his promise of two, and that chapter is primarily made up of the raftsman passage from *Huck Finn*. "Old Times" is converted from the seven sketches into fourteen chapters that make up the flush-times epoch. And the actual travel book, detailing the "tranquil present epoch," comprises chapters 18 to 60. His casual declaration of structure, accentuated by repeated references to writing as speaking ("say a word about," "so to speak," and "talk about"), points up the fact that the first two stages—the physical history and the historical history—take up all of 16 pages of the total 496 in the Author's National Edition. The other three stages, which Mark Twain inversely calls epochs, convert the history of the river into the life of Mark Twain.

But that is only the beginning. The two epochs that precede the travel-book account of the tranquil present epoch, constituted (as they are) of the manuscript episode of Huck Finn and the wholesale importation of "Old Times," show that even as Mark Twain was doubly capitalizing on his past published writing he was also looting his future masterpiece. Nor is that all. If we did not know that the raftsman episode had been taken out of *Huckleberry Finn*, we would never miss it; moreover, it can be inserted wholesale into that book without disturbing the narrative sequence. Of course, arguments can be and have been made as to whether the episode should be left out or put into *Huckleberry Finn*,[7] but the fact that it can be either in or out tells us more about the nature of *Huckleberry Finn* than a host of critical elucidations about its place in or out of the narrative. And beyond that, if we did not know that the chapters constituting "Old Times" were previously published as a unit, I am not at all sure that we would or could so confidently say that these chapters are the exquisite sections of the book. Knowing so much keeps us, in a real sense, subtracting from the structure and art of the book in order to add to the figural myth of Mark Twain. The only comfort I can see in this nice problem is that if we participate in making Mark Twain somehow larger than his books, we are doing just what Mark Twain himself did.

So much for the declared structure and the enlarged Mark Twain. We are still left with the devalued travel book. By way of showing how we might look at the material of the book, I want to quote its opening paragraph. Unlike the famous river-as-text passage, previously alluded to, or the "When-I-was-a-boy" passage opening "Old Times," or the "You-don't-know-about-me" beginning of *Huckleberry Finn*, this passage has never, to my knowledge, been singled out for attention.

> The Mississippi is well worth reading about. It is not a commonplace river, but on the contrary is in all ways remarkable. Considering the Missouri its main branch, it is the longest river in the world—four thousand three hundred miles. It seems safe to say that it is also the crookedest river in the world, since in one part of its journey it uses up one thousand three hundred miles to cover the same ground that the crow could fly over in six hundred and seventy-five. It discharges three times as much water as the St. Lawrence, twenty-five times as much as the Thames. No other river has so vast a drainage basin; it draws its water-supply from twenty-eight states and territories; from Delaware on the Atlantic seaboard, and from all that country between that and Idaho on the Pacific slope—a spread of forty-five degrees of longitude. The Mississippi receives and carries to the Gulf water from fifty-four subordinate rivers that are navigable by steamboats, and from some hundreds that are navigable by flats and keels. The area of its drainage basin is as great as the combined areas of England, Wales, Scotland, Ireland, France, Spain, Portugal, Germany, Austria, Italy, and Turkey; and almost all this wide region is fertile; the Mississippi valley proper, is exceptionally so.

The resonance of the passage—with its array of facts, its grandly marshaled parallelisms, and its imposing quantitative crescendo—obscures what seems a grand joke. For right at the center of this first paragraph, and as a culminating fact about the great river's size, Mark Twain climactically announces that the Mississippi drains Delaware. This "fact," set in the majestic current of an imposing list of seemingly scientific and geographic measurements, is difficult to see precisely because it is in such a *current* of prose. If we take the passage and juxtapose it against the celebrated passage on reading the river, I think we can see how, implicitly, we are challenged to read a text.

That joke in the center of the first paragraph is equivalent to a snag in the river big enough to tear the bottom right out of a steamboat. If we have missed the snag on our first or second or third reading, seeing it instantaneously exposes what has been mere absence of vision as humiliating stupidity, and at the same time converts the feeling of humiliation into an enormous gain of pleasure as we recognize ourselves in the act of becoming master pilots. The sudden glory of our pleasure in this new-found identity shouldn't blind us to the fact that we both have and need the ignorant and complacent cub in us.

But I want to make more of this initial joke in *Life on the Mississippi* in the return visit to the book. It shows that if the Mississippi is a mighty current, so is language. The reason we miss the joke or "stretcher" is that the effect of the parallel clauses extending the size of the Mississippi carries us right by the snag. To see this force of language working is to be at the heart of narrative deception; it is also to see the function of the snag, which is nothing less than Mark Twain's deliberate deviation from a sequence of "truths" to which we have too complacently become adjusted. Those who miss the snag won't be killed, as they might be if they were pilots on the other current. They will just be comfortable jackasses, of which the world of readers is already full. Those who "get it," while they won't be sold, had better remember that they didn't always get it, and so will have a humiliatingly complacent past they have to convert into the pleasure of looking at others miss what they have lately come to see. Then there will be those who always got it—some of whom will of course be lying, whereas others will too much lie in wait, always on the lookout for every lie and every joke. And of course there will be those who insist that it wasn't much of a joke anyway, some of whom never had, and never will have, a sense of humor, and others who will be inwardly miffed that they had to have it shown them. Finally, there will be those adamant few who contend there is no joke. After all, they could say, the passage *means* to say that the Mississippi draws its water from the twenty-eight states and territories *between* Delaware and Idaho.

Read with that determination, "from Delaware on the Atlantic seaboard" is what we might call Mark Twain's redundant stutter in preparing himself to assert the area of the river's drainage basin. Against such resistance, I can't claim with arrogant assurance that this *isn't* Mark Twain's intention; I merely want to retain a skeptical eye on the passage, keeping the possibility that it might be—just *might* be—a joke.[8] It would not be a big joke, since Delaware is after all a small state; and, considering the geographical centrality I have claimed for Mark Twain, there is a rich conclusiveness in seeing him have the Mississippi "suck in" an Eastern Seaboard state. But the more important point is to see all these enumerated responses to the passage, including this last contention, as constituting an expansive humorous consciousness in Mark Twain's audience.

Seen from such a perspective of expansion, the book becomes what it is: an accumulating of every kind of narrative—Mark Twain's past, masquerading as present narrative; his importation of what he calls the emotions of European travelers as they confront the Mississippi; the broadly humorous tall tales the pilots tell him in order not so much to deceive him as to draw him out of the incognito with which he futilely tries to conceal his identity; the bogus letter of a supposedly reformed criminal preying upon the charity of gullible do-gooders wishing to believe lies (the letter, actually written by a Harvard confidence man, dressed out in the form of sentimentally appealing illiteracy); the fake narratives of spiritualists claiming to have conversations with the dead; the self-advertising lies of salesmen hawking oleomargarine and cottonseed oil as manufactured replacements for traditional substances; the intruded yarns of gamblers conning other gamblers; the romantic guide-book legends of Indian maidens (and on and on). Yet all along the way there is penetrating information, exquisite criticism of other books on the Mississippi, pungent observations of the culture of the great valley, acute commentary on the society, literature, and art of both pre– and post–Civil War America.[9] Information and history are so interlaced with tall tales, intruded jokes, and seemingly irrelevant "loitering and gab" that truth and exaggeration scarcely can be told apart. Finally there are the episodes that Mark Twain recounts of his boyhood as he reaches Hannibal— narratives which biographers have all too often taken as the traumatic, true experience of Mark Twain's childhood, although they have about them the aspect of indulgent (as well as invented) guilt fantasies.

A way of seeing it all, in a bit of nubbed down compression, would be to remember that the pilot whom Mark Twain meets on the *Gold Dust* is called Rob Styles (the actual name was Lem Gray, and he was killed in a steamboat explosion while Mark Twain was writing the book). How right a name to be waiting for Mark Twain as he hopelessly tries to hide his own identity! For Mark Twain does indeed *rob styles*, showing us, by implication, our outlaw writer operating as a literary highwayman, ready to raid even his own work to flesh out his book. How much of the King and the Duke he has in him! No wonder he comes back to that name of his in this part of the book, showing that it had first been used by Isaiah Sellers (and here what is presumably the true name is nonetheless perfect), a veritable Methuselah among riverboat pilots.

Samuel Clemens had thoughtlessly yet irreverently parodied the old man's river notes and the lampoon had, according to Mark Twain, silenced the old captain, leaving him to sit up nights to hate the impudent young parodist. And so Mark Twain says that when, on the Pacific Coast, he had set up as a writer, he *confiscated* the ancient captain's pen name. He concludes his account by saying that he has done his best to make the name a "sign and symbol and warrant that whatever is found in its company may be gambled on as being the petrified truth."[10]

Never mind that Samuel Clemens didn't first use his *nom de guerre* on the Pacific Coast (we experts see *that* joke).[11] The point is that, if in "Old Times" Mark Twain had shown the memory, skill, anxiety, courage, humiliation, and the joke attending the leadsman's call, he now shows the aggression, theft, parody, and comic guilt attending the act of *displacing* the ancient mariner of the river. Having confiscated the old man's pen name, he makes his own life and writing identical with the *epochs* of the river's emergence from the sleep of history.

The "petrified truth," which the name Mark Twain is said to signify, is itself the broadest of jokes. The actual truth is as elusive as the shape of the river that Horace Bixby had said the pilot must know with such absolute certainty that it lives in his head. Through all the shifts of perspective in this book, through all the changes of direction, the abrupt compression of space, and wayward digressions to kill time, there is yet a single writer whose shape seems somehow in *our* head, rather than in the shifting book before us. That figure is of course the myth of Mark Twain, growing out of and beyond the book that cannot contain him. We might devalue, and have devalued, this book, but in devaluing it we are already preparing to use it as a foil for *Huckleberry Finn*, the book that was waiting to be finished even as Mark Twain brought this one to an abrupt conclusion.

And this mythic figure, always materializing above his books, whose shape is in our heads, seems in his way as real as the great river—seems, indeed, to be that river's tutelary deity. He is the figure who, more than any of our writers, knows the great truth that Swift exposed in the fourth book of *Gulliver's Travels*: that if man cannot tell the truth, neither can language. Language can only lie.

In this connection, it is well to remember those Watergate days when Richard Nixon said that he would make every effort to find out "where the truth lies." Apparently, Nixon never saw the joke in his assertion,[12] but Mark Twain would certainly have seen it since he knew that the truth lies everywhere, and nothing can really lie like it. Being our greatest liar, he knew how much he believed in and needed the beautiful and powerful and deceptive river at the center of his country. It was a muddy river—the river he knew—so that you couldn't see the bottom, which was always so near, and it ran south into slavery just as man's life runs down into the slavery of adulthood. It rolled from side to side, wallowing in its valley as it shifted landmarks and state boundaries. It could hardly be bridged, and to this day has few bridges on it between New Orleans and St. Louis. It was, and still is, a lonely river for anyone upon its current. Lonely as it is, and monotonous too, it remains a truly wild river. Even now it may burst its banks and head through the Atchafalaya Bayou, leaving New Orleans high and dry. For it is a living river, always changing, always giving the lie to anyone who counts on its stability.

If Mark Twain grows out of the lie that language can't help telling, the great river grows out of some force that language cannot name. To begin to study the current of Mark Twain's prose in this book is to begin to sense the power of that other current that his discontinuous narrative displaces more than it represents. How good it is that Mark Twain does not spend all his time—he actually spends quite little—in describing, analyzing, or celebrating the river. If his book is not a great book, as great books go, it is well worth revisiting.

Revisiting it makes me know that it is time for the present generation of critics to take up Mark Twain. With their problematics, their presences-become-absences, and their aporias, they will be able to see the river as the genius loci of Mark Twain's imagination. I very much believe that this newer criticism, dealing as it can and does with discontinuity and open-ended forms, should be able to give a better account of Mark Twain's structure and language than the generation of New Critics who relied on the closed structures of lyric, drama, and novel. In the gap—I had almost said aporia—between Samuel Clemens and Mark Twain, these critics may see, as if for the first time, the writer's two I's which yet make one in sight.

NOTES

1. See my *Mark Twain: The Fate of Humor* (Princeton: Princeton University Press, 1966), pp. 105–26, 161–67.

2. The most penetrating and suggestive treatments of this passage that I know are by Henry Nash Smith, *Mark Twain: The Development of a Writer* (Cambridge, Mass.: Harvard University Press, 1962), pp. 77–81, and Larzer Ziff "Authorship and Craft: The Example of Mark Twain," *Southern Review*, 12 n.s. (1976), 256–60.

3. For interesting discussions relating the art of piloting to the art of writing, see Edgar J. Burde, "Mark Twain: The Writer as Pilot," *PMLA* 93 (1978), 878–92; Sherwood Cummings, "Mark Twain's Theory of Realism; or the Science of Piloting," *Studies in American Humor*, 2 (1976), 209–21; and Larzer Ziff, "Authorship and Craft," 246–60.

4. Anyone interested in the conception, composition, and interpretation of *Life on the Mississippi* will find Horst H. Kruse's *Mark Twain and "Life on the Mississippi"* (Amherst: University of Massachusetts Press, 1981) indispensable. For a briefer account which corrects many prior errors and misconceptions concerning the composition of *Life on the Mississippi*, see Guy A. Cardwell, "Life on the Mississippi: Vulgar Facts and Learned Errors," *Emerson Society Quarterly*, 46 (1973), 283–93.

5. Walter Blair's "When Was *Huckleberry Finn* Written?" *American Literature*, 30 (1958), 1–20, remains the most succinct and authoritative effort to establish the chronology of composition of *Huckleberry Finn*. For the full account of Mark Twain's composition of *Life on the Mississippi* during the summer of 1882, see Kruse, pp. 43–91.

6. I use the Author's National Edition because it is the text most readily available in libraries to the general reader.

7. For a thorough account of this issue, see Peter D. Beidler, "The Raft Episode in *Huckleberry Finn*," *Modern Fiction Studies*, 14 (Spring 1968), 11–20.

8. But contenders for a serious reading will have to contend with the fact that Mark Twain repeats the claim that the Mississippi drains Delaware: "A few more days swept swiftly by, and La Salle stood in the shadow of his confiscating cross, at a meeting of the waters from Delaware, and from Itasca, and from the mountain ranges close upon the Pacific, with the waters of the Gulf of Mexico, his task finished, his prodigy achieved (*Life on the Mississippi*, Author's National Edition, p. 16). I suppose it would be possible to argue that Mark Twain was so stupid that he didn't know that the Mississippi *doesn't* drain Delaware!

9. Stanley Brodwin's "The Useful and Useless River: *Life on the Mississippi Revisited*," *Studies in American Humor*, 2 (1976), 196–208, is a splendid interpretation of the structure and meaning of the continuity, as well as the discontinuity, of these episodes.

10. Because of Mark Twain's notorious penchant for unreliability, the scholarship devoted to his account of acquiring his pen name is necessarily extensive. The most authoritative treatment of this episode, at once summarizing and correcting prior scholarship, is in Kruse, pp. 82–90.

11. Samuel Clemens' first known use of "Mark Twain" occurred on 3 February 1863 in the Virginia City *Territorial Enterprise*, well before he left Nevada for California.

12. There was an earlier occasion when Nixon became the unwitting victim of his own speech. In the campaign of 1960 he repeatedly told the nation, "We can't stand pat," presumably forgetting that his wife's name was Pat—or is it possible that he was the victim of a malicious speechwriter?

SUSAN GILLMAN

Introduction: Mark Twain in Context

Ever since William Dean Howells insisted in his memoir *My Mark Twain* on defying his own title and calling his friend "Clemens ... instead of Mark Twain, which seemed always somehow to mask him," the peculiarly double personality Samuel Clemens/Mark Twain has continued both to elude and to fascinate.[1] A critical language of twinning, doubling, and impersonation has subsequently developed around this writer, in part fostered by what James Cox calls "the primal creative act of inventing Mark Twain."[2] There is also all the fascination with alternate selves in his writing: the paired and disguised characters, the mistaken, switched, and assumed identities, the confidence men and frauds that everyone remembers as part of Twain's fictional world, even if they have read only *Tom Sawyer* and *Huckleberry Finn*. Gender and genetic twins seem especially to proliferate: lookalikes (*The Prince and the Pauper*), putative half-brothers (*Pudd'nhead Wilson*), Siamese twins (*Those Extraordinary Twins*), and characters such as Huck and Tom Driscoll who through imposture become twin selves of both genders. The writer also doubles himself through autobiographical projections within the fictions and by his pseudonym. As Howells recognized, though, the problem with these writerly doubles (as with the treatment of doubles/twins) is that they tend not only to multiply confusingly but to entangle one another in complex ways. Mark Twain presses his investigations of twinness to the point

---

From *Dark Twins: Imposture and Identity in Mark Twain's America.* © 1989 by The University of Chicago.

where coherent individual identity collapses: it ceases to be possible to separate one brother from the other, or to punish one-half of a pair of Siamese twins, or even to determine whether a housemaid is female and pregnant or male and larcenous.[3] Similarly, Samuel Clemens himself invents a persona that not only becomes a second self but after a time enslaves the first, so that the twin Twain eclipses Clemens. "Mark the Double Twain" Dreiser once entitled a short critical piece on Samuel Clemens.[4]

The proliferating doubles therefore seem frustratingly as much to mask as to reveal the self they also project. No wonder that the language of doubling used by Howells and others since has sought to identify the overlapping series of masks that constitute the writer's invented personae—funny man, satirist, public performer/reformer—and to situate these roles in the context of his life and times. The primacy of his biography was of course encouraged by Mark Twain himself as a writer of autobiographical fiction. Certain biographical explanations are repeatedly, almost ritualistically cited as evidence that Twain felt himself to be a man divided: he was a southerner living in the North; a frontier bohemian transplanted to urban life in genteel Hartford; an American who lived in Europe for at least ten years of his life; a rebel who criticized, inhabited, and even named the world of the Gilded Age.

The most insightful of Mark Twain's biographers, Justin Kaplan, recognizes that these biographical versions of dividedness were inflated by Mark Twain himself into the kind of legend that hides its subject by flaunting only a spectacular composite of his personality. In the suggestively titled *Mr. Clemens and Mark Twain*, Kaplan argues that even before the pseudonym Mark Twain had become an identity in itself and "swallowed up" Samuel Clemens, he was "already a double creature. He wanted to belong, but he also wanted to laugh from the outside. The Hartford literary gentleman lived inside the sagebrush bohemian." At the center of the Kaplan biography, the whole issue of duality is represented as Clemens's "wrestling" "with the enigma of dual personality"—by which Kaplan means personal, psychological problems often worked out in, or placed in parallel relationship to, Twain's writing.[5] This broad biographical approach has provided powerful accounts of, and explanations for, the problematic authorial identity summed up in the *nom de plume* that Mark Twain sometimes called a *nom de guerre*.[6] Or as Leslie Fiedler once described the particular dilemma that Kaplan addresses so perceptively: "From the moment he gave himself the telltale pseudonym Mark Twain, Samuel L. Clemens was haunted by that second self, and his last words were inchoate murmurings about Jekyll and Hyde and dual personality."[7]

No one would deny that the figure "Mr. Clemens and Mark Twain" of the Kaplan biography has his own idiosyncratic and urgently personal claims on problems of identity. But as his reference to Robert Louis Stevenson's popular novel *Dr. Jekyll and Mr. Hyde* suggests, Mark Twain is also very much of a representative man, given to thinking and speaking in nineteenth-century colloquialisms. Thus to pick only two examples from contemporary popular culture, Twain's allusions to Jekyll and Hyde and to Siamese twins bespeak a fascination, beyond Twain's personal predicament, with things that in themselves embody questions about the boundaries of human identity. My approach to the subject that might be called by its nineteenth-century name of "duality" is to (re)create the dialogue between Twain's language of identity and the cultural vocabularies available to him.[8] Such a dialogue would reflect the complex interplay between personal insights and cultural tradition. My own method also depends on the dialogue of cultural history informed by and emerging from literary analysis, or literary analysis of cultural history. This kind of "historical criticism," Jane Tompkins points out, is not merely "backdrop" for the writer's individual genius. Instead, literary texts are read for the "cultural work" they do as "agents of cultural formation," "a means of stating and proposing solutions for social and political predicaments."[9]

Such contextualizing allows us to broaden our conception of the subject beyond the conventions of literary dualities traceable to Mark Twain's own unstable personal identity. The problem of identity and imposture— that is, of a unitary, responsible self—led Twain to become interested in potential solutions embodied in the processes of identification and legitimation, primarily legal and scientific, that were available in the world around him. Thus we will see how Twain's most apparently unique and idiosyncratic representations of problematic identity engage with late-nineteenth-century efforts to classify human behavior within biological, sexual, racial, and psychological parameters. At the same time, Mark Twain's America is also representative in its denials and silences, in what he, like his culture, dismissed as trivial, disguised, or concealed, or simply did not acknowledge. By reading Twain, for example, in the context of writings (his own and that of others, journalistic, scientific, legal) that have been considered, then and now, as "nonliterary," we may open up the canon in terms of how we understand both Mark Twain and late-nineteenth-century questions of identity.

In identifying the predicament and its solutions, of course, it will be *my* Mark Twain and *my* nineteenth century that emerge, but they share both the features and the non-canonical sources of what several cultural historians have already recounted of the man's class and his time. Drawing on a heterogeneous set of texts, both public and private utterances, Peter Gay premises his first volume of *The Bourgeois Experience: Victoria to Freud* on "a broad band of far-reaching cultural shifts between, for the most part, the 1850s and the 1890s." Mark Twain's writing career, from 1865–1910, not only happens to span those critical decades, but as I will argue, registers intimately their cultural transformations. Among the heady and anxiety-producing changes, Gay focuses in this volume on sexuality: patterns of courtship and marriage, fears about masturbation, concepts of childbirth, and the psychological images of "offensive women and defensive men" generated by feminist movements. Although Mark Twain is generally seen as a writer reluctant or unable to address issues of adult sexuality, I will show, through a number of Twain's little-known or unpublished writings, mostly from the 1890s and concerning the subjects of pregnancy and legal paternity, that he was indeed a child of the "Age of Nervousness"—the time, as Gay points out, christened at the end of the century at a meeting of physicians, psychologists, and sociologists.[10]

The period has also been characterized as an age of "weightlessness," "marked by hazy moral distinctions and vague spiritual commitments, ... [such that] personal identity itself came to seem problematic." "Weightlessness" is Nietzsche's term, here mediated through Jackson Lears's reinterpretation in his penetrating analysis of a broad "anti-modernist" impulse at the turn of the century.[11] Mark Twain's late, so-called "dream writings" of the 1890s and after—science fiction and fantasy tales—reflect some of the kinds of reaction formations Lears identifies in Henry Adams and others: paradoxical efforts to master, through repeated flights into nostalgia and other regressive fantasies, what is perceived as the increasingly uncontrollable social and natural world. Among the changing nineteenth-century realities that induced the sensation of weightlessness in Mark Twain, the most important centered around man's often contradictory efforts to ground his environment through technological and corresponding social inventions: the creation of a culture industry through massive increases in book and journal output, paralleled by increases in population and literacy; the twin movements of immigration and imperialism that, along with civilization's "triple curse" of railroad, telegraph, and newspapers, made the world seem simultaneously smaller and more alien;[12] and, finally, the curves of scientific thought, especially the proliferation of conceptual systems, such as Darwin's, Marx's, and Freud's, that applied self-consciously and self-critically the scientific, classificatory analysis in which so much modern faith was put. Out of all of this, a nineteenth-century "culture" constructs itself as a time, in Peter Gay's words, "of progress and for confidence, but also one for doubt, for second thoughts, for bouts of pessimism, for questions about identity."[13] It is those questions of identity, framed in terms of their economic, legal, social, psychological, and metaphysical dimensions, that I will address in Mark Twain.

Although Mark Twain writes obsessively about twinness, doubling for him was always less a literary than a social issue. Whether these lookalikes are random and contingent (such accused innocents as Muff Potter; the prince mistaken for a pauper; Huck Finn "born again" as Tom Sawyer) or willful and exploitative (the unexposed criminal Injun Joe; all Twain's confidence men), they raise a fundamental question: whether one can tell people apart, differentiate among them. Without such differentiation, social order, predicated as it is on division—of class, race, gender—is threatened. Thus Mark Twain, champion of the subversive, also championed the law as one agent of control that resolves confusions about identity, restoring and enforcing the fundamental distinctions of society. A number of legal premises particularly fascinated him: that innocence and guilt are two distinct categories; that proofs in the form of legal evidence exist to back up that distinction; and that legal evidence is so rigorously defined as to constitute nearly "absolute" knowledge.

In Mark Twain's fiction throughout the seventies and eighties, the law solves problems of identity by sorting out the captor/captive confusions in "Personal Habits of the Siamese Twins" (1869); by exonerating the falsely accused Muff Potter in *Tom Sawyer* (1876); and by rectifying the exchange of social identities in *The Prince and the Pauper* (1882). The problem, at once literary, social, economic, and legal, might better be called imposture than twinning or doubling, for by 1890 Twain is replacing the more legitimately confused, switched, or mistaken identities, which spill over in his fiction of the seventies and eighties, with the impostor, a figure of potentially illegitimate, indeterminate identity.

Yet imposture is a slippery term. Whereas twinning or doubling suggests merely mathematical division, imposture leads to a kind of logical vicious circle. Since "posture" already implies posing or faking, "imposture" is the pose of a pose, the fake of a fake: the word implies no possible return to any point of origin. Synonyms for imposture complicate this ambiguity by distinguishing degrees of intentionality on the part of the impostor. "Deceit," for example, is "strongly condemnatory" because it refers to "purposeful" deceiving or misleading, whereas "counterfeit" and "fake" may or may not condemn "depending on culpable intent to deceive."[14] Thus imposture raises but does not resolve complex connections between morality and intentionality. Its multiple confusions leave room for lawyers, confidence men, and, ultimately, the writer himself to erase boundaries and circumvent the law, making suspect the premise that knowledge is possible—by legal or any other means.

P.T. Barnum, an artist at turning humbug into big business, recognized the difficulties in confining imposture to clear-cut boundaries. "Many persons have such a horror of being taken in," he noted shrewdly, "that they believe themselves to be a sham, and in this way are continually humbugging themselves."[15] Mark Twain began his career by trading humorously on that horror, representing for entertainment the fictional impostors, including the deadpan narrators of frontier humor, that he observed in the world around him; he ended by getting entangled in the process of representation and convicting himself and his writing of imposture. In short, Twain initially assumed that imposture is a social problem that he could expose through the neutral lens of the writer's eye, but ended by turning that eye inward on himself and his own art. In the art of humor he discovered the same capacity for deception that he sought to expose in life. For imposture is intimately related to his art: the early journalistic hoaxes, the humor of the tall tale, even the humor of irony that works by making language itself duplicitous.

Clemens's extraordinarily successful self-creation as the humorist "Mark Twain" testifies both to his grasp of showmanship and to his exposure of all the attendant "anxieties of entertainment."[16] In nineteenth-century America humor was perceived as a "popular" rather than a "serious" mode, and fame as a humorist was not easy to transcend. Still worse, the role of humorist, which Mark Twain alternately exploited and railed against, put him in the ambiguous position of being lionized by his own targets of derision. Telling tales about people being duped, Mark Twain reflects his own ambivalent relationship to his audience, those he entertained quite literally at their own expense. Kenneth Burke's comment on irony helps to discriminate the tangled boundaries among Twain, his art, and his audience: "True irony is based upon a sense of fundamental kinship with the enemy, as one *needs* him, is *indebted* to him, is not merely outside him as an observer but contains him *within*, being consubstantial with him."[17] Mark Twain, wearing the mask of the ironic stranger observing the human race of "cowards," ultimately unmasks himself and discovers that he is "not only marching in that procession but carrying the banner."[18]

The term "imposture" with all its inherent ambiguities thus captures not only the problem of identity that Twain both observed and embodied, but also the problem of his representing that problem: the tendency of conscious intentions to entangle and expose unconscious ones and of public voices and vocabularies to emerge from and merge with the private. Some of these particular cultural vocabularies are clearly articulated by Twain himself. He was bitterly aware, for example, of the double bind of his success as an artist. "Playing professional humorist before the public" gave him a voice and an audience, he reflected late in life in his autobiography, but it was to the exclusion of other, more serious voices and at the cost of other, more serious audiences (*MTE*, 201). Even as early as 1874, he wrote to William Dean Howells that his preferred audience was that of the highbrow *Atlantic Monthly*, "for the simple reason that it don't require a 'humorist' to paint himself striped & stand on his head every fifteen minutes."[19] It was in part the ambiguities of his status as an artist—humorist or serious writer? master of audiences or their slave?—that led Twain to his most explicit formulation of what he called in a January 1898 notebook entry the "haunting mystery" of "our duality."[20]

This long and complex notebook entry, to which I will return in detail in the next chapter, demonstrates how Mark Twain's own awareness of problems of identity, or duality, to use his word, tended to shift radically, according in part to the cultural vocabularies available to him. In the entry he identifies, explicitly or implicitly, several particular vocabularies and contexts that helped to give voice to his various "new 'solutions' of a haunting mystery." Yet the notebook also confirms that Twain's omissions, silences, and elisions can be traced to cultural as well as to personal blind spots. While he drew quite self-consciously on the findings and language of psychology, for example, the metaphors of the law and criminality, conventionalized through actual trials and in detective fiction, were appropriated more unintentionally, as part of the world around him. And the entry alludes to a link between racial identity and sexuality that is, in the explicit theory of duality formulated in the notebook, not acknowledged at all.

Using the 1898 notebook entry's rough outline, I have followed suit in the shape and sequence of my own argument, mapping out Mark Twain's "solutions" to the "haunting mystery" of human identity and tracing their complex, shifting relationships to the culture whose vocabularies he alternately appropriated and quibbled with, exploited and subverted, inhabited and ironized, but which were always enabling. Reading his whole career in the light of what he self-consciously articulated only in the 1890s and after, I argue that Twain's early reliance on literal, literary conventions of external, consciously divided identity becomes entangled with a social conception that treats identity as culturally controlled and then gives way to an imposture that is increasingly internal, unconscious, and therefore uncontrollable: a psychological as opposed to social condition. Finally, though, even these distinctions—external/internal, conscious/unconscious, waking/dreaming—collapse into an undifferentiated darkness, as Mark Twain, during the much-debated dark period of "pessimism" and artistic "failure," confronted the impossibility of his arriving at any foundation of self and other—and yet continued to produce a poignant series of half-finished writings, his effort to create an abstract, ahistorical metaphysics of identity.

Each chapter in this book identifies a group of diverse Mark Twain materials—newspaper and magazine pieces, fiction, journals, letters, speeches—which I believe bear on the different rough stages I have outlined and which I situate in dialogue with a specific cultural context. The second chapter begins by exploring Twain's attitudes toward authorship, his own authorial control, and the authority of the humorist, since the whole issue of identity for Twain always involved his art, even as it broadened out to include social, legal, and psychological dimensions. The increasing professionalization of authorship in the nineteenth century, especially the role of machinery and technology in making literature a consumable product and the role of the lecture platform in making the writer a public performer and property, generated deep conflicts that Mark Twain both sprang from and helped to shape.

The third chapter, centered on the bifurcated stories *Pudd'nhead Wilson* and *Those Extraordinary Twins* (1893–94), argues that those novels draw on Twain's earliest literary conceptions of twinning and mistaken identity in order to explore the historical actualities of slavery. Thus Mark Twain was led to the serious social, psychological, and moral issue of racial identity, a genealogy that I argue must be understood against the context of turn-of-the-century racism: legal discourse on issues of blood, race and sex, miscegenation; Jim Crow laws and Negrophobic mob violence; the ideologies of imperialism and racial Darwinism. There are also barely articulated implications here about sexual identity that I pursue in the following chapter, through materials that I alluded to earlier, a series of largely unknown writings on the law and sexuality. Although some of these pieces date from Mark Twain's early period—*A Medieval Romance*, for example, from 1870—most were written during the last two decades of his life—1890–1910—when popular Darwinian debates over heredity and environment informed Twain's representations of both racial and sexual difference. In the trials that culminate (but often without concluding) many of these tales as well as *Pudd'nhead Wilson*, legal determination of identity becomes a metaphor for questioning to what extent difference, both of race and of gender, is as much culturally as biologically constituted. Thus Mark Twain discovered in a very graphic context, rooted in the historical actualities of race slavery, how social fictions assume not the pose but the power of unalterable realities; he exposed human bondage to cultural categories and historical circumstances.

Once these concepts had been called into question, Twain began questioning his own basic assumptions about selfhood and reality. *Pudd'nhead Wilson* directly initiated the confused and confusing writings of 1895–1910, the dream narratives and science-fiction fantasies that are frequently incoherent, some only half-finished. Chapter five argues that these formless, inchoate works—it is hard to tell where one begins and another ends—express poignantly Twain's late struggle to find a new form, emptied of history and divorced from social reality, whose only referent is to itself, and whose only subject is the dreamer and the problem of his artistic imagination. The tales begin with narrators dreaming themselves into a nightmarish reality from which neither they nor the story ever emerges. Even these fantasies of escape from history, however, bear explicit cultural marks. As the author himself recognized in his January 1898 notebook entry and elsewhere in the notebooks and letters, his conception of the unconscious dream-self crystallized only in the context of turn-of-the-century psychology: not only Freud's dream analysis, but Charcot's experiments with hypnosis and William James's with spiritualism and psychical research. So, too, did Twain's late, rather crude, philosophical essays on human nature—*What Is Man?*, for example—take full shape (for they were variations on earlier themes) in the context of popular debates about the "pseudoscience" of spiritualism and the "science" of psychology. Thus Mark Twain turned ironically to the popular sciences in writing his late dream narratives, which repeatedly turn on inversions of scale, time, and space to create their fantasies of disorientation and escape from reality.

The teleology outlined here is somewhat too neat, since Mark Twain was fascinated not just at the end of his life but throughout by the vocation of the artist and the sources of his creativity. Even in his early writings there is a kind of duplicity in the narrative strategy. The deadpan mask of the narrator derived from frontier humor is a complex convention, difficult to penetrate. Simon Wheeler's appearance of unconscious artistry, for example, is never exposed as either genuine or fraudulent. The audiences of the "Jumping Frog" (1865) cannot tell if Wheeler is only posing, consciously assuming the mask of innocence, or if his innocence extends inward, part of his unconscious personality. Similarly, Mark Twain's letters and notebooks strike different poses at different times toward contemporary scientific and pseudoscientific research in the human imagination, ranging from the stance of the would-be believer in his eldest daughter Susy's faith in "mind cure," to that of the sceptic *malgré lui* during seances when he and his wife Livy tried futilely to contact the dead Susy's spirit, to the analytical sceptic in his polemic on Mary Baker Eddy, *Christian Science* (1907). The rough chronological progression of my argument is thus only rough, not meant to be enshrined, as the curve of Twain's life, from humorist to nihilist, optimist to pessimist, has tended by now to be rigidified in Mark Twain studies. Although the book moves forward in time, within each chapter I draw on materials from various periods of Twain's life, because that is how his own investigation proceeded: erratically, in fits and starts, gaining new terrain by retracing old ground.

My argument also follows the overall drift of Mark Twain's writing toward incompleteness. Much of the material I discuss in the second half of the book remains unfinished, and because of their aesthetic incoherence, some manuscripts have not yet been published, or even if available, have not received much sustained, sympathetic attention.[21] But in spite of this, I argue that they are an important, perhaps essential, part of the picture. The incoherent, fragmentary state of both the sexual manuscripts and the dream writings makes them resistant, even inaccessible, to conventional literary analysis; an interdisciplinary approach helps to make their silences speak, in part because it is receptive to the cultural realities on which these works so ostentatiously turn their backs. Indeed, even grouping the pieces as I have done itself constitutes the beginning of my argument. No single one of the tales of sexual identity makes much sense in isolation; only putting all of that material together defines it as belonging among Twain's "solutions" to the "haunting mystery" of "duality." He himself never speaks directly or indirectly of the "sexual writings" in these terms at all, and surely would have disavowed any role to sexuality in his various solutions to the problem of establishing a criterion of the self. It is I who argue that such a context enables otherwise apparently incoherent, vestigial, and even rather silly texts to begin to articulate themselves. Mark Twain's views of sexuality were never formulated as consciously or self-consciously as they were on the (for him) closely allied subject of race, certainly in part reflecting the cultural vocabularies available and the collective denial in force. But when sex was wedded to race, as in antebellum legal regulation of miscegenation and in turn-of-the-century popular fiction justifying Negrophobia on the grounds of uncontrollable black sexuality, the pair was obsessively returned to, in a kind of cultural return of the repressed. In this context, Mark Twain was very much a representative man.

Given these multiple voices and glaring silences, my approach is to speak both *through* Mark Twain as a conscious, articulate critic of and spokesman for his culture, and *for* Mark Twain when he is less aware and more disguising, displacing, or denying of his own subject. At times this means permitting oneself to be constrained by one's materials. I have tried to adhere to the usual convention of using "Clemens" to refer to Samuel L. Clemens in his extra-authorial identity and "Twain" to refer to the authorial self. Unfortunately, the two selves do not remain fixed in their proper categories, making it difficult to maintain the linguistic distinction consistently. But, then, that is the problem with all the dual taxonomies that might be used to label Mark Twain, by himself or others—and, indeed, that conflict is the theme of this book. In addition, it is not I but Mark Twain who takes the term "fraud" as a *locus classicus*. He relies astonishingly often on the language of "fraud" and its cognates—swindle, humbug, sham, pretense—to convey a vision of the broadest array of social beings, events, and conventions, thus ironically giving unintentional voice to the wish that a world without fraud is either possible or desirable.

Just the reverse, however, seems to apply to Mark Twain's America. As he saw it, nothing and no one were immune from charges of imposture. Individuals could be frauds: George Carleton, a publisher who rejected a collection of early Mark Twain pieces, including the "Jumping Frog," was, the author wrote a friend, "a Son of a Bitch who will swindle him." The old European masters whose art Mark Twain observed in 1867 on the *Quaker City* excursion are "dilapidated, antediluvian humbugs," but so, too, are some American masters, such as the three "impostors" posing in Mark Twain's "Whittier Birthday Dinner Speech" as the "littery" men "Mr. Longfellow, Mr. Emerson, and Mr. Holmes." Even a whole geographical and cultural region, the South, for example, may fall "in love with ... the sham grandeurs, sham gauds, and sham chivalries of a brainless and worthless long-vanished society," also known as "the Walter Scott Middle-Age sham civilization." In sum, anyone who, like Mark Twain, has been through the "mill" of the world must know it "through and through and from back to back—its follies, its frauds and its vanities—all by personal *experience* and not through dainty *theories* culled from nice moral books in luxurious parlors where temptation never comes."[22]

But finally, perhaps precisely because Mark Twain, by his own admission, has so intimately and personally known the frauds of the world, he sets out to expose fraudulence through the art of humor. "Ours is a useful trade," he said of humor in 1888 when he accepted an honorary M.A. from Yale:

> With all its lightness and frivolity it has one serious purpose, one
> aim, one specialty, and it is constant to it—the deriding of shams,
> the exposure of pretentious falsities, ... and whoso is by instinct
> engaged in this sort of warfare is the natural enemy of royalties,
> nobilities, privileges and all kindred swindles, and the natural
> friend of human rights and human liberties.[23]

The problem, of course, as Kenneth Burke's comment on irony suggests, is
that such a war of exposure may expose the self in "fundamental kinship with
the enemy," and thus end by confusing the distinctions between friend and
enemy, self and other, the authentic and the fraudulent, the observer of sham
and the participant in it. It is exactly these risks that Mark Twain ran
throughout his life, alternately succumbing to and resisting them. And it is
that process of continual self-construction and destruction by someone who
is both critic and child of his culture that I hope to represent in this book.

NOTES

1. William Dean Howells, *My Mark Twain: Reminiscences and Criticisms*, ed. Marilyn
Austin Baldwin (Baton Rouge, La., 1967), p. 6.

2. James M. Cox, *Mark Twain: The Fate of Humor* (Princeton, 1966), p. 21, n. 12.

3. For this last predicament, see the various versions of "Wapping Alice," ed. Hamlin
Hill, number 29 of the "Keepsake" series, The Friends of the Bancroft Library, University
of California (Berkeley, 1981). I discuss this story in detail in chapter 4.

4. Theodore Dreiser, "Mark the Double Twain," *The English Journal* 24 (1935)
615–27.

5. Justin Kaplan, *Mr. Clemens and Mark Twain* (New York, 1966), pp. 36, 18, 211.

6. See Twain's account of how he won his *nom de guerre* in *Life on the Mississippi*, vol.
12 of *The Writings of Mark Twain*, Definitive Edition, 37 vols. (New York, 1922–25), pp.
401–3; further references to works in this collection will be abbreviated *DE* and cited by
volume and page numbers.

7. Leslie Fiedler, *Freaks: Myths and Images of the Secret Self* (New York, 1978), p. 270.
Fiedler's source for this deathbed account is Albert Bigelow Paine, *Mark Twain: A
Biography*, 3 vols. (New York, 1912), 3: 1575; further references to this work will be
abbreviated *MTB* and cited by volume and page numbers.

8. On "duality" as a nineteenth-century term, see Karl Miller, *Doubles: Studies in
Literary History* (Oxford, 1985), p. 38. Miller describes the eighties and nineties as "an age
tormented by genders and pronouns and pen-names, by the identity of authors" (p. 209).

9. Jane Tompkins, *Sensational Designs: The Cultural Work of American Fiction,
1790–1860* (New York, 1985), pp. xv–xvii.

10. Peter Gay, *Education of the Senses*, vol. I of *The Bourgeois Experience: Victoria to Freud*
(New York, 1984), pp. 3, 110, 67–68.

11. T.J. Jackson Lears, *No Place of Grace: Antimodernism and the Transformation of
American Culture, 1880–1920* (New York, 1981), pp. 32, 41–47.

12. *MTB*, 2:591–92. This comment was made in the context of a trip to Bermuda with a Clemens family friend and neighbor, the Reverend Joseph Twichell, in May 1877 (described in *A Tramp Abroad* [1880]). There Twain was dazzled by the whiteness of the houses, but was certain that this Eden too would be ruined by the "triple curse."

13. Gay, *Education of the Senses*, p. 8.

14. *Webster's Third New International Dictionary of the English Language Unabridged* (Springfield, Mass., 1976), s.v. "imposture."

15. P.T. Barnum, *The Humbugs of the World* (New York, 1865), p. 102.

16. The phrase is Judith Fetterly's in "Mark Twain and the Anxiety of Entertainment," *Georgia Review* 33 (1979): 388.

17. Kenneth Burke, *A Grammar of Motives* (New York, 1952), p. 514.

18. See epigraph, dated 4 September 1907, to *Mark Twain in Eruption*, ed. Bernard DeVoto (1940; rpt. New York, 1968); further references to this work will be abbreviated *MTE*.

19. Clemens (hereafter SLC) to Howells, 8 December 1874, *Mark Twain–Howells Letters*, ed. Henry Nash Smith and William Gibson, 2 vols. (Cambridge, Mass., 1960), 1: 49–50; further references to this collection will be abbreviated *MTHL* and cited by volume and page numbers.

20. *Mark Twain's Notebook*, ed. Albert Bigelow Paine (New York, 1935) pp. 348–52; further references to this work will be abbreviated *MTN*.

21. On the unpublished material concerning sexuality that I refer to here, see Hamlin Hill's provocative treatment of the last ten years of Twain's life, *Mark Twain: God's Fool* (New York, 1973).

22. *MTHL*, 1: 1331 *Mark Twain to Mrs. Fairbanks*, ed. Dixon Wecter (San Marino, Ca., 1949), pp. 18–21; "The Whittier Birthday Dinner Speech" in *Selected Shorter Writings of Mark Twain*, ed. Walter Blair (Boston, 1962), pp. 151–55; *DE*, 12: 375; *The Love Letters of Mark Twain*, ed. Dixon Wecter (New York, 1949), p. 26.

23. In a letter of appreciation from SLC to Yale President Timothy Dwight, 29 June 1888; quoted in *Mark Twain Speaking*, ed. Paul Fatout (Iowa City, 1976), p. 237.

SHELLEY FISHER FISHKIN

Jimmy: Chapter One

> Been a listening all the night long,
> Been a listening all the night long[1]

Twentieth-century American criticism abounds in pronouncements about how Twain's choice of a vernacular narrator in *Huckleberry Finn* transformed modern American literature. Lionel Trilling, for example, felt that

> The prose of *Huckleberry Finn* established for written prose the virtues of American colloquial speech.... It has something to do with ease and freedom in the use of language. Most of all it has to do with the structure of the sentence, which is simple, direct, and fluent, maintaining the rhythm of the word—groups of speech and the intonations of the speaking voice.... [Twain] is the master of the style that escapes the fixity of the printed page, that sounds in our ears with the immediacy of the heard voice....[2]

"As for the style of the book," Trilling concluded, "it is not less than definitive in American literature."[3] As Louis Budd noted in 1985, "today it is standard academic wisdom that Twain's central, precedent-setting achievement is Huck's language."[4]

From *Was Huck Black? Mark Twain and African-American Voices*. © 1993 by Shelley Fisher Fishkin

Before Twain wrote *Huckleberry Finn*, no American author had entrusted his narrative to the voice of a simple, untutored vernacular speaker—or, for that matter, to a child. Albert Stone has noted that "the vernacular language ... in *Huckleberry Finn* strikes the ear with the freshness of a real boy talking out loud."[5] Could the voice of an actual "real boy talking out loud" have helped Twain recognize the potential of such a voice to hold an audience's attention and to win its trust?

Twain himself noted in his autobiography that he based Huck Finn on Tom Blankenship, the poor-white son of the local drunkard whose pariah status (and exemption from school, church, etc.) made him the envy of every "respectable" boy in Hannibal.[6] Twain wrote,

> In *Huckleberry Finn* I have drawn Tom Blankenship exactly as he was. He was ignorant, unwashed, insufficiently fed; but he had as good a heart as any boy had. His liberties were totally unrestricted. He was the only really independent person—boy or man—in the community, and by consequence he was tranquilly and continuously happy, and was envied by all the rest of us. We liked him, we enjoyed his society. And as his society was forbidden us by our parents, the prohibition trebled and quadrupled its value, and therefore we sought and got more of his society than of any other boy's.[7]

What demands our notice is that although Tom Blankenship may have been the model for Huck's place in society, Twain never suggested that there was anything memorable about the nature of his "talk." Huck's talk, on the other hand, as many critics have noted, is the most memorable thing about him.[8] I suggest that there was another "real boy talking out loud" whose role in the genesis of *Huckleberry Finn* has never been acknowledged.

On 29 November 1874, two years before he published *Tom Sawyer* or began *Adventures of Huckleberry Finn*, Mark Twain published an article called "Sociable Jimmy" in the *New York Times*.[9] *"Sociable Jimmy" takes the place of honor as the first piece Twain published that is dominated by the voice of a child.* This fact alone would seem to mark it as deserving of scholars' attention. Strangely enough, however, it has been almost totally ignored.[10]

In this article, Twain says he originally sent the sketch of "Jimmy" home in a letter in the days when he was a public lecturer. Although this initial letter has disappeared, subsequent letters Twain wrote home to his wife allow us to determine that the encounter he relates happened in December 1871 or January 1872, in a small town in the Midwest, probably

Paris, Illinois, and that the child in question definitely existed.[11] Twain reports that he had supper in his room, as was his habit, and that a "bright, simple, guileless little darkey boy ... ten years old—a wide-eyed, observant little chap" was sent to wait on him. The intensity of Twain's response to the child is striking. He notes that he wrote down what the child said, and sent the record home because he

> ... wished to preserve the memory of *the most artless, sociable, and exhaustless talker I ever came across*. He did not tell me a single remarkable thing, or one that was worth remembering; and yet he was himself so interested in his small marvels, and they flowed so naturally and comfortably from his lips, that his talk got the upper hand of my interest, too, and *I listened as one who receives a revelation*. I took down what he had to say, just as he said it— without altering a word or adding one.[12]

Twain's "revelation" involved his recognition of the potential of a "bright, simple, guileless ... wide-eyed, observant" child as narrator. I suggest that the voice of Jimmy, the "most artless, sociable, and exhaustless talker" Twain had ever come across, became a model for the voice with which Twain would change the shape of American literature.

It was a voice that Twain contained within himself, a language and set of cadences and rhythms he could generate fluently on his own, having been exposed to many such voices in his youth. Jimmy triggered his recollection of those voices, and sparked his apprehension of the creative possibilities they entailed. We can view the remarkable impression Jimmy made upon Twain, then, as connected to Twain's awareness of the ease with which he could speak in that voice himself. As he put it in a letter to Livy written shortly after he met Jimmy, "*I think I could swing my legs over the arms of a chair & that boy's spirit would descend upon me & enter into me.*"[13] It was a crucial step on the road to creating Huck.

"Sociable Jimmy" consists mainly of what Twain presents as a transcription of Jimmy's engaging conversation. Twain had been intrigued for several years by the possibilities of a child as narrator, but this was the first time that he developed this perspective at any length in print."[14] Along with "A True Story," which ran in the *Atlantic Monthly* the same month "Sociable Jimmy" ran in the *Times*, it also represented one of Twain's first extended efforts to translate African-American speech into print. Indeed, to the extent that critics took notice of the piece at all, it was as an experiment in African-American dialect. Jimmy's defining characteristic for critics seemed to be the fact that he was black. For Twain, however, Jimmy was mainly a charming and delightful *child* who captured his heart and captivated his imagination.

In the "Explanatory" with which *Huckleberry Finn* begins,[15] Twain enumerates seven dialects used in the book, one of which is "Missouri negro dialect." Critics have debated whether Twain did, in fact, use seven dialects, or more, or fewer; but they have generally assumed that the only "negro dialect" in the book is that spoken by African-American characters. On a phonological level, that assumption is correct: only African-American characters, for example, say "dat," as opposed to "that." But phonology alone does not describe a *voice*, as the voluminous criticism about what makes Huck's voice distinctive clearly shows. Voice involves syntax and diction, the cadences and rhythms of a speaker's sentences, the flow of the prose, the structures of the mental processes, the rapport with the audience, the characteristic stance as regards the material related.

The cadences and rhythms of Jimmy's speech, his syntax and diction, his topics of conversation, attitudes, limitations, and his ability to hold our interest and our trust bear a striking resemblance to those qualities of speech and character that we have come to identify indelibly with Huck. Both boys are naive and open, engaging and bright. They are unpretentious, uninhibited, easily impressed, and unusually loquacious. They free-associate with remarkable energy and verve. And they are supremely self-confident: neither doubts for a minute that Twain (in Jimmy's case) or the reader (in Huck's) is completely absorbed by everything he has to say. I am not suggesting that Twain was being intentionally misleading either in his "Explanatory" or in his comments about the roots of Huck in Tom Blankenship: rather, I put forth the far from controversial notion that artists are notoriously unreliable critics of their own work. As I point out later on, Twain's blending of black voices with white to create the voice we know as Huck's may well have been unconscious.

On a linguistic level, my discussion of what Huck and Jimmy have in common is indebted to the work of three critics whose sophisticated analyses of Huck's characteristic speech patterns provide invaluable points of departure: Richard Bridgman, Janet Holmgren McKay, and David Carkeet.

One of the key elements Richard Bridgman identifies as emblematic of Huck's speech patterns and of Twain's organizing structure in the novel is *repetition*. Bridgman comments that repetition reaches a particularly "conscious structural function in extended passages where phrases are repeated." Huck:

We got a LICKING every time one of our snakes come in her way, and she allowed these LICKINGS warn't NOTHING to what she would do if we ever loaded up the place again with them. I DIDN'T MIND THE LICKINGS because they didn't amount to NOTHING; but I MINDED the trouble we had to LAY IN another lot. But we got them LAID IN.[16]

The same subtle repetition of key words and phrases characterizes Jimmy's speech in "Sociable Jimmy," as the following examples show:

1. But de res' o' de people, *DEY* HAD A GOOD TIME— mos' all uv 'em HAD A GOOD TIME. DEY ALL GOT DRUNK. DEY ALL GITS DRUNK heah, every Christmas, and carries on and has AWFUL GOOD TIMES.... Pa used to GIT DRUNK, but dat was befo' I was big—but he's done quit. He don' GIT DRUNK no mo' now.

2. Dat's an AWFUL BIG church—AWFUL HIGH STEEPLE. An' it's all solid stone, excep' jes' de top part—de STEEPLE.... It's gwine to kill some body yit, dat STEEPLE is. A man—BIG man, he was—BIGGER'n what Bill is—he tuck it up dare and fixed it again—an' he didn't took no BIGGER'n a boy, he was so HIGH up. Dat STEEPLE's AWFUL HIGH.[17]

In a passage Bridgman does not cite but that makes the point about repetition as well as the one he does cite, Huck says,

I set down again, a shaking all over, and got out my pipe for a smoke; for the house was all STILL as death, now, and so the widow wouldn't know. Well, after a long time I HEARD the clock away off in the town go BOOM—BOOM—BOOM— twelve licks—and all STILL again—STILLER than ever. Pretty soon I HEARD a twig snap, down in the dark amongst the trees—something was a stirring. I set STILL and LISTENED.[18]

In a similarly repetitive passage in "Sociable Jimmy," Jimmy characterizes the sound made by a clock in town with the identical onomatopoetic construction.

It mus' be awful to stan' in dat steeple when de CLOCK is STRIKIN'—dey say it is. BOOMS and jars so's you think the

world's a comin' to an end. *I* wouldn't like to be up dare when de
CLOCK'S A STRIKIN'. Dat CLOCK ain't just a *STRIKER*, like
dese common CLOCKS. It's a *BELL*—jist a reglar *BELL*—and
it's a buster. You kin hear dat BELL all over dis city. You ought to
hear it BOOM, BOOM, BOOM ...[19]

Another dimension of Huck's vernacular speech that Bridgman
identifies as particularly significant is Twain's willingness to "invest words
with new meaning."

> The surface of his prose is littered with queer ore quarried from
> Huck's mine. A melodeum is "pretty *skreeky*," ... Huck "*smouches*"
> a spoon, he has "*clayey*" clothes ... he speaks of an undertaker's
> "soft *soothering* ways," ... the king inquired what he was "*alassing*
> about" ... he guts a catfish by "*haggling*" it open with a saw; and
> finally he says that a certain surprise would make "most anybody
> *sqush*."[20]

"The effect of these words," Bridgman writes,

> —dialect, nonce, slang—is that of poetry. Carrying expository
> meaning, they flash out with a light unique for prose. They are
> employed less to build an effect cumulatively, more to make an
> effect immediately. And they contribute to the gradually
> accumulating feeling in American literature for the importance of
> the single word....[21]

Jimmy's lexicon is, in its own way, equally creative. When his
employer's daughters catch a cat in the house, "dey jis' *scoops* him." The clock
Jimmy admires "ain't just a striker, like dese common clocks ... it's a *buster*."
The brother named Bob "don't git drunk much—jes' *sloshes*, roun' de s'loons
some, an' takes a dram sometimes."[22]

Bridgman also notes "the frequent use of present participles in Huck's prose."

> Huck uses participial constructions especially when there is a
> violent or otherwise memorable action.... "They swarmed up the
> street towards Sherburn's house, A-WHOOPING and
> YELLING and RAGING like Injuns.... Lots of women and girls
> was CRYING and TAKING ON, scared most to death."[23]

Jimmy, too, favors participial constructions to describe memorable actions: "You don't never see Kit A-RAIRIN an' A-CHARGIN' aroun' an' KICKIN' up her heels like de res' o' de gals in dis fam'ly does gen'ally."[24] Linguist Janet Holmgren McKay observes, as well, that "frequently, Twain adds the colloquial 'a-' prefix to Huck's present participles, and he couples these forms with two-syllable adverbials for even greater rhythm." Jimmy does the same.[25]

Finally, Bridgman notes that "the participle and the reiterated conjunction of a long list 'and ... and ... and ... and ... and ...'—are two of the least evident yet most pervasive forms of repetition to be found in Huck's version of the vernacular."[26] "Huck's remembering mind," Bridgman writes, "lays in these details one after the other without any urge toward subordination."[27] McKay also comments on Twain's propensity to make Huck's sentences "seem simple by a lack of overt indications of subordination between clauses and phrases. For example, Huck characteristically uses the conjunction *and* to link any number of subordinate and coordinate ideas, a practice that suggests a lack of linguistic sophistication."[28]

"And" is a common conjunction in Jimmy's speech as well: "He tuck de bottle AND shuck it, AND shuck it—he seed it was blue, AND he didn't know but it was blue mass ... AND so he sot de bottle down, AND drat if it wa'n't blue vittles...." Or, as he says elsewhere, "Dey all gits drunk heah, every Christmas, AND carries on AND has awful good times." The particularly long list of names Jimmy rattles off, also connected by "and"— "Bill, an' Griz, an' Duke, an' Bob, an' Nan, an' Tab, an' Kit, an' Sol, an' Si, an' Phil, an' Puss, an' Jake, an' Sal," and so on—so impresses Twain that he quickly scribbles it all down on "the flyleaf of Longfellow's *New England Tragedies* presumably the closest thing handy on which to write.

McKay enumerates several other dimensions of Huck's voice, virtually all of which characterize Jimmy's voice, as well. "The kinds of errors that Huck makes are by no means haphazard," McKay writes. "Twain carefully placed them to suggest Huck's basic illiteracy but not to overwhelm the reader." McKay notes that "nonstandard verb forms constitute Huck's most typical mistakes. He often uses the present form or past participle for the simple past tense ... and he often shifts tense within the same sequence."[29] She identifies "the frequent occurrence of double negatives" as the second most prominent nonstandard feature in Huck's speech other than the verb forms.[30] McKay underlines "a redundancy of subjects" as characteristic of Huck's speech patterns. Each of these nonstandard features characterizes Jimmy's speech as well.[31]

Yet another dimension of Huck's style that McKay emphasizes is his "skillful use of ... verbal imagery of all sorts, particularly hyperbole, metaphor and onomatopoeia." McKay cites such similes as "like the whole world was asleep," and such onomatopoeia as thunder "rumbling, grumbling, tumbling down the sky."[32] Jimmy, too, is no stranger to simile (the drowned cat is "all swelled up like a pudd'n") or to onomatopoeia (the clock "booms and jars so's you think the world's comin' to an end," and "Bob ... jes' sloshes roun' de s'loons").

McKay notes Huck's preference for using adjectives in place of adverbs.[33] Interestingly, two of the specific adjectives Huck uses most frequently in this way—"powerful" and "considerable"—are also in Jimmy's lexicon.[34] Jimmy says, "He's powerful sickly." Huck says, "I was most powerful sick"; "he got powerful thirsty"; "I was powerful lazy and comfortable"; "[they] had such a powerful lot to say about faith"; and "I was powerful glad to get away from the feuds." Jimmy says, "Some folks say dis town would be considerable bigger ..." Huck says, "I read considerable to Jim about kings, dukes and earls and such"; "This shook me up considerable"; "I beat it and hacked it considerable"; "He hopped around the cabin considerable"; and "We've heard considerable about these goings on."[35]

Jimmy and Huck both use "snake" rather unconventionally as a verb. Jimmy says, "Dey snake him into de cistern," and Huck asks, "What do we want of a moat, when we're going to snake him out from under the cabin?"[36] The words "particular" (as in "choosy" or "discriminating") and "reckon" (as in "think") are standard elements in both boys' speech patterns, and both boys end sentences for negative emphasis with their dialect variant of the word "scarcely": Jimmy says, "she don't make no soun', scasely," while Huck says, "there warn't no room in bed for him, skasely."[37] Both boys use the word "disremember" for "forget" in contexts that are virtually identical in the two texts. Jimmy says, "he's got another name dat I somehow disremember ..." while Huck says, "I disremember her name."[38]

Huck's style, McKay writes, "is so colloquial and seemingly unaffected and unrehearsed that we frequently feel as if he is carrying on a conversation with us"—a quality that is less surprising if we accept the basic point I'm making here: that it was real conversation that inspired Huck's voice in the first place. This sense, McKay continues, "is heightened by [Huck's] liberal use of direct addresses to 'you,' the reader."[39] Jimmy, too, in Twain's rendition of his conversation, frequently uses the direct address, "you," to his listener—although Twain's responses in the conversation are largely superfluous: all that was needed to spark Jimmy's monologue was Twain's presence. Both boys' use of the word "you" helps establish the conversational intimacy that McKay rightly finds so memorable in Huck's case.

Victor Doyno has observed that Huck's "self-interrupting style" creates the illusion that we are watching and listening to him "thinking aloud."[40] Jimmy's talk, in Twain's rendition of it, is characterized by this same "self-interrupting" quality, often established through sentences that spurt fitfully across the page in a breathless blur of dashes. "Because he interrupts himself for clarification or for qualification," Doyno notes, Huck "seems open-minded, as if he is not enshrining his own statements. Because we hear the thought process, not the final product of the thought-to-language development, we tend to trust the thinking as honest. Yet we should realize that in his rush of statements we find little subordination, and that he verifies his remarks mostly by repetition."[41] This description applies equally well to Jimmy.

Clearly, Twain is experimenting with African-American dialect in "Sociable Jimmy," just as he was in "A True Story, Repeated Word for Word as I Heard It," which appeared in the *Atlantic Monthly* the same month that "Sociable Jimmy" appeared in the *New York Times*. But although on the phonological level Jimmy's dialect bears some obvious resemblances to the speech of black characters in the novel, particularly Jim's, in a number of other ways his speech is closer to that of Huck.[42] It is not just linguistically, however, that Jimmy and Huck have much in common.[43] Even more striking than the similarities between Jimmy and Huck on the level of cadence, syntax, and diction, are the similarities between the two boys' character traits and topics of conversation.

The adult world remains rather confusing and cryptic to both Jimmy and Huck, who are blissfully oblivious to the gaps in their understanding. Part of the humor in both "Sociable Jimmy" and *Huckleberry Finn* stems from the reader's awareness that sometimes neither Jimmy nor Huck understands that a joke is being perpetrated. Twain finds Jimmy's "dense simplicity" so engaging that he devotes a bracketed aside in the piece to explicating it:

> "Some folks say dis town would be considerable bigger if it wa'n't on accounts of so much lan' all roun' it dat ain't got no houses on it." [This in perfect seriousness—dense simplicity—no idea of a joke.]

Huck, too, sometimes fails to "get" a joke. At the circus, for example, the "drunk" who had argued with the ringmaster until he gave him a chance to ride jumps on a charging horse, pulls off his outer clothes, and turns out to be one of the regular circus performers in disguise. Huck says, then the ring-master he see how he had been fooled, and he was the sickest ring-master you ever see, I reckon. Why, it was one of his own men! He had got up that joke all out of his own head, and never let on to nobody. Well, I felt sheepish enough, to be took in so, but I wouldn't a been in that ring-master's place, not for a thousand dollars.[44]

Huck has been taken in even more than he realizes, of course, since he is oblivious to the fact that the ringmaster's "embarrassment" is part of the circus routine as well. His typical stance is dead earnestness, particularly in the face of circumstances that would strike most readers as funny. As Walter Blair put it, "since he was almost completely humorless, he was bound to be incongruously naive and somber on many laugh-provoking occasions."[45] (It is interesting that in "Sociable Jimmy," written early in his career, Twain felt the need to flag the gaps in the child's understanding for the reader; by *Huckleberry Finn*, he would allow that character trait to emerge without authorial comment.) A year or so before Twain met Jimmy, in "Disgraceful Persecution of a Boy" (1870), Twain had experimented with creating a narrator too bigoted to understand the full import of what he related. In "Sociable Jimmy," Twain gave his reader an early glimpse of a narrator too innocent to understand the meaning of all he said. By the time he wrote *Huckleberry Finn*, of course, Twain had figured out how to use a narrator's naive responses to the world around him to unmask the hypocrisy and pretensions of that world, a strategy with which he had begun to experiment in 1870 and 1871 in "Goldsmith's Friend Abroad Again." Although Jimmy's naïveté, as conveyed by Twain, serves no satirical purpose, it is completely convincing. That totally believable, authentic innocence would be a crucial component of what readers would find compelling about Huck.[46]

Both Jimmy and Huck casually pepper their conversation with accidents that are simultaneously bizarre, grisly, and preposterous. In Jimmy's case, it is the cow that got skewered by the church steeple:

I reckon you seed dat church as you come along up street.... [I]t's all solid stone, excep' jes de top part—de steeple, I means—dat's wood. It falls off when de win' blows pooty hard, an' one time it stuck in a cow's back and busted de cow all to de mischief.... You see dat after on top o' dat steeple? Well, Sah, dat arrer is pooty nigh as big as dis do' [door]. I seed it when dey pulled it outen de cow.

For Huck, it is the flattening of Hank Bunker:

> ... I've always reckoned that looking at the new moon over your left shoulder is one of the carelessest and foolishest things a body can do. Old Hank Bunker done it once, and bragged about it; and in less than two years he got drunk and fell off of the shot tower and spread himself out so that he was just a kind of a layer, as you may say; and they slid him edgeways between two barn doors for a coffin, and buried him so, so they say, but I didn't see it. Pap told me. But anyway, it all come of looking at the moon that way, like a fool.[47]

As David Sloane notes, "Effortlessly blended into Huck's comments on omens of bad luck, this anecdote disappears in the run of his talk."[48] Jimmy's anecdote slips unobtrusively into his talk, as well. Both boys apparently wish to be scrupulously accurate about whether their reports are first—or secondhand, reinforcing, in the process, the reader's trust in the candor of their narratives.

Another element Jimmy and Huck have in common is an aversion to violence and cruelty. Both boys have bad dreams about cruel and violent acts they've witnessed, and have difficulty talking about the subject. Jimmy tells us,

> I can't kill a chicken—well, I kin wring its neck off, cuz dat don't make 'em no sufferin scacely; but I can't take and chop dey heads off, like some people kin. It makes me feel so—so—well, I kin see dat chicken nights so's I can't sleep.

After the mindless killings during the feud, Huck comments:

> It made me so sick I most fell out of the tree. I ain't agoing to tell *all* that happened—it would make me sick again if I was to do that. I wish I hadn't ever come ashore that night, to see such things. I ain't ever going to get shut of them—lots of times I dream about them.[49]

While Jimmy's comments involve chickens and Huck's involve human beings, the visceral rejection of violence and cruelty in each case is similar, as is each child's reluctance to talk about it, and the expression of personal anguish with the barely understood sleep disturbance of a child.

When either Jimmy or Huck is truly determined to fascinate his listener he launches into a long, name-filled family narrative. In neither case is the family his own. Jimmy talks about the family that runs the inn in which he works, and Huck about an invented family designed to make convincing whatever identity he has chosen (for pragmatic reasons) at that moment. "Dey's fo'teen in dis fam'ly," Jimmy notes,

> —all boys an' gals. Bill he suppo'ts 'em all—an he don' never complain—he's *real* good, Bill is.... Dat was Nan dat you hearn a cuttin' dem shines on de pi-anah while ago.... *Tab* can't hole a candle to her, but Tab kin *sing* like de very nation. She's de only one in dis family dat kin sing. You don't never hear a yelp outen Nan. Nan can't sing for shucks. I'd jes lieves hear a tom-cat dat's got scalded. Dey's fo'teen in dis fam'ly 'sides de ole man and de ole looman—all brothers an' sisters ... Dey all gits drunk—all 'cep Bill.... Dey's all married—all de fam'ly's married—'cep some of de gals. Dare's fo'teen. It's de biggest family in dese parts, dey say. Dare's Bill—Bill Nubbles—Nubbles is de name; Bill, an' Griz, an' Duke, an' Bob, an' Nan, an' Tab, an' Kit, an' Sol, an' Si, an' Phil, an' Puss, an' Jake, an' Sal—Sal she's married an' got chil'en as big as I is—an' Hoss Nubbles, he's de las'. Hoss is what dey mos' always calls him, but he's got another name dat I somehow disremember, it's so kind o' hard to git the hang of it.

Jimmy is convinced that all of these details will intrigue his listener—and, as it turns out, they do. Twain interjects,

> [Then, observing that I had been taking down the extraordinary list of nicknames for adults, he said]: "But in de mawnin' I can ask Bill what's Hoss's other name, an' den I'll come up an' tell you when I fetches yo' breakfast. An' may be I done got some o' dem names mixed up, but Bill, he kin tell me. Dey's fo'teen." ... By this time he was starting off with the waiter, (and a pecuniary consideration for his sociability), and, as he went out he paused a moment and said: "Dad—fetch it, somehow dat other name don't come. But, anyways, you jes' read dem names over an' see if dey's fo'teen." [I read the list from the flyleaf of Longfellow's *New-England Tragedies*.] "Dat's right, sah. Dey's all down. I'll fetch up Hoss's other name in de mawnin', sah. Don't you be oneasy."

[Exit, whistling "Listen to the Mocking Bird."]

Jimmy's concern that Twain might lose sleep over the fact that Jimmy hadn't been able to recall all the names reveals a blithe self-assurance that Twain found utterly charming and delightful.

Similarly, when the Grangerfords quiz Huck on who he is, he tells them a tale about "pap and me ... and Mary Ann ... and Bill ... and Tom and Mort." Huck offers the fugitive-slave-hunters a family narrative about "pap, and mam, and sis, and Miss Hooker," and regales the king and the duke with a tale about "Pa and my brother Ike ... [and] uncle Ben [and] our nigger, Jim." The language Huck uses in one such tale echoes Jimmy's precise phrasing. Huck says, "All of us was saved but Bill Whipple—and oh, he *was* the best cretur![50] As Jimmy had put it years earlier, "Bill, he's de oldest. An he's de bes', too."

The only "real" family that each boy has is "Pa" or "Pap" and in both cases the father has a history of alcohol problems that both children describe with unembarrassed frankness. In both cases (despite Jimmy's assertion that Pa's drinking days are over), the problem is ongoing.[51]

Jimmy and Huck also share some matters of taste: each boy is especially awed by a particular clock, and both set themselves up as judges of refinement.[52] Jimmy and Huck are both easily impressed by other things as well—Jimmy by the size of the church steeple and the weather vane at its top, Huck by the Grangerfords' fake plaster fruits and Emmeline's dreadful poetry.[53]

Finally, Jimmy and Huck are both at home with dead animals—dead cats, dead fish. These are simply a part of their world and they wouldn't dream of omitting them from their chatty conversation. They bring them in casually and comfortably, unaware that details about the dead animal might disrupt their listener's equilibrium or digestion. Jimmy entertains Twain at dinner, apropos of nothing in particular, with an anecdote about the dead cat in the well that supplied Twain's drinking water:

> Bill's down on cats. So is de gals—waiter gals. When dey ketches a cat bummin' aroun' heah, dey jis' *scoops* him—'deed dey do. Dey snake him into de cistern—dey's been cats drownded in dat water dat's in yo' pitcher. I seed a cat in dare yistiddy—all swelled up like a pudd'n. I bet you dem gals done dat.

With similarly jarring candor, Huck fails to edit out of his lyrical description of dawn on the river a decidedly pungent dead fish:

then the nice breeze springs up, and comes fanning you from
over there, so cool and fresh, and sweet to smell, on account of
the woods and the flowers; but sometimes not that way, because
they've left dead fish laying around, gars, and such, and they do
get pretty rank ...[54]

Perhaps Jimmy's sociable chatter about the dead cats remained in
Twain's subconscious, when, a few years after his encounter with Jimmy, he
introduced Huck Finn to the world in Tom Sawyer carrying a dead cat.

> Tom hailed the romantic outcast:
> "Hello, Huckleberry!"
> "Hello yourself, and see how you like it."
> "What's that you got?"
> "Dead Cat."[55]

Dead cats enter the scene in *Huckleberry Finn* as well, this time *en masse*, when
the Bricksville crowd is gunning for the king and the duke at their third
performance of "The Royal Nonesuch." Huck says,

> If I know the signs of a dead cat being around, and I bet I do,
> there was sixty-four of them went in.[56]

Both Jimmy and Huck are proud that they "know the signs of a dead cat
being around" and are only too glad to share their knowledge.

Twain had long admired the artful presentation of many of those
qualities Jimmy so fully embodied. For example, referring to a story James
Whitcomb Riley told, Twain commented,

> The simplicity and innocence and unconsciousness of the old
> farmer are perfectly simulated, and the result is a performance
> which is thoroughly. charming and delicious. This is art—and
> fine and beautiful.[57]

If "simplicity and innocence and unconsciousness" are to be desired, who
better to embody these traits than a child?

"Sociable Jimmy" was Twain's first published work in which the voice
of a child took center stage.[58] In the years that immediately followed its
publication, Twain became increasingly aware of the distinctive possibilities
of the choice of a child narrator. As he once put it, "Experience has taught

me long ago that if ever I tell a boy's story ... it is never worth printing.... To be successful and worth printing, the imagined boy would have to tell the story *himself* and let me act merely as his amanuensis."[59] That was, of course, precisely the role in which Twain placed himself as he copied down Jimmy's speech that evening. It is the same role Twain assumed in his imagination when he began writing *Huckleberry Finn*. In the recently discovered manuscript of the beginning of the novel, Huck's opening lines, "You don't know about me ..." are preceded by the words,

> Huck_∧^{leberry} Finn
> reported by Mark Twain[60]

Asked to explain his writing process, Twain said to an interviewer in 1907,

> I never deliberately sat down and "created" a character in my life. I begin to write incidents out of real life. *One of the persons I write about begins to talk this way and another*, and pretty soon I find that these creatures of the imagination have developed into characters, and have for me a distinct personality. These are not "made," they just grow naturally out of the subject. *That was the way Tom Sawyer, Huck Finn and other characters came to exist.*[61]

Twain's comment that his characters develop from their "talk" adds credence to the idea that the "revelation" that Twain experienced listening to Jimmy speak was a vital part of the process by which Huck Finn came into being. Whenever we encounter a sentence we like, Twain wrote, "we unconsciously store it away in our model-chamber; and it goes with the myriad of its fellows to the building, brick by brick, of the edifice which we call our style...."[62] Reading over his transcription of the encounter with Jimmy, Twain may have stored away in his "model-chamber" some of the texture of the child's speech.

It would not have been unusual for Twain to have taken some of Jimmy's topics of conversation, habits of expression, and turns of phrase (as recorded in his own rendition of them) and unknowingly recycled them as Huck's. For Twain had a habit, as he recognized himself, of unconsciously borrowing ideas and phrases from others. Walter Blair notes,

> In 1869, as [Twain] put it, he had "stolen" the dedication of a book by Oliver Wendell Holmes "almost word for word" quite unconsciously, and on apologizing had been reassured by Holmes

of the "truth" that we all unconsciously work over ideas gathered in reading and hearing, imagining they were original with ourselves. Midway in *Tom Sawyer* he again caught himself committing "unconscious plagiarism." In a letter of 1876, the year *Tom Sawyer* appeared, he indicated that he often unknowingly transplanted ideas from stories by others into stories of his own.[63]

Later in life Twain would express the doubt that "there was much of anything in human utterance *except* plagiarism!"

> The kernel, the soul—let us go further and say the substance, the bulk, the actual and valuable material of *all* human utterances—is plagiarism. For substantially all ideas are second-hand, consciously and unconsciously drawn from a million outside sources, and daily used by the garnerer with a pride and satisfaction born of the superstition that he originated them.[64]

If Twain found himself "garnering" some of Jimmy's ideas and expressions for Huck's world, his comments here suggest he felt that such a process was central to the production of his art.[65]

What enabled Twain to transform the voice of a black child into the voice of a white one so effortlessly, confidently, and, possibly, unconsciously? A good deal of the puzzle may be explained by the element of class. As contemporary accounts testify, there were many similarities between the speech of Southern whites and blacks at the lower reaches of the economic spectrum in the nineteenth century. A traveller in the South shortly after the Civil War observed, for example, that "the language of the lower class of the whites is so much like that of the negroes that it is difficult to say where the English ends and the African begins."[66] Although we know nothing whatsoever about Tom Blankenship's patterns of speech, his rock-bottom economic status as the offspring of "paupers and drunkards"[67] suggests that the dividing line between his speech and the speech of blacks in his community may have been quite faint. Twain could thus have plausibly borrowed habits of speech from Jimmy and put them in the mouth of Tom Blankenship or Huck without any sense of incongruity, without violating his own "pains-taking" efforts to have his characters speak in accurate (as well as accurately rendered) dialect. Although Twain distinguishes between the speech of white and black characters in the novel on a phonological level, on the level of syntax and diction, Jimmy's speech and Huck's speech are similar, as we have shown.

There may be another reason, however, for the ease with which Twain was able to blend elements of black and white experience in Huck: Tom Blankenship, the boy on whom Twain says he modeled Huck, had a black sidekick. On 22 August 1917, an old playmate of Twain's, John W. Ayres (who is mentioned in the *Autobiography*), wrote a letter to the *Palmyra Spectator* that was published under the headline, "Recollections of Hannibal." A clipping of it appears in a scrapbook owned by the Mark Twain Museum in Hannibal."[68] Here one "Black John" makes the following, rather startling appearance—startling because this is the only reference to him that we have. Ayres writes, "I spent part of my early childhood with my grandmother and many a day have chased rabbits over 'The Broadax'" [an open tract of land occupied by "squatters"]

> with "Black John," a half grown negro belonging to my grandmother, and Tom Blankenship. My grandmother told us that Tom Blankenship was a bad boy and we were forbidden to play with him, but when we went on a rabbit chase he joined us. Tom Blankenship was in fact "some kid." He was not subject to laws of conventionality and did not have to go to school and "behave himself" as the rest of us boys did, and therefore was much envied. Black John and Tom Blankenship were naturally leading spirits and they led us younger "weaker" ones through all our sports. Both were "talented," bold, kind, and just and we all "liked" them both and were easily led by them....

Ayres adds that he saw Clemens frequently in those days.

We know tantalizingly little about this slave named Black John, a "'talented,' bold, kind, and just" young man with natural leadership qualities who was at Tom Blankenship's side in "all our sports," and to whom Ayres refers in the same breath when Blankenship's name comes up.[69] But it is tempting to think that a fleeting memory of this high-spirited black companion of Tom Blankenship's, this "black Huck Finn," may have encouraged Twain to forge ahead with his daring project of blending, in Huck Finn, the voice of a black child (Jimmy) with the status and actions of a white child (Tom Blankenship).[70]

Can we assume that Twain's meeting with "Sociable Jimmy" actually happened and that Jimmy really existed—that neither was an invention on Twain's part? I believe we can. The most compelling evidence for Jimmy's existence is a letter Twain wrote to his wife on 10–11 January 1872, while on the lecture circuit. The letter reads, in part, as follows:

... If I had been at Mrs. Stowe's reading & they wanted any help,
I would have read about "Fat-Cholly Aithens" & the rest of my
little darkey's gossip. I think I could swing my legs over the arms
of a chair & that boy's spirit would descend upon me & enter into
me. I'm glad Warner likes the sketch. I must keep it for my
volume of "Lecturing Experiences"—but I'm afraid I'll have to
keep it a good while, for I *can't* do without those unapproachable
names of the Aithens family—nor "Tarry Hote,"—nor any of
those things—& if I were to print the sketch now I should have
the whole "fo'teen" after me.[71]

Twain evidently changed the family name from "Aithens" to "Nubbles"
when he published the sketch in the *Times* two years later, and Jimmy's name
may have been changed, as well. He also masked some details about the
scene's locale (no reference to "Tarry Hote" survives in the published sketch).
But Twain's references to the "boy" and the "fo'teen" members of the family
for whom he worked (and Twain's fear of the "fo'teen" coming after him if
he published the sketch) clearly establish that Jimmy was a real child whom
Twain met in late December 1871 or early January 1872.

Even without this documentary proof of Jimmy's existence, textual and
contextual evidence lend support to the idea that Jimmy was real. The
manner in which Twain framed his transcription of Jimmy's speech echoes
his transcription/re-creation during this period of the speech of two notable
vernacular speakers, in "The Jumping Frog" (1865) and "A True Story"
(1874). In both of these latter cases, the specific individuals who served as
models for the speakers in the story have been identified.

Twain introduces Simon Wheeler, the narrator in "Jumping Frog," as
follows:

... I found Simon Wheeler dozing comfortably by the bar-room
stove of the dilapidated tavern in the decayed mining camp of the
Angel's, and I noticed that he was fat and bald-headed, and had
an expression of winning gentleness and simplicity upon his
tranquil countenance.... He never smiled, he never frowned, he
never changed his voice from the gentle-flowing key to which he
tuned his initial sentence, he never betrayed the slightest
suspicion of enthusiasm; but all through the interminable
narrative there ran a vein of impressive earnestness and sincerity,
which showed me plainly that, so far from his imagining that

there was anything ridiculous or funny about his story, he regarded it as a really important matter, and admired its two heroes as men of transcendent genius in *finesse*. I let him go on in his own way, and never interrupted him once.[72]

Simon Wheeler was based on an Illinois river pilot named Ben Coon,[73] whom Twain had met at Angel's Camp, Calaveras County, California, in the company of his friend Jim Gillis in December 1864 or January 1865. As Albert Bigelow Paine described it, "one dreary afternoon, in his slow, monotonous fashion, [Coon] told them about a frog—a frog that had belonged to a man named Coleman, who trained it to jump, but that failed to win a wager because the owner of a rival frog had surreptitiously loaded the trained jumper with shot."[74] Twain entered a brief reminder of Coon's story in his notebook.[75] His own version of the story, "Jim Smiley and His Jumping Frog" (as it was originally called), appeared in the *Saturday Press* on 18 November 1865, and brought him immediate national fame.

Twain's introduction of Aunt Rachel resembles his initial presentations of both Ben Coon and Jimmy. He presented Aunt Rachel, the narrator in "A True Story, Repeated Word for Word as I Heard It," in this manner:

> It was summer-time, and twilight. We were sitting on the porch of the farmhouse, on the summit of the hill, and "Aunt Rachel" was sitting respectfully below our level, on the steps—for she was our servant, and colored. She was of mighty frame and stature; she was sixty years old, but her eye was undimmed and her strength unabated. She was a cheerful, hearty soul, and it was no more trouble for her to laugh than it is for a bird to sing. That is to say, she was being chaffed without mercy, and was enjoying it. She would let off peat after peal of laughter, and then sit with her face in her hands and shake with the throes of enjoyment which she could no longer get breath enough to express. At such a moment as this a thought occurred to me, and I said:
>
> "Aunt Rachel, how is it that you've lived sixty years and never had any trouble?"[76]

From that point on, Twain allows Aunt Rachel to tell her moving story in her own words.[77] The result Twain's first contribution to the *Atlantic Monthly*, whose editor, William Dean Howells, credited Twain with having successfully put "the best and reallest kind of black talk in it."[78] Twain was paid at the highest rate the magazine had ever offered.

The model for Aunt Rachel, as Twain and others readily acknowledged, was Mary Ann Cord, an ex-slave who worked as a servant at Quarry Farm, the Clemenses' summer home in Elmira, New York. Several sources corroborate the accuracy of Twain's description of Mary Ann Cord, in terms of both her character and her physical presence.[79] As Twain himself put it in 1906,

> she was cheerful, inexhaustibly cheerful, her heart was in her laugh & her laugh could shake the hills. Under emotion she had the best gift of strong & simple speech that I have known in any woman except my mother. She told me a striking tale out of her personal experience, once, & I will copy it here—& not in my words but her own. I wrote them down before they were cold. (Insert "A True Story.")[80]

On 18 November 1875, Twain presented a copy of the first edition of *Sketches New and Old* to Mary Ann Cord with the following inscription,

> The author of this book offers it to Aunty Cord with his kindest regards, and refers her to page 202 for a well-meant but libelous portrait of herself & also the bit of personal history which she recounted to him once at "Quarry Farm."[81]

Mary Ann Cord is buried in the same Elmira cemetery as Mark Twain.[82] In 1986, her great grandson, Leon W. Condol, of Silver Springs, Maryland, presented Twain's inscribed volume to the University of Maryland.[83]

Both of Twain's national successes through 1874 involving vernacular speech were thus based on real and identifiable people. His introduction of these speakers in these pieces resembles his introduction of Jimmy, supporting the belief that Jimmy was, indeed, a real child. In "A True Story," Twain was proud of having told the tale "not in my words" but in those of Mary Ann Cord. It is quite possible that some three years earlier he did just what he said he did and wrote down Jimmy's words, too, "before they were cold."

A fair amount has been written on Ben Coon and Mary Ann Cord, but no scholar has persisted enough to track down Jimmy, presumably because until now his significance has not been recognized.[84] There is no record of any letters or response to "Sociable Jimmy," Twain never reprinted it, and he never referred to it elsewhere. All the evidence indicates that he was probably unaware of the role this material could play in his career. He was initially blind to the significance of "A True Story," as well, minimizing its importance as he casually slipped it in the envelope when he mailed another manuscript to William Dean Howells.[85]

"Sociable Jimmy" seemed so obscure and trivial to George Hiram Brownell, editor of the *Twainian*, that in 1937 when Irving S. Underhill sent him a "photostat copy of ['Sociable Jimmy'] as it appears in printed form on the page of a magazine, name, date and place of publication unknown," Brownell casually filed it away for six years before printing it. When in February 1943 he finally reprinted the piece in the *Twainian*, he noted that when he was given "Sociable Jimmy,"

> In an accompanying letter, Mr. Underhill explains that the magazine page was pasted, without any identification data whatever, in a scrapbook purchased by him from a printer who had worked in Chicago during the period 1870–1875; and other clippings on the same page of the scrap-book were taken from newspapers and magazines published during the year 1874.[86]

He urged readers to come forth with any information about where the article had initially appeared. In April, Brownell announced that no readers had written the *Twainian* with any leads.[87]

By the time Paul Fatout reprinted "Sociable Jimmy" in *Mark Twain Speaks for Himself* in 1978, he was able to identify it as having run in the *New York Times*. Neither after its first republication in 1943, nor after its second in 1978, did the piece elicit any additional critical comment. In the brief note that Fatout appended to the piece, he wrote that Twain "may have been attuning his ear to the variations of Negro dialect and attempting to get it down credibly on paper." Fatout suggests that "perhaps Mark Twain wrote 'Sociable Jimmy' partly as an exercise in vernacular language."[88] The challenge of rendering speech in print had long intrigued Twain, and it is indeed quite possible that he used his encounter with Jimmy as an occasion for linguistic experimentation. It is, of course, impossible to determine precisely which phrases and sentences Twain heard and which he created in this as in other pieces rooted in real encounters. In "A True Story," for example, when Twain changed "'I ain't no hound dog mash to be trod on by common trash'" in the manuscript to "'I wa'nt bawn in de mash to be fool' by trash'" in the printed version, was he improving on Mary Ann Cord's original story, or merely revising his record of it to read more accurately?[89]

Jimmy's speech may have reminded Twain of voices from his childhood. Twain himself was candid about his preference for black playmates throughout his youth. He recalled, "I was playmate to all the niggers, preferring their society to that of the elect...."[90] As Twain noted in his *Autobiography*, "All the negroes were friends of ours, and with those of our own age we were in effect comrades."[91] Bernard DeVoto observed of the atmosphere in which Twain was raised,

> Black and white children grew up together, without distinction except that when wills crossed blacks must yield.... They investigated all things together, exploring life.[92]

Some reminiscences of summers on the Quarles farm by Twain's favorite cousin, Tabitha Quarles Greening, that were published around 1917 mentioned, for example, "the slave girl, Mary, little Sam's playmate" as an important companion of Twain's.[93] Throughout the article Greening emphasized the central role Twain's "darky playmates" played in his childhood and her own and in their memories.[94]

The unquestioned, important presence of black children in Hannibal as well as at the Quarles farm in Florida, Missouri, is captured by Twain in the pump scene in *Tom Sawyer*. When Tom Sawyer is forced to whitewash the fence on a sunny Saturday morning, he tries to switch chores with one of the servants who has been sent to fetch water:

> Bringing water from the town pump had always been hateful work in Tom's eyes, before, but now it did not strike him so. He remembered that there was company at the pump. White, mulatto and negro boys and girls were always there waiting their turns, resting, trading playthings, quarreling, fighting, skylarking.[95]

Whether Jimmy's voice belonged solely to the ten-year-old black child Twain met in 1871 or 1872, or whether it also drew on voices from Twain's past, it was rooted, as are all of Twain's most memorable creations, in real events and real people: "I confine myself to life with which I am familiar, when pretending to portray life ..." he wrote in 1890. "[T]he most valuable capital, or culture, or education usable in the building of novels, is personal experience."[96] In his journal in late 1887, Twain wrote,

> If you attempt to create & build a wholly imaginary incident, adventure or situation you will go astray, & the artificiality of the thing will be detectable. But if you found on a fact in your

personal experience, it is an acorn, a root, & every created adornment that grows up out of it & spreads its foliage & blossoms to the sun will seem realities, not inventions. You will not be likely to go astray; your compass of fact is there to keep you on the right course....[97]

Further, as he told an interviewer in 1895,

I don't believe an author, good, bad or indifferent, ever lived, who created a character. It was always drawn from his recollection of someone he had known. Sometimes, like a composite photograph, an author's presentation of a character may possibly be from the blending of ... two or more real characters in his recollection. But, even when he is making no attempt to draw his character from life, ... he is yet unconsciously drawing from memory.[98]

Did Twain's meeting with Jimmy take place as he described it? A number of contextual clues suggest that it did. The scene Twain recreated in "Sociable Jimmy" matches other scenes during his lecture tours, as described by his daughter and others. We know, for example, that after several years of being irritated with the lack of privacy when he stayed in people's homes while on the lecture circuit, Twain preferred to stay in obscure inns, where he often took meals in his room in an atmosphere resembling the one he describes in "Sociable Jimmy."[99]

We also have outside corroboration of the fact that Twain did, indeed, take a copy of Longfellow's *New England Tragedies* on his lecture tour that year. "To relieve the tedium of long train rides he always carried with him literary classics that had come to his attention, books by prominent literary contemporaries, and such things as Livy wanted him to read."[100] One book Livy urged on him was Longfellow's *New England Tragedies*, which came out in 1868. On 9 January 1872, Twain wrote Livy from Steubenville, Ohio, that he had "read & sent home" that particular volume.[101] The book was listed in the MTLAcc entry #2055, as a volume donated from Twain's library to the Mark Twain Library in Redding in 1910 by his daughter Clara Clemens Gabrilowitsch. Clara and her father donated 1,751 documented volumes to the Redding Library, but by 1977, when Alan Gribben prepared *Mark Twain's Library: A Reconstruction*, only 240 books that could be identified as having been donated by Twain or his daughter remained. The other books had been lost through circulation or "unwittingly sold to provide more shelf space for newer books."[102] Unfortunately, Twain's copy of Longfellow's *New England Tragedies* was evidently one of the volumes that had disappeared, for when Mark Twain's library was transferred to the Stowe-Day Library of the Mark Twain Memorial and later to the Watkinson Library of Trinity College, Hartford, this volume was missing. The book may turn up yet, in some Connecticut garage or estate sale, with Twain's list of names on the flyleaf.

It is also entirely plausible that Twain would have taken "down the extraordinary list of nicknames for adults" on the flyleaf of the nearest book he had at hand. Twain had the habit, throughout his life, of scribbling miscellaneous notes to himself on the flyleaves of books he owned when they were the most convenient things on which to write.[103]

If we assume that Twain met Jimmy while on tour some time shortly before 9 January 1872, when Longfellow's book still would have been in his room, we can narrow down somewhat where Jimmy may have lived. After a twenty-month absence from the platform, Twain had begun that season's lecture tour on 16 October in Bethlehem, Pennsylvania.[104] His tour took him to Washington, D.C., Wilmington, Delaware, and numerous cities and towns in Pennsylvania, Massachusetts, Connecticut, New York, New Hampshire, Vermont, Maine, New Jersey, Michigan, Indiana, Illinois, and Ohio.[105] From mid-December through early January, Twain's lecture dates were concentrated in the Midwest. The encounter, as we have noted, probably took place in Paris, Illinois.[106] Jimmy's boast that he had been as far as halfway to the town that was about 60 miles away (probably Decatur)[107] suggests that he had probably lived all of his life in the same small Midwestern town in which he was born. This assumption is consistent with his dialect, as Twain transcribed it, and helps explain why his speech is quite different from that of other black speakers whose voices Twain recreated in his fiction, most of whom hailed from Missouri or points farther south.

When he met Jimmy, some time between October 1871 and January 1872, Twain, who had just finished *Roughing It*, was in a good frame of mind to appreciate the child's innocence and exuberance. Jeffrey Steinbrink writes of Twain's persona on the lecture circuit that season: "Twain had ceased for the most part to be an innocent himself and had become instead a commentator on innocence, frequently the innocence of his earlier life."[108] Twain may have had only the vaguest notion, at this point, of where that role would take him. But a note he wrote his wife while he was on the lecture circuit suggests that he knew he was on the verge of something "big." "When I come to write the Mississippi book," he wrote Livy, "*then* look out!"[109]

What happened between Twain's first encounter with Jimmy in 1871 or 1872 and his decision to let a voice much like Jimmy's be the narrator of a novel some four years later, when he began *Huckleberry Finn*? For one thing, Mary Ann Cord told her story. That evening in 1874 when Mary Ann Cord captivated Twain and Livy on the porch of Quarry Farm may have been almost as important a step on the road to Huckleberry Finn as Twain's encounter with Jimmy two years earlier. For, while Jimmy's vernacular speech intrigued Twain, Mary Ann Cord showed Twain the possibilities of combining vernacular speech with accomplished narrative skill. She told her story so artfully that Twain felt he had to do little to its structure other than start it at the beginning rather than in the middle. Her story impressed Twain as a "curiously strong piece of literary work to come unpremeditated from lips untrained in literary art."[110] Quite possibly, the "curiously strong" nature of Cord's "literary work" may have been as much of a "revelation" to Twain in 1874 as the vitality of Jimmy's vernacular speech had been two years earlier.[111] It may be no accident that several months after hearing Cord tell her story, and after recording it on paper himself, Twain decided to return to the story his "little darkey" had told him two years earlier, change the names and places, and put it into print. Perhaps Cord's example, and Howells's unexpected enthusiasm for Twain's rendition of it, helped Twain recognize the great potential that lay in vernacular storytelling. Cord's narrative power in that vein, combined with Jimmy's cadences, rhythms, innocence, good-heartedness, and ebullient loquaciousness, may have moved Twain gradually closer to *Huckleberry Finn*.

Critics have long insisted that Huck Finn was a direct literary descendant of such earlier vernacular figures as Johnson J. Hooper's "Simon Suggs," Augustus Baldwin Longstreet's "Clown," George W. Harris's "Sut Lovingood," David Ross Locke's "Petroleum V. Nasby," and Charles Farrar Browne's "Artemus Ward."[112] Fine scholars including Kenneth Lynn, Walter Blair, Pascal Covici, Jr., and David Sloane developed the idea that Twain knew and admired the work of these popular newspaper humorists who preceded him, that these authors played a role in shaping his own career as a writer, and that they left their mark on Twain's writing in *Huckleberry Finn*. There are major differences, however, between Huck and these early comic "precursors" that scholars have never fully explained.

Twain's earliest sketches are clearly indebted to the work of many of the Southwestern humorists and Northeastern literary comedians. Browne left his mark on *Innocents Abroad* and *Roughing It*,[113] and Longstreet left his on *Tom Sawyer*.[114] These newspaper humorists played a role in the creation of

Huckleberry Finn, as well. For example, Twain drew on Johnson J. Hooper's "Simon Suggs Attends a Camp-Meeting" when he created the character of the dauphin,[115] and "Aunt Polly" bore such a close resemblance to B. P. Shillaber's "Mrs. Partington" that "Mrs. Partington's" picture was actually used to represent her in *Tom Sawyer*.[116]

One can easily see political satirist David Ross Locke's "Petroleum V. Nasby" as a forerunner to "Pap":

> ... Deekin Pogram sed he'd bore with them niggers til his patience wuz gin out. He endoored it till last Sunday. After service he felt pensive, ruther, and walked out towards Garrettstown, meditatin, as he went, on the sermon he hed listened to that mornin on the necessity uv the spread of the Gospil. Mournin in spirit over the condition of the heathen, he didn't notis where he wuz till he found hisself in the nigger settlement, and in front uv one uv their houses. There he saw a site wich paralyzed him. There wuz a nigger, wich wuz wunst his nigger,—which Linkin deprived him uv,—settin under his porch, and a profanin the Holy Bible by teachin his child to read it! "Kin this be endoored?" the Deekin asked.[117]

Twain knew and liked Locke, and it is quite possible that he took some tips from him on how to let his most blatantly racist character shoot himself in the foot. Locke's (Nasby's) "Ethnology at Confedrit x Roads: 'Possibly the Seat uv the Intelleck Is in the Heel,'" published in 1867, bears a strong resemblance to Pap's "Call this a govment!" speech in *Huckleberry Finn*.[118]

But what of Huck himself? Kenneth Lynn considers Harris's "Sut Lovingood" a major precursor. But Huck neither sounds, acts, nor feels like Sut Lovingood does. Listen, for a moment, to Sut Lovingood's speech:

> I seed a well appearin man onst, ax one ove em [the proprietors of taverns, evidently carpetbaggers] what lived ahine a las' year's crap ove red hot brass wire whisters run tu seed, an' shingled wif har like onto mildew'd flax, wet wif saffron warter, an' laid smoof wif a hot flatiron, ef he cud spar him a scrimpshun ove soap? The "perpryiter" anser'd in soun's es sof an' sweet es a poplar dulcimore, tchuned by a good nater'd she angel in butterfly wings an' cobweb shiff, that he never were jis' so sorry in all his born'd days tu say no, but the fac' were the soljers hed stole hit.... When the devil takes a likin tu a feller, an' wants tu

make a sure thing ove gittin him he jis' puts hit intu his hed to open a cat-fish tavern, with a gran' rat attachmint, gong 'cumpanimint, bull's neck variashun, cockroach corus an' bed-bug refrain, an' dam ef he don't git him es sure es he rattils the fust gong....[119]

Sut's cadences, lexicon, and syntax are worlds apart from Huck's. His long, dense, convoluted sentences do not manifest the repetition or serial verb construction that characterize Huck's speech, and Sut's sentences contain much more subordination. Sut uses no redundancy of subjects and does not use adjectives in place of adverbs.

Sut Lovingood's character and stance toward life are as far from Huck's as the language in which he describes them:

Every critter what hes ever seed me, ef he has sence enuff to hide from a cummin kalamity, ur run from a muskit, jis' knows five great facks in my case es well es they knows the road to their moufs. *Fustly*, that I hain't got nara a soul, nuffin but a whiskey proof gizzard, sorter like the wus half ove a ole par ove saddil bags. *Seconly*, that I'se too durn'd a fool to cum even onder millertary lor. *Thudly*, that I hes the longes' par ove laigs ever hung to eny cackus.... *Foufly*, that I kin chamber more cork-screw kill-devil wisky, an' stay on aind, than enything 'sceptin' only a broad bottum'd chun.[120]

Whereas Jimmy and Huck had a clear aversion to cruelty, Sut was, in Edmund Wilson's words, "always malevolent and always excessively sordid." "His impulse," Wilson maintains, "is avowedly sadistic."[121]

An' yere's anuther human nater: ef enything happens to sum fetter, I don't keer ef he's yure bes' frien, an' I don't keer how sorry yu is fur him, thars a streak ove satisfackshun 'bout like a sowin thread a-runnin all thru yet sorrer. Yu may be shamed ove hit, but durn me ef hit ain't thar....[122]

When Sut sees a "littil long laiged lamb ... dancin' staggerinly onder hits mam a-huntin fur the tit, ontu hits knees," his first impulse—indeed, he asserts it as a universal impulse—is

to seize that ar tail an' fling the little ankshus son ove a mutton over the fence amung the blackberry briars, not tu hurt hit, but jis' tu disapint hit.[123]

Sut's sadism isn't limited to "littil long laiged lambs." Affronted by innocence, he also welcomes the thought of kicking a calf fifteen feet in the air when it's trying to suck at its mother's breast, and would relish the chance to wallop a nursing human baby, too, "tu show hit what's atwixt hit an' the grave."[124]

In "Simon Suggs," another Southwestern character cited as a precursor to Huck,[125] we see a similar strain of selfishness, malevolence, and sadism. Summarizing one episode in his adventures, Kenneth Lynn writes,

Deciding that his parents are of no use to him ... he laughs aloud at the thought that he has secretly stuffed his mother's pipe with gunpowder instead of tobacco, and that soon she will be lighting it.[126]

Simon Suggs's character is as different from Huck's as Sut Lovingood's is. Franklin J. Meine describes Suggs as "a sharp, shrewd swashbuckler," whose whole philosophy "lies snugly in his favorite aphorism—'it is good to be shifty in a new cuntry'—which means that it is right and proper that one should live as merrily and as comfortably as possible at the expense of others...."[127]

Critics who place Twain in the tradition of the Southwestern humorists note that he "had the advantage of having been born later as well as innately superior to the rest of them."[128] But when it came to the crafting of Huck's voice, the gaps between Twain's art and theirs must be explained by something more than birth order or innate superiority. While Huck may have been related to Simon Suggs or Sut Lovingood or Petroleum V. Nasby on Pap's side of the family, that literary genealogy is woefully incomplete.

Something else helped make Huck who he was, helped catapult him beyond the ephemeral popularity these other characters enjoyed, to immortality. That "something else" may turn out to have been Jimmy and the memories of African-American speech he helped Twain recall.[129] Although Kenneth Lynn and others may see enough of a family resemblance to call a character like Sut Lovingood "a prototypical Huck Finn," the resemblances between Huck and Jimmy—on the level of both language and character—are infinitely stronger.[130]

NOTES

1. Mark Twain shared W.E.B. DuBois's intense and passionate appreciation of the beauty and eloquence of African-American spirituals. In recognition of the power this music had to move and inspire Twain, I reprise DuBois's practice of printing, "before each chapter ... a bar of the Sorrow Songs" (DuBois, *Souls of Black Folk*, 359). Both DuBois and Twain considered these songs "the most beautiful expression of human experience born this side of the seas" (*Souls*, 536–37). The bars of music and fragments of lyrics with which I begin each chapter come from songs Twain was likely to have heard the Fisk Jubilee Singers perform; they are taken from Anon., *Jubilee Songs: Complete. As Sung by the Jubilee Singers, of Fisk University* (1872) and Frederick J. Work, ed., *New Jubilee Songs, As Sung by the Fisk Jubilee Singers of Fisk University* (1902). They are, in order of appearance, Chapter 1: "Been a Listening" (Anon., *Jubilee*, 25); Chapter 2: "By and By" (Work, 45); Chapter 3: "Go down, Moses" (Anon., *Jubilee*, 22–23); Chapter 4: "Go down, Moses" (Anon., *Jubilee*, 22–23); Chapter 5: "O, Nobody Knows Who I Am" (Work, 39); Chapter 6: "Give Me Jesus" (Anon., *Jubilee*, 19); Chapter 7: "I Know the Lord's Laid His Hands On Me" (Work, 7); Chapter 8: "My Good Lord's Done Been Here" (Work, 11); Chapter 9: "I'm A-Going to Join the Band" (Work, 12). As John Lovell, Jr.'s "The Social Implications of the Negro Spiritual" makes clear, the spirituals expressed in coded language the slaves' deepest aspirations for freedom. "The spiritual," Lovell writes, "was a language well understood in all its burning import by the slave initiate, but harmless and graceful to an unthinking outsider" (462). As Frederick Douglass noted, "every tone was a testimony against slavery, and a prayer to God for deliverance from chains" (*Narrative*, 58). See also Sylvia Holton, *Down Home and Uptown: The Representation of Black Speech in American Fiction*, 48–49, and Gates, Jr., "Dis and Dat: Dialect and the Descent," 174–76.

2. Lionel Trilling, "The Greatness of Huckleberry Finn," 91–92.

3. Trilling, "The Greatness of Huckleberry Finn," 90–91. Philip Fisher, who calls "the novel told in the uniquely honest and vital voice of Huck Finn" the "most important first-person narrative in American literature," adds, "In Huck Twain invented a richer autobiographical voice than the comparatively weak first-person voices of Dickens" (Fisher, "Mark Twain," 636).

4. Louis J. Budd, "Introduction," *New Essays on "Huckleberry Finn,"* 15.

5. Albert Stone, *The Innocent Eye: Childhood in Mark Twain's Imagination*, 151–52.

6. Twain also drew on an experience that had occurred to Tom's brother Bence, who had helped a runaway slave hiding on a nearby island with deliveries of food.

7. Mark Twain *Autobiography*, ed. Paine, 2:174–75.

8. Tony Tanner, for example, observed in 1965 in *Reign of Wonder* that "Huck remains a voice..." (181); and Keith Opdahl noted in 1990 in "'The Rest Is Just Cheating,'" "Huck comes to life for us not as a physical being, since his appearance is barely described in the book (we know only that he dresses in 'rags' and fidgets at the dinner table) but as a voice ..." (277).

9. "Sociable Jimmy" ran on page 7 of the *New York Times*, 29 November 1874, over Mark Twain's by-line. All my quotations from the piece are taken from the original publication. Twain had begun to write *Tom Sawyer* the preceding summer.

10. On pp. 31–32 I describe in more detail the obscurity of this sketch among Twain scholars. The only critical attention the sketch has received is an eleven-line note Paul Fatout appended to the sketch when he reprinted it in *Mark Twain Speaks for Himself* (92)

and a brief, dismissive reference in Arthur G. Pettit's *Mark Twain and the South* (198 n. 14).

11. A letter Twain wrote to Livy on 10–11 January 1872 in which he refers to the previously sent sketch suggests that he was lecturing in the Midwest when he wrote the letter enclosing the sketch, possibly near Terre Haute, Indiana (there is a reference to "Tarry Hote" in the letter). Twain's first letter and original copy of the sketch have disappeared. The second letter indicates that Livy showed or sent a copy of the sketch to Charles Dudley Warner (*SLC to OLC*, 10–11 January 1872, *Mark Twain Papers*). Another letter lends further support to the idea that Twain met Jimmy in late December 1871 or early January 1872 (*SLC to OLC*, 9 January 1872, Mark Twain Papers). (See p. 35.) The working copy of Twain's lecture calendar for 1871 (being prepared as part of *Letters, vol. 4: 1870–1871*), which Victor Fischer of the Mark Twain Papers was good enough to share with me, allows us to narrow down the towns in which Twain met Jimmy to the following: in Illinois: Sandwich, Aurora, Princeton, Champaign, Tuscola, Danville, Matoon, and Paris; in Indiana: Logansport and Richmond; in Ohio: Wooster and Salem. (This list rules out the large cities Twain lectured in during this period, since "Sociable Jimmy" is clearly set in a less populous setting.) Victor Fischer believes the reference to Terre Haute in Twain's extant letter about "Sociable Jimmy" would make Paris, Illinois, a town thirty miles from Terre Haute, the most likely setting for the encounter (personal communication).

Another potential signpost is Jimmy's comment, "I ben mos' halfway to Dockery" and Twain's interjection, "[thirty miles]." Karla Holloway has suggested to me that "Dockery" may actually be "Decatur," a town whose "halfway" distance from Paris, Illinois, is some forty miles (not that far off from Twain's estimated thirty). Holloway notes, "Phonetically, 'Dockery' only replaces the vowel sounds and maintains the syllabic as well as the major consonant patterns. In linguistic change, even intentional change as Twain might have done, vowel shift (especially the front to back (and reverse) as happens if Decatur becomes Dockery) is still the most flexible" (personal communication). Holloway's insight lends further credence to the speculation that the encounter took place in Paris, Illinois. The name of the family for which Jimmy worked was "Aithens" (Twain changed it to "Nubbles" in the published sketch); evidence of an Aithens family in Paris, Illinois, in 1871 or 1872 may yet be found.

12. Mark Twain, "Sociable Jimmy." Emphasis added.

13. *SLC to Olivia Langdon Clemens*, 10–11 January 1872, *Mark Twain Papers*. Quoted with permission. Emphasis added. I am grateful to Victor Fischer and Louis J. Budd for having brought this letter to my attention.

14. A child's perspective surfaces briefly in his presentation of the letter he allegedly received from his niece Annie in "An Open Letter to the American People" (1866). Twain also experimented with a child narrator in his unpublished fragment, "Boy's Manuscript" (1868). See note 58.

15. Mark Twain, *Adventures of Huckleberry Finn*, Walter Blair and Victor Fischer, eds. [lvii]. Unless otherwise indicated, all citations refer to this edition. The "Explanatory" is quoted in full on page 103.

16. Huckleberry Finn, Chapter 39, cited in Bridgman, *The Colloquial Style in America*, 124–25. Capitals added by Bridgman.

17. Twain, "Sociable Jimmy." Capitals added.

18. Twain, *Huckleberry Finn*, 5. Capitals added.

19. Twain, "Sociable Jimmy." Capitals added.

20. Bridgman, *The Colloquial Style in America*, 117–118. Emphasis added.

21. Bridgman, *The Colloquial Style in America*, 118.

22. Emphasis added. Interestingly, although Bridgman cites these examples of Twain (and Huck's) investing words with "new meaning," the *Oxford English Dictionary* documents several of these usages—in particular, "smouches," "clayey," "soothering," and "haggling"—as having been employed before 1884 in precisely the same manner as Twain uses them (*OED* 15:815; 3:291; 16:4; 6:1014). This does not mean that the usage is the most common, however, and Bridgman's general point may still hold. "Skreeky," "alassing," and "sqush," on the other hand, seem to be genuinely original. "Skreeky" and "alassing" are in neither the *OED* nor the *Dictionary of American Slang*, and the entry for "sqush" in the *OED*, which notes that the word is "U.S. colloq. and dial. rare," cites Twain's use of the word in *Huckleberry Finn* as the first known usage (*OED* 16:427). Jimmy's use of the verb "sloshes" turns out to be a creative amalgam of the three definitions listed for "slosh" as an intransitive verb. The closest is the second definition: "U.S. To move aimlessly; to hang or loaf about." The first example provided, dating from 1854, refers to the expression "sloshing around" as a "Louisiana negro" usage. But when Jimmy has the "sloshing" taking place in saloons, he is creatively blending the idea of aimless loafing with the two definitions associated with splashing liquids and flowing streams (*OED* 15:735). Jimmy's use of the word "buster" resembles the first OED definitions, which are "slang (chiefly U.S.)" (*OED* 2:699). However, both *The Dictionary of American Slang* (80) and the *OED*'s earliest citations of the word (1850 and 1860) involve references to persons rather than things, suggesting that Jimmy's use of the word to refer to a clock may be somewhat fresh, if not wholly original. Perhaps Jimmy's most creative innovation in usage among the words on this list is "scoops": "When dey ketches a cat bummin' aroun' heah, dey jis' *scoops* him—'deed dey do" (italics Twain's). The usual usage of the verb requires the word "up" or some equivalent (*OED* 15:669). Could Jimmy (unwittingly) or Twain (quite wittingly) be punning on or playing with the phrase "to scoop the kitty," a gambling expression meaning "to win all the money that is staked" (*OED* 14:669)?

23. Bridgman, *The Colloquial Style in America*, 123–24. Capitals added by Bridgman.

24. Twain, "Sociable Jimmy." Capitals added.

25. Janet Holmgren McKay, "'An Art So High': Style in Adventures of Huckleberry Finn," 63. "During the thunderstorm, Huck glimpses 'tree-tops a-plunging about away off yonder.' At the circus, the bareback riders go 'a-weaving around the ring'" (McKay, 65, quoting from *Huckleberry Finn*, Chapter 22; emphasis added). Another example of Huck's double use of the "a-" prefix is "he set there a-mumbling and a-growling" (*Huckleberry Finn*, 24, emphasis added). As Twain characterizes his voice, Jimmy, too, employs the alliterative double "a-" in "You don't never see Kit a-rairin an', a-chargin'" ("Sociable Jimmy," emphasis added).

26. Bridgman, *The Colloquial Style in America*, 124.

27. Bridgman, *The Colloquial Style in America*, 122.

28. McKay, "'An Art So High': Style in Adventures of Huckleberry Finn," 67.

29. McKay, "'An Art So High,'" 64.

30. McKay, "'An Art So High,'" 66.

31. Nonstandard verb forms: Huck says, "I seen somebody's tracks" (19). Jimmy, in a related vein, says, "I seed it, when dey pulled it outen de cow" or, "I seed a cat in dare." Double negatives: Huck says, "I hain't got no money" (25); Jimmy says, "We ain't got no cats" or "dey ain't got no bell like dat in Ragtown." Redundancy of subject: Huck says,

"Tom he showed him how unregular it would be" (309). This feature characterizes virtually all of Jimmy's constructions as well: *"Bill he* don't like 'em," *"De res' o' de people dey* had a good time," *"Bill he's* real good," *"De ole man he* gits drunk, too," *"Bob, he* don't git drunk much," *"Bob he's* next to Bill," *"Sal she's* married," *"Hoss Nubbles, he's* de las." Emphasis added.

32. McKay, "'An Art So High,'" 70.

33. McKay, "'An Art So High,'" 66.

34. This particular use of the word "powerful" was noted by Thomas L. Nichols in 1864 as characteristic of Southern speech in general. "The Southerner," Nichols wrote, "is apt to be 'powerful lazy' and 'powerful slow'" (Thomas L. Nichols, *Forty Years of American Life*, Vol. I, 387). In *Huckleberry Finn*, however, the only character besides Huck who uses the word "powerful" in this way is Jim (who uses it twice, as compared with Huck's sixteen times). Villy Sorensen *"Huckleberry Finn* Concordance" in the *Mark Twain Papers* reveals that Huck uses the word "powerful" sixteen times in the novel, on the following pages and lines: 27.13; 45.17; 81.30; 92.3; 147.34; 149.10; 155.1; 192.7; 200.3; 204.37; 232.22; 235.2; 254.4; 264.22; 336.28; 345.1). In every case, the word is used as a synonym for "very" or "extremely." (Jim uses "powerful" on page 53, line 23 and on page 176, line 10.) I am grateful to Sterling Stuckey for having pointed out to me that Elma Stuckey, an accomplished poet and a granddaughter of slaves, uses the word "powerful" in the same manner in her poem "Defense": "De fence they keep on talking 'bout / Must gonna be powerful strong. / Done taken all them soldier boys, / Must gonna be powerful long" (Elma Stuckey, *Collected Poems*, 163).

35. Twain, *Huckleberry Finn*, 336, 27, 45, 147, 155, 93, 31, 40, 34, 69. Demonstrative of how characteristic the word "considerable" is in Huck's lexicon is the fact that he uses it no fewer than twenty-eight times in the book, as Sorensen's "Concordance" shows. (Huck uses it on the following pages and lines: 2.17; 4.12; 14.5; 31.30, 36; 34.26; 40.16; 52.13; 60.34; 68.24; 69.9; 93.26; 104.10; 137.14; 164.11; 166.1,28; 172.28; 181.31; 183.35; 187.25; 204.8; 239.6; 271.34; 284.25; 288.37; 314.3; 319.14.) Curt Rulon notes that "uninflected intensifiers" including "considable, considerble, tolable, tolerble, pow'ful, powful occur pervasively without -ly" in all the dialects spoken in the book (Rulon, "Dialect Areas," 220). This fact does not lessen the significance of these terms as characteristic of Huck's speech, however, since all speech in the book is ostensibly filtered through Huck and passed on to us in his version of it. Other similarities in Jimmy's and Huck's lexicons include both boys' use of the words "pison" and "truck" to refer to "poison" and "things" (or "substances"). Jimmy says, "Ain't it dish-yer blue vitties dat's pison?—ain't dat it?—truck what you pisons cats wid?" Huck says, "If I had a yaller dog that didn't know more than a person's conscience does, I would pison him" (290), and "... we turned over the truck the gang had stole off the wreck" (93).

36. Twain, *Huckleberry Finn*, 299.

37. Twain, *Huckleberry Finn*, 330. If Twain is inconsistent in his spelling of this word in "Sociable Jimmy" (Jimmy says both "scacely" and "scasely"), Twain will remain inconsistent in *Huckleberry Finn*, where, on one page, Huck says both "there warn't no real *scarcity* of snakes," and "there warn't no room in bed for him, *skasely*" (emphasis added), 330.

38. Twain, *Huckleberry Finn*, 90. Emily Budick has noted that Toni Morrison uses the word "disremember" in a somewhat similar manner in Beloved (274) (Budick, personal communication).

39. McKay, "'An Art So High,'" 70–71.

40. Victor A. Doyno, *Writing "Huck Finn": Mark Twain's Creative Process*, 43.

41. Doyno, *Writing "Huck Finn,"* 43.

42. Twain's use of nonstandard spelling, or "eye-dialect," to render vernacular speech, for example, places Jimmy closer to Huck than to Jim. Words that are phonologically identical are transcribed by one set of rules for Jimmy and Huck, and by another set of rules for Jim. Jimmy and Huck say "was," while Jim more frequently says "wuz." Jim's speech is generally characterized by more "eye-dialect" than either Jimmy's or Huck's. As Victor Fischer has observed, Twain's distinctions on this front were often refinements he added to the manuscript as he revised (personal communication). On page 111, line 19, for example, the manuscript originally had Jim saying "was," and Twain changed it, in the first American edition of the book, to "'uz." (Victor Fischer, "*Huckleberry Finn*: Mark Twain's Usage," n.p.). Twain eventually changed "was" to "wuz" on four occasions, and "was" to "'uz" on three occasions (Jim sometimes says "was," as well, but extremely rarely) (Blair and Fischer, "Textual Introduction," 510). Jimmy and Huck say "reckoned" and Jim says "reck'n'd."

There are some strong resemblances between Jimmy and Huck on the grammatical level, as well. David Carkeet's linguistic analysis in "The Dialects in *Huckleberry Finn*" provides the most elaborate effort to differentiate among the various patterns of speech in the novel. Taking Huck's dialect as the norm, Carkeet isolates those elements of Jim's dialect, for example, that differ from Huck's. Although "grammatically, Huck's and Jim's dialects are very similar," he notes, "Jim's dialect additionally shows the done-perfect construction (*she done broke loose*), deletion of the copula, and an *s* suffix on second-person present-tense verbs" (317). Jimmy uses a *done*-perfect construction only once; otherwise, his speech, like Huck's, characteristically manifests none of these features.

Whereas Jimmy's speech may be closer to Huck's than to Jim's grammatically, there are strong resemblances between Jimmy and Jim on the phonological level.

> Phonologically Jim shows widespread loss of *r* (*do* door, *heah* here, *thoo* through), palatalization (i.e., the insertion of a palatal glide—the initial sound of yes—in certain environments: *k'yer* care, *dish-yer* this here, (a) *gwyne* as the present participle of go, and substitution of voiceless *th* with *f* (*mouf* mouth) of voiced *th* with *d* (*dese* these) and of the negative prefix *un-* with *on-* (oneasy). (Carkeet, "Dialects," 317)

Huck's speech, unlike Jimmy's and Jim's, has none of these features. But even from a phonological standpoint, I would argue, several elements make Jimmy's dialect closer to Huck's than to Jim's. Jimmy and Huck say "considerable" while Jim says "considable." Jimmy and Huck usually preserve the final *t* in contractions even when the next word begins with a consonant, but Jim usually drops it. As James Nathan Tidwell observed, for example (based on his analysis not of the manuscript or first edition, but, as Blair and Fischer note, on the "heavily styled Harper's 'Mississippi Edition'"), "Jim tends to drop the final *t* of a contraction when the next word begins with a consonant (as in 'ain' dat'), but to retain the *t* when the next word begins with a vowel or is emphatic ..." (Tidwell, "Mark Twain's Representation of Negro Speech," 175; Blair and Fischer, "Textual Introduction," 508). Jimmy, by way of contrast, usually *keeps* the final *t* in contractions followed by consonants: "we ain't got no cats heah," "I wouldn't like to count all dem people," "Dey ain't got no bell," "De bell ... don't make no soun', scasely," "I don't think." (The one exception to this rule in Jimmy's speech is "I don' never git drunk.") Jimmy and Huck say "an'" or "and"—in fact, Jimmy says "and" nine times, while Jim almost always says "en'."

43. An occasional quality that Bridgman and McKay isolate as characteristic of Huck's speech, and that I have shown to be characteristic of Jimmy's speech, may also be found in other vernacular speakers Twain created. On 18 December 1869, for example, Twain published the story of Dick Baker's cat in the *Buffalo Express* (he would include the story in Roughing It in 1872). It was a revised and expanded version of an earlier sketch, which he had probably written in California (Twain, "Explanatory Notes," *Roughing It*, 600). The original sketch, "Remarkable Sagacity of a Cat," was written in standard English, but Twain's 1869 revision told the story in a vernacular voice (Dick Baker's), and included some of the qualities that Twain would later find or make central to Jimmy's speech and Huck's, including irregular verb forms, double negatives, "and" as a connector, and repetition (*Roughing It*, 390–91). Although these qualities are present on occasion in Baker's speech, they are not as essential to it as they will be to Jimmy's and Huck's speech. Twain's recognition in 1869 that the original "Cat" sketch held more interest and was more dramatic when told in the vernacular may be viewed as a step toward his recognition of the power of vernacular voices. Double negatives, "and" as a connector, and the use of "considerable" as an adjective are also found in Simon Wheeler's speech in "Jim Smiley and His Jumping Frog" (1865), and repetition appears in the speech of Coon in "An Unbiased Criticism" (1865). For all their vitality, however, the voices of Dick Baker, Simon Wheeler, and Ben Coon are not Huck's the way Jimmy's voice is Huck's. The striking correspondences between Jimmy's and Huck's basic syntax, diction, and cadences, as well as between the two boys' defining character traits, confirm the importance Jimmy played in revealing to Twain the narrative potential of that distinctive brand of vernacular speech.

44. Twain, *Huckleberry Finn*, 193–94. Drawing humor from a narrator who is oblivious to the implications of his own comments was, of course, a stock feature of literary humor and folklore, as well.

45. Walter Blair, *Mark Twain and "Huck Finn,"* 75.

46. Peter Messent notes that

> When Bakhtin speaks of the "radical character" of a naive narrator who completely fails to understand the usual ways of looking at the world, he could have had Huck Finn in mind. Bakhtin uses the word *estrangement* (his closeness to Russian Formalist conceptions of "defamiliarization" is obvious here) to suggest what happens when a fixed way of looking at and speaking about the world meets a narrator who is uncomprehendingly naive; who "by his very uncomprehending presence ... makes strange the world of social conventionality. (Messent, The "Clash of Language: Bakhtin and *Huckleberry Finn*," 217)

47. Twain, *Huckleberry Finn*, 65.

48. Sloane, *Mark Twain as a Literary Comedian*, 132.

49. Twain, *Huckleberry Finn*, 153.

50. Twain, *Huckleberry Finn*, 135, 89, 166, 90.

51. Jimmy tells us, "Pa used to git drunk, but dat was befo' I was big—but he's done

quit. He don' git drunk no mo' now. Jis' takes one nip in de mawnin', now cuz his stomach riles up, he sleeps so soun'. Jis' one nip—over to de s'loon—every mawnin'." With similar nonchalance, Huck notes that the judge who tried to reform Pap "reckoned a body could reform the ole man with a shot-gun, maybe, but he didn't know no other way" (28).

52. Jimmy enthusiastically admires the clock on the local church: "Dat clock ain't just a striker, like dese common clocks. It's a *bell*—jist a reglar *bell*—and it's a buster." Huck is just as impressed by the clock he encounters on the Grangerford mantelpiece: "It was beautiful to hear that clock tick; and sometimes when one of these peddlers had been along and scoured her up and got her in good shape, she would start in and strike a hundred and fifty before she got tuckered out. They wouldn't took any money for her" (136). Both Jimmy and Huck on occasion set themselves up as judges of refinement, unaware of the irony that their taking this role inevitably entails. Thus Jimmy passes judgment on the manners of the women in his house, and Huck on the wall markings left by some rough characters. Jimmy pronounces, "All dem brothers an' sisters o' his'n ain't no 'count—all ceptin' dat little teeny one dat fetched in dat milk. Dat's Kit, Sah. She ain't only nine year ole. But she's de mos' lady-like one in de whole bilin'." And Huck tells us, "There was heaps of old greasy cards scattered over the floor, and old whisky bottles, and a couple of masks made out of black cloth; and all over the walls was the ignorantest kind of words and pictures, made with charcoal" (61). The incongruity of a speaker who uses the word "ignorantest" while passing judgment on whether or not something is "ignorant" is lost on Huck. Similarly, Jimmy sees nothing amiss about putting himself forth as an authority on female refinement.

53. Twain, *Huckleberry Finn*, 137, 140.

54. Twain, *Huckleberry Finn*, 157.

55. Twain, *Tom Sawyer*, 74. Also on Huck's tongue shortly after he enters *Tom Sawyer* is the nickname "Hoss" (he refers to "Hoss Williams" on page 76; later in the book the Judge calls this person "Horse Williams"). "Hoss" is the nickname Jimmy expatiates on at some length in "Sociable Jimmy." Huck in *Tom Sawyer* shares some characteristic sentence constructions with Jimmy, as well. Huck, for example, says, "A body can't be too partic'lar how they talk about these-yer dead people" (*Tom Sawyer*, 93, emphasis added); Jimmy says, "People *can't be too particlar* 'bout sich things," and frequently says, "*dish-yer*," as well (emphasis added). Huck (in *Tom Sawyer*, 177–78) and Jimmy (in "Sociable Jimmy") both use the word "gal," while Tom makes it clear to Huck that (at least when referring to Becky Thatcher) he prefers the word "girl."

56. Twain, *Huckleberry Finn*, 198.

57. Twain, quoted in Walter Blair and Hamlin Hill, *America's Humor*, 322.

58. In a sketch written in 1868, which remained unpublished until Bernard DeVoto included it in *Mark Twain at Work* in 1942, Twain had experimented with telling a story from a boy's point of view. Twain presented the sketch as the diary of a boy named Billy Rogers. The sketch is, in some ways, a preparation for *Tom Sawyer*, and Billy is a precursor of Tom. The diary is dominated by Billy's admiration for "a heroine named Amy who inflicts on the hero the same agonies and ecstasies that Becky Thatcher was to inflict on Tom" (DeVoto, *Mark Twain at Work*, 6). But, as DeVoto comments, "It is Tom Sawyer untouched by greatness, and Tom Sawyer ... without Huck Finn. It is crude and trivial, false in sentiment, clumsily farcical, an experiment in burlesque with all its standards mixed" (DeVoto, *Mark Twain at Work*, 7). The "Boy's Manuscript" is reprinted in Dahlia Armon and Walter Blair, eds., *Huck Finn and Tom Sawyer Among the Indians and Other*

Unfinished Stories, 1–19. Armon and Blair assign 1868 as its date of composition ("Explanatory Notes," 265–66).

Although "Sociable Jimmy" is Twain first published piece dominated by the perspective of a child narrator, he had shown an interest as early as 1866 in children's tendency to be oblivious to the import of what they reveal. In a letter Twain presents as being from his eight-year-old niece "Annie," for example, Twain had the child sociably prattle on about a range of news items, including the fact that "Sissy McElroy's mother has got another little baby. She has them all the time. It has got little blue eyes, like Mr. Swimey that boards there, and looks just like him" (Twain, "An Open Letter to the American People," 1). I am grateful to Victor Fischer for bringing this piece to my attention. For more on Twain's interest in the speech patterns of real children, including his own, see Doyno, *Writing "Huck Finn,"* 41–42, 131–32.

59. Twain, quoted in Blair and Hill, *America's Humor*, 327.

60. Doyno, *Writing "Huck Finn,"* 40.

61. Anon., "Mark Twain Tells the Secrets of Novelists," *New York American*, 26 May 1907, in Neider, ed., *Life as I Find It*, 388. Emphasis added.

62. Mark Twain, "The Art of Composition," 227.

63. Blair, *Mark Twain and "Huck Finn,"* 59. In addition to being the year *Tom Sawyer* appeared, 1876 was, of course, the year Twain began writing *Huckleberry Finn*. During that year, Blair tells us, Twain showed particular interest in a chapter on plagiarism in Henry H. Breen *Modern English Literature: Its Blemishes and Defects.*

> On page 218 Breen scornfully quotes a statement of Alexander Dumas, whom he calls, rather sweepingly, "the most audacious plagiarist of any time or country." Says Dumas: "The man of genius does not steal; he conquers, he annexes to his empire. He makes laws for it, peoples it with subjects, and extends his golden scepter over it. And where is the man who, in surveying his beautiful kingdom, shall dare to assert that this or that piece of land is no part of his property?" Though Breen calls this a barefaced plea for literary thievery, Clemens agrees with Dumas in a marginal comment: "A good deal of truth in it. Shakespeare took other people's quartz and extracted the gold from it—it was a nearly valueless commodity before." (Blair, *Mark Twain and "Huck Finn,"* 59–60)

In other marginal comments Twain voiced his conviction that, as Blair put it, "an author might make materials his own by adapting them to the fictional world he was creating" (60).

64. *SLC to Helen Keller*, St. Patrick's Day 1903, *Mark Twain's Letters*, ed. Paine, 2:731. Twain's comments here are echoed by Bakhtin, who, as Peter Messent notes, "stresses so importantly, our language is not our own. In everyday speech 'of all words uttered ... no less than half belong to someone else'.... We constantly use the speech of another. Prior discourse ... invades our language at every turn" (Bakhtin, *Problems of Dostoevsky's Poetics*, 339, quoted in Messent, "The Clash of Language," 223).

65. Huck's voice, of course, will be more complex than Jimmy's, and much of that complexity will stem from the fact that two languages are, in effect, warring within him. Messent writes that one is "the words the dominant culture has given him to use concerning the slave," the "language of the authorities which has helped form him," and

the other is "that language which has emerged during and out of the conversation with Jim on the raft—that of equality and friendship, one rooted in pragmatic experience of doing and acting." Although the "latter language, celebrating 'an affirmation of a friendship among equals' wins out (in terms of the way Huck will act) in the contest of both language and values ... and leads to Huck's famous decision to tear up the letter and 'go to hell,'" by the same token, "Huck cannot overthrow the monoglossic discourse which has formed (part of) him. He is caught within its terms, its judgments, even as he decides to act in a way which counters its commands" (Messent, "The Clash of Language," 233). Messent feels that Huck "increasingly finds ... his language too weak to oppose those dominant voices which take over the raft, take over his and Jim's lives. That element of his voice which has emerged—hesitantly and sporadically—to find positive expression within the context of that community of two on the raft, is muted to greater and greater extent" (235). Although "Huck has the final word in the novel," Messent feels that "the implications of those last words are, in Bakhtinian terms, bleak" (238).

66. Sidney Andrews, *The South Since the War: As Shown by Fourteen Weeks of Travel and Observation in Georgia and the Carolinas* [1866], 229. See Walt Wolfram, "The Relationship of White Southern Speech to Vernacular Black English." Also, David Carkeet notes that in Twain's time and in the present century as well, "the speech of lower-class rural whites in the South shares a great deal with the speech of blacks" (Carkeet, "The Dialects in *Huckleberry Finn*," 332). These parallels often led dialect geographers to assume that African-American speech was identical with the speech of Southern whites, a premise most linguists today reject. As George Townsend Dorrill notes in a 1986 review article updating Raven McDavid, Jr., and Virginia McDavid 1951 article, "The Relationship of the Speech of American Negroes to the Speech of Whites," Ralph W. Fasold "states that many of the features claimed to be unique to blacks are shared with whites in the South, but that there is still a residue of features unique to the English of blacks" (Dorrill, *Black and White Speech in the Southern United States: Evidence from the Linguistic Atlas of the Middle and South Atlantic States*, 16). J.L. Dillard notes,

> Dialect geographers, in keeping with their preconception (almost, at times, an obsession) that the dialects of American English must be basically regional in distribution, continued to assert that Black dialects were—or, at least, had been in earlier times—identical with those of Southern whites. Since any specifically Black forms must represent "archaisms," the pidgin-creole tradition was felt to be unnecessary as an explanation of Black dialects in the United States. But the dialect geographers further asserted that these differences were solely a matter of a few relics, hardly enough to constitute a true dialect difference. The historical records did not, of course, bear them out. Neither did the evidence of listener perception tests...." (J.L. Dillard, "General Introduction: Perspectives on Black English," 13)

For a fuller discussion of the controversies surrounding this issue, see Holton, *Down Home and Uptown*, 24–41; John Baugh, *Black Street Speech: Its History, Structure and Survival*, 15–19; George Townsend Dorrill, *Black and White Speech in the Southern United States*, 1–17; and Ila Wales Brasch and Walter Milton Brasch, *A Comprehensive Annotated Bibliography of Black English*, ix.

67. Mark Twain, "Villagers of 1840–3," 96.

68. A photocopy of the page from *Morris Anderson Scrapbook* is in the Mark Twain Papers at the Bancroft Library at Berkeley.

69. Victor Doyno observed to me that the phrase "naturally leading spirits" suggests figures whose leadership qualities come from "nature," as opposed to the social world, with all its hierarchy and fixity (personal communication).

70. In Jay Martin's provocative and controversial psychoanalytic essay, "The Genie in the Bottle: Huckleberry Finn in Mark Twain's Life" (an essay that focuses on Twain's "persistent feelings of loss, guilt, despair, and insignificance and ... his momentary masked disclosure and transcendence of these feelings in" the novel), the following intriguing sentence appears: "To oppose his father, then, was to identify with the black—to imagine that Uncle Dan'l or Uncle Ned and Jennie were his real parents and that, like Tom and Valet in *The Tragedy of Pudd'nhead Wilson*, he too was divided; his selves were interchangeable, but *his real self was a black child disguised as a white man*" (Martin, 60, emphasis added; summary of essay from Sattelmeyer and Crowley, eds., *One Hundred Years of "Huckleberry Finn,"* 14). Twain's personal identification with the experience of black slaves is also apparent from the metaphor he uses in *Life on the Mississippi* to describe how it felt to escape unscathed from Brown, an abusive riverboat pilot to whom Twain, as a young apprentice, had been lent by his "master," Horace Bixby: "I know how an emancipated slave feels; for I was an emancipated slave myself" (160).

71. SLC to Olivia Langdon Clemens, 10–11 January 1872, in Mark Twain Papers. Quoted with permission.

72. Mark Twain, *Sketches New and Old*, 30.

73. Edgar Marquess Branch and Robert Hirst, eds., Mark Twain, *Early Tales and Sketches* II, 265.

74. Albert Bigelow Paine, *Mark Twain: A Biography* 1:217.

75. Twain's notebook entry read, "Coleman with his jumping frog—bet stranger $50—stranger had no frog, and C. got him one:—in the mean time stranger filled C.'s frog full of shot and he couldn't jump. The stranger's frog won" (Paine, *Mark Twain, A Biography*, 1:273).

76. Twain, *Sketches New and Old*, 240.

77. No one has given a more illuminating and insightful reading of the scene on the porch when Mary Ann Cord told her tale than Sherwood Cummings in *Mark Twain and Science*, 126–29.

78. William Dean Howells, *Twain-Howells Letters*, 1:195. In *My Mark Twain* he added, "The rugged truth of the sketch leaves all other stories of slave life infinitely behind, and reveals a gift in the author for the simple, dramatic report of reality which we have seen equalled in no other American writer" (Howells, *My Mark Twain*, 124).

79. I am grateful to Sherwood Cummings for generously sharing his fine paper about Mary Ann Cord with me:

> Research by Elmira scholar Herbert Wisbey has endorsed the essential accuracy of the story. Twain did change Auntie Cord's first name, which was Mary Ann rather than Rachel, and he got her age wrong. She was 76 rather than 60, a mistake testifying to the vigor in which she lived until, at age 90, she died from complications resulting from failing down a well. She had, indeed, been reunited with son Henry, who had become and remained a barber in Elmira until he died there in 1927 at age 82. There is a striking

corroboration from three sources concerning the commanding presence of
Rachel, or Mary Ann, Cord. In the story Rachel is "of mighty frame and
statute," and in her telling how as a slave for sale she was chained and put on
a scaffold, Rachel, the story-teller, "towered above us, black against the
stars." Twain described Mary Ann in a letter to Howells three years later as
"very tall, very broad, very fine in every way" (*MT-H*, 195). And in
photographs recently discovered by Herbert Wisbey she appears as a
handsome, tall, broad-shouldered woman.... (Cummings, "The
Commanding Presence of Rachel Cord," 2)

See also Herbert A. Wisbey, Jr., "The True Story of Auntie Cord."

80. Mark Twain, photocopy of manuscript of "A Family Sketch," 39. Mark Twain
Papers. Original in Mark Twain Collection, James S. Copley Library, La Jolla, Ca. Quoted
with permission.

81. Photostat of inscription reproduced in Angela Gambill, "UM Receives Rare,
Signed Twain Book," 13.

82. Wisbey, "The True Story of Auntie Cord," 4.

83. Gambill, "UM Receives Rare, Signed Twain Book," 1, 13; Molly Sinclair, "Mother
and Son's Amazing Reunion," 1.

84. Louis J. Budd, who plans to reprint "Sociable Jimmy" in an edition of Mark Twain's
social and political writings to be published by the Mark Twain Project, tried hard, more than
ten years ago, to identify the town in which Jimmy lived (Budd, personal communication).

85. Additional material, however, may yet appear. The letter Twain wrote pledging his
support of Warner McGuinn, one of the first black law students at Yale, was lost for a
hundred years before it resurfaced in 1985, reminding us that "lost" chapters of history
may continue to reveal themselves unexpectedly. See Edwin McDowell, "From Twain, a
Letter on Debt to Blacks," 1.

86. George Brownell, ["Request for Information about Sociable Jimmy'], 3.

87. He stated that "the proof of Twain's authorship of the "Sociable Jimmy" tale can
be established only by the discovery of a complete copy of the magazine containing it.
(Note: Despite Mr. Underhill's statement that the clipping in his scrapbook was taken
from a magazine, the photostat reproduction of it presents evidence that the clipping *might*
have been cut from a newspaper.)" (George Brownell, "Home," 1.)

88. Fatout, *Mark Twain Speaks for Himself*, 92. Fatout's note and another note in Pettit
Mark Twain and the South comprise the entirety of published critical comment that
"Sociable Jimmy" has received. Fatout's note reads as follows:

Mark Twain may have been attuning his ear to the variations of Negro
dialect and attempting to get it down credibly on paper. As Arthur G. Pettit
observes in *Mark Twain & the South* (1974), the notebooks of the 1880s and
1890s are full of dialect fragments, as well as folk expressions, as if Mark
Twain were testing accuracy by the sound and experimenting with spelling
to make print convey the sound correctly. In *Huckleberry Finn*, he explains,
there are seven varieties of dialect, black and white. Furthermore, "The
shadings have not been done in a haphazard fashion, or by guesswork; but
painstakingly, and with the trustworthy guidance and support of personal
familiarity with these several forms of speech." Perhaps Mark Twain wrote

"Sociable Jimmy" partly as an exercise in vernacular language. (Fatout, *Mark Twain Speaks for Himself*, 92)

While Fatout deserves credit for making this important article available to scholars, it should be noted that the transcription that appears in *Mark Twain Speaks for Himself* is unreliable: there are twenty-nine discrepancies between it and the original article that ran in the *New York Times* in 1874.

Pettit's reference to "a long and tedious sketch about a ten-year-old black boy named Sociable Jimmy" is brief, dismissive, and riddled with erroneous conjectures based on faulty chronology (Pettit, *Mark Twain and the South*, 198 n. 14). *Pettit* gives the sketch slightly more attention in his unpublished dissertation, but still dismisses it as "long and tedious" and generally without significance. He complains about Jimmy's "repetitiousness," failing to see any prefiguring of that same quality in Huck's speech. He uses "Sociable Jimmy" to bolster his case for "Twain's inability, or disinclination ... to account for deeper character traits in the black man than superlative ignorance, innocence, and gullibility," failing to recognize how positive and important these very qualities will become when transmuted into the voice and character of Huck (Arthur G. Pettit, "Merely Fluid Prejudice," 118–19).

89. Photocopy of manuscript of "A True Story." Mark Twain Papers. Original in Mark Twain Collection (#6314), Clifton Waller Barrett Library, Manuscripts Division, Special Collections Department, University of Virginia. Quoted with permission.

90. Dixon Wecter, *Sam Clemens of Hannibal*, 75; Mark Twain Papers DV 206.

91. *Mark Twain's Autobiography*, ed. Paine, 1:100. Twain followed this statement with the comment, "I say in effect, using the phrase as a modifier. We were comrades, and yet not comrades; color and condition interposed a subtle line which both parties were conscious of and which rendered complete fusion impossible" (*Autobiography* 1:100).

92. Bernard DeVoto, *Mark Twain's America*, 65.

93. The affection Twain and his cousin felt toward black childhood playmates was not unusual. Eugene Genovese notes, "Sometimes, lifelong friendships grew out of these early years. 'When I's a chile we'uns played togedder,' Betty Farrow said of her childhood with her master's three girls and four boys, 'and we'uns 'tached to each other all our lives'" (Genovese, *Roll, Jordan, Roll*, 516).

94. In July–August 1952, the *Twainian* reprinted an article containing Tabitha Quarles Greening's recollections that the editor identifies as having appeared in print some 35 years ago and reveals valuable information concerning Mark's environment during his youth" (Anon., "Mark Twain's Cousin, His Favorite, Tabitha Quarles," *The Twainian*, 1). In the article she recalled that

> The folk tore and strange African legends of "Daddy Ned" and Uncle Dan'll [*sic*] with the weird distorted superstitions of the slave girl, Mary, Little Sam's playmate developed the romantic nature that he inherited from his visionary father. The captivating stories that made Mark Twain famous were founded on the stories of Uncle Dan'l and Daddy Ned. Uncle Dan'l is the Nigger Jim [*sic*] of *Tom Sawyer*. The pages of *Huckleberrey Finn* [*sic*] show picture after picture of the life on the Quarles farm.
>
> We children had a mighty easy life. You see the negroes did the work and we roamed the hills gathering flowers, picking nuts, tapping the trees for

sugar and at night gathered around the fire place and heard the darkies tell
their ghost stories. Sam just repeated those tales Uncle Dan'l and Uncle Ned
told and folks said he was smart CA.)

In a little while I will go Away and if it is to a reunion with father and
mother, Uncle John and Aunt Martha, Sam and Margaret, Pamela and
Brother Fred, that place, wherever it may be, will be heaven. I do not think
we will be altogether happy unless we have Uncle Dan'l and Jinny the slave
girl who was sold down south. They are the imperishable part of our
childhood days and Sam with all the honors that came to him never forgot
"Puss" and his darky playmates. ["Puss" was Tabitha Quarles's nickname.]
(Anon., "Mark Twain's Cousin," *The Twainian*, 1–2)

According to the 1840 census, Quarles "owned, or at least recorded" two female slaves
under age ten, who would have been Twain's contemporaries (Twain being five years old
in 1840); the 1850 census (when Twain was fifteen) showed Quarles owning or recording
female slave children who were eight and twelve years old. (There were younger and older
slaves, as well, but these were the ones who were closest to Twain in age. All of these
children were probably the children of "Uncle Dan'l." Census data from Ralph Gregory,
curator of the Mark Twain Memorial, Florida, Missouri, cited in Pettit, *Mark Twain & the
South*, 192 n. 23). There is no record of Quarles having owned male slaves Twain's age. But
this information does not rule out the possibility that there were other slave children on
the farm, or on surrounding farms, with whom Twain may have played.

95. Mark Twain, *Tom Sawyer*, 46.

96. Mark Twain, in letter to unidentified person, quoted in Blair, *Mark Twain and
"Huck Finn,"* 9.

97. Mark Twain, *Notebooks and Journals*, vol. 3, ed. Robert Pack Browning, Michael B.
Frank, and Lin Salamo, 343.

98. (Lute J Pease "Mark Twain Talks," Portland *Oregonian*. 11 August 1895, 10.
Reprinted in Louis Budd, "A Listing of and Selection from Newspaper and Magazine
Interviews with Samuel L. Clemens, 1874–1910," 51–53; and quoted in Blair and Fischer,
"Explanatory Notes," *Adventures of Huckleberry Finn*, 372.

99. Fred W. Lorch, *The Trouble Begins at Eight*, 129. Citing Clara Clemens, *My Father,
Mark Twain*, 50, Lorch notes, "To escape any interference with his privacy Mark Twain
sometimes deliberately chose obscure hotels and occasionally employed the pseudonym
'Samuel Langhorne' while on tour" (Lorch, *The Trouble Begins at Eight*, 129).

100. Lorch, *The Trouble Begins at Eight*, 129.

101. SLC to Olivia Langdon Clemens, 9 January 1872, rpt. in *Love Letters of Mark
Twain*, ed. Dixon Wecter, 172.

102. Alan Gribben, *Mark Twain's Library: A Reconstruction*, 1:xxvii.

103. For example, while the front free endpaper of Meredith White Townsend's *Asia
and Europe* was torn out (perhaps something to do with jottings that had been on it?), the
front paste-down endpaper includes a note about having taken out fire insurance, and
another about comments made by a palmist. Twain scribbled penciled notes about the
dearth of cheap American books on the front and rear endpapers of Émile Zola's *Rome*, and
his assorted arithmetical computations appear on the last page of *A Story of the Golden Age*,
on the back cover of a pamphlet entitled *The Beecher Trial: A Review of the Evidence*, and
elsewhere (Gribben, *Mark Twain's Library* 1:41, 56; 2:709, 787).

104. Paul Fatout, *Mark Twain on the Lecture Circuit*, 151.

105. His speaking engagements included Allentown, Wilkes-Barre, Easton, Reading, Norristown, Washington, D.C., Wilmington, Great Barrington, Milford, Brattleboro, Boston, Hartford, Worcester, Manchester, Haverhill, Portland, Lowell, Philadelphia, Brooklyn, Rondout, Bennington, Albany, Newark, Oswego, Homer, Geneva, Auburn, Warsaw, Fredonia, Erie, Jackson, Lansing, Grand Rapids, Kalamazoo, Chicago, Aurora, Sandwich, Princeton, Champaign, Tuscola, Danville, Matoon, Paris, Indianapolis, Logansport, Richmond, Dayton, Columbus, Wooster, Salem, and Steubenville (Fatout, *Mark Twain on the Lecture Circuit*, 152–70).

106. See note 11. Twain lectured in Paris, Illinois, on 30 December 1871, and remained there through at least part of the next day.

107. See note 11.

108. Jeffrey Steinbrink, *Getting to Be Mark Twain*, 190.

109. SLC to Olivia Langdon Clemens, 27 November 1871, in *Love Letters*, ed. Wecter, 166.

110. Typescript of notebook 35, May–Oct 1895, 8. Mark Twain Papers. Quoted with permission.

111. I am very grateful to William Andrews for making this astute observation and for suggesting to me this promising line of reasoning (personal communication).

112. See, for example, Lynn, *Mark Twain and Southwestern Humor*; Sloane, *Mark Twain as a Literary Comedian*; Covici, Jr., *Mark Twain's Humor*; Walter Blair, *Native American Humor*; M. Thomas Inge, ed., *The Frontier Humorists*. Although Henry Nash Smith (*Mark Twain: The Development of a Writer*) rejects the idea that Twain was influenced by Charles Farrar Browne's Artemus Ward, David E.E. Sloane (*Mark Twain as a Literary Comedian*) makes a convincing case for a closer connection between Ward and Twain.

113. Sloane, *Mark Twain as a Literary Comedian*, 95–103; 133.

114. Lynn, *Mark Twain and Southwestern Humor*, 69.

115. Lynn, *Mark Twain and Southwestern Humor*, 81; Covici, Jr., *Mark Twain's Humor*, 13–14; Sloane, *Mark Twain as a Literary Comedian*, 134.

116. Blair, *Mark Twain and "Huck Finn*," 62–64; Sloane, *Mark Twain as a Literary Comedian*, 134.

117. Petroleum V. Nasby [Locke], "Presumptuous Freedman: 'Ef It Hadn't Bin for Their Black Faces, They Wood Have Passed for Folks'" [1866], in Locke, *The Struggles of Petroleum V. Nasby*, 75.

118. Nasby [Locke], "Ethnology at Confedrit x Roads: 'Possibly the Seat uv the Intelleck Is in the Heel,'" in Locke, *The Struggles of Petroleum V. Nasby*, 208–13; Twain, *Huckleberry Finn*, 37–39. Other characters in *Huckleberry Finn* may have been indebted to contemporary dialect writers, as well. Since Twain completed the book in the early 1880s, he may have modeled the white women's gossip scene at the Phelps's plantation on a similar episode Joel Chandler Harris included in "At Teague Poteet's: A Sketch of the Hog Mountain Range," which appeared in *Century Magazine* in 1883. See David Carkeet, "The Source for the Arkansas Gossips in Huckleberry Finn," 90–92.

119. Sut Lovingood, quoted in Edmund Wilson, "Sut Lovingood," 149–50.

120. "Sut Lovingood Yarns," quoted in Franklin J. Meine, "Tall Tales of the Southwest," 22. Huck would never break down categories in this manner, as Susan Harris has observed (personal communication).

121. Wilson, "Sut Lovingood," 149, 148.

122. "Sut Lovingood," quoted in Wilson, "Sut Lovingood," 148.

123. "Sut Lovingood," quoted in Wilson, "Sut Lovingood," 148.

124. "Sut Lovingood," quoted in Wilson, "Sut Lovingood," 148–49.

125. Covici, Jr., *Mark Twain's Humor*, 40.

126. Lynn, *Mark Twain and Southwestern Humor*, 80.

127. Meine, "Tall Tales of the Southwest," 21.

128. John Donald Wade, "Southern Humor," 35.

129. It is also important to note, of course, that that "something else" involved Twain's genius for narrowing the gap between oral and written communication. Twain's dialect writing is more readable and poses fewer obstacles for the reader than any that came before him.

130. In Twain's sequels to *Huckleberry Finn* in which Huck reappears, a number of the resemblances between Huck and Jimmy still hold. In *Tom Sawyer, Detective*, for example, Huck retains in his vocabulary words he had shared with Jimmy—such as "reckon," "snake," and "powerful." And the repetition characteristic of both boys' voices is still a part of Huck's voice in *Tom Sawyer Abroad*:

> All around us was a *ring*, a perfectly round ring, where the sky and the water come together; yes a monstrous big ring, it was, and we right in the dead *centre* of it. Plum in the *centre*. We was racing along like a prairie fire, but it never made any difference, we couldn't seem to git past that *centre* no way. I couldn't see that we ever gained an inch on that *ring* (24). (Emphasis added)

Huck in *Tom Sawyer Abroad* occasionally sounds like the "old" Huck, using words like "considerable" and "lonesome," employing irregular verb forms, double negatives, and frequent "and"s as connectors, and making up effective new words ("homeful"):

> We set scrunched up together, and thought considerable, but didn't say nothing, only just a word once in a while when a body had to say something or bust, we was so scared and worried. The night dragged along slow and lonesome. We was pretty low down, and the moonshine made everything soft and pretty, and the farm houses looked snug and homeful, and we could hear the farm sounds, and wished we could be down there.... (14)

In *Tom Sawyer Abroad*, Huck manifests the same aversion to cruelty that he and Jimmy had shown earlier:

> ... I see a bird setting on a dead limb of a high tree, singing, with his head tilted back and his mouth open, and before I thought I fired, and his song stopped and he fell straight down from the limb, all limp like a rag, and I run and picked him up, and he was dead, and his body was warm in my hand, and his head rolled about, this way and that, like his neck was broke, and there was a white skin over his eyes, and one little drop of blood on the side of his head, and laws! I couldn't see nothing more for the tears; and I hain't ever murdered no creature since, that warn't doing me no harm, and I ain't going to. (32)

In general, however, there is a real falling off in these works. Gratuitous eye-dialect intrudes, as in "I was just as cam, a body couldn't be any cammer" (*Tom Sawyer Abroad*, 19), and Huck's comments are often rather wooden. Huck's voice is substantially diminished, and, as the titles of the volumes suggest, it is Tom's agenda and perspective that take over despite the fact that Huck is the ostensible narrator.

HENRY B. WONHAM

Joyous Heresy:
Travelling with the Innocent Abroad

Americans expended considerable energy attempting to answer criticism from European travellers in the New World during the late eighteenth and early nineteenth centuries. In their defense, writers such as Royall Tyler were understandably prone to grasp at whatever advantage they could claim, with the result that many of the earliest responses to European criticism probably provoked more amusement than respect on the other side of the Atlantic. As one of the first and best known patriots to brandish a pen in the nation's defense, Tyler helped to initiate a tradition of American response to European censure by producing his own observations of travel in England, published anonymously in 1808 as *The Yankey in London*. In a typical passage, the American writer condemns what he considers the pernicious habit among members of the most polite British society of polluting their language with "evanescent vulgarisms of fashionable colloquy," or slang. He goes on to object that "there are a number of words now familiar, not merely in transient converse, but even in English fine writing, which are of vulgar origin and illegitimate descent, which ... degrade their finest modern compositions by a grotesque air of pert vivacity."

The Yankee is especially rankled by the word "clever," which the British frequently employ to mean "skillful" or "adroit." He observes that

From *Mark Twain and the Art of the Tall Tale* © 1993 Oxford University Press.

Englishmen, from the peer to the peasant, cannot converse ten minutes without introducing this pert adjunct. The English do not, however, use it in the same sense we do in New England, where we apply it to personal grace, and call a trim, well-built young man, clever—which signification is sanctioned by Bailey's and the elder English dictionaries.

Had America's cultural sovereignty depended on the effectiveness of such attacks, it might have been a much longer and ultimately less successful struggle. Not surprisingly, a proposed second volume of Tyler's travel observations never appeared in print, possibly indicating that his strategy for out-Britishing the British was not terribly effective at bolstering the national pride.

Fortunately for America, more resourceful writers fashioned other weapons with which to answer the charge of cultural depravity in the New World. If the former colonists could not speak more correctly than their European critics, at least they could speak differently, in fact so differently that no degree of Old World refinement and polish could decipher the full meaning of an American's idiom. Hence when a character named Jonathan Peabody made a fictional journey to London as part of James Kirke Paulding's 1813 production of *The Bucktails; or Americans in England*, he was full of unmistakably native pride, whistling "Yankee Doodle" and bragging in defiance of his foreign critics: "I'm half horse, half alligator, and a little bit of the Ingen, I guess." Paulding's foppish British characters were thoroughly subdued by such figurative boasting, and they seemed equally befuddled by the American gift for spinning out formulations like "I guess," "I reckon," and "I calculate." Royall Tyler would have been embarrassed to hear his fictitious countryman Sam Slick brag in a similar vein of his peculiar advantage over the British in Thomas Chandler Haliburton's *The Attaché; or Sam Slick in England* (1843). Sam admits he may be inferior to his English hosts in manners and refinement, but he knows "a leetle, jist a leetle, grain more, p'r'aps," about the British "than they [know] of the Yankees." More specifically, Sam finds that "they're considerable large print are the Bull family," "you can read 'em by moonlight," whereas the narrator warns of Sam himself that "it was not always easy to decide whether his stories were facts or fictions." After "shampooing the English" in one episode, the champion of Yankee slang exclaims, "Oh dear! how John Bull swallows this soft sawder, don't he?"

Paulding, as usual, played an important role in establishing the yarn spinner's art as a national trait capable of asserting American democratic values against criticism from Europe. His *John Bull in America; or, The New Munchausen* (1825) satirized Britain's thirst for confirmation of its already firm belief that the liberated colonies were populated by wild animals and even wilder humans. The mock editor of this purportedly unfinished manuscript explains that, despite the title he has chosen, readers should be prepared to enjoy "a work of incomparable veracity." The manuscript's author, according to the editor, was an Englishman, probably a staff writer for London's *Quarterly Review*, a journal famous for its denunciations of America. While gathering observations of American life, the author disappeared without a trace, leaving only a tattered notebook behind. Finding the mysterious Englishman's work to be "of severe and inflexible truth," despite its author's occasional willingness to "stretch his belief into the regions of the marvellous," the editor has decided to publish the unclaimed manuscript. Predictably, the new Munchausen's narrative often verges on the fantastic, although in his eagerness to confirm a cultural bias, the Englishman is the last to suspect that his accounts of American brutality and vice are even partially exaggerated.

> The Governor told me a story of a man, who tied his black servant naked to a stake, in one of the neighboring canebrakes, near the city, which abound with a race of moschetoes that bite through a boot. He was left one night, in the month of December, which is a spring month in this climate, and the next morning was found stone dead, without a drop of blood in his body. I asked if this brutal tyrant was not brought to justice? The Governor shrugged his shoulders and replied, that he was now a member of Congress!

Paulding's caricature of the hopelessly credulous Englishman proved a far more convincing response to British attitudes than had Royall Tyler's haughty critique of London slang. The tall tale was readily available as a weapon that could be used against unsuspecting European travellers in America, and it was not long before American globe-trotters like J. Ross Browne, Samuel Fiske, and Mark Twain were arriving in foreign lands, armed with this slender superiority. In their dispatches to readers at home, America's travelling humorists declared their independence from traditional romantic and associationist approaches to descriptive writing about foreign cultures. Browne, for example, warned in *Yusef* (1853) that readers would find his account of experiences in Palestine more cheerful and less profound than other books on the Holy Land: "it will be seen that I have not felt it to be my duty to make a desponding pilgrimage through the Holy Land; for upon a careful perusal of the Scriptures, I can find nothing said against a cheerful frame of mind." Samuel Fiske, another popular dissenter from the "desponding" school of travel correspondence, published a memoir of his journey through Europe, North Africa, and the Holy Land in 1857 under the title *Mr. Dunn Browne's Experiences in Foreign Parts*. A typical passage tended to demystify European experience for American readers by adopting a yarn spinner's figurative and hyperbolic language:

> A German bed is a sort of coffin about five feet long and two wide, into which a body squeezes himself and passes the night completely buried in feathers, and digs himself out in the morning.... I never endured the thing but one night, during which I dreamed of undergoing no less than four distinct deaths, one by an anaconda necklace, one by a hempen ditto, one by the embrace of a grizzly bear, and a fourth by the press of a cider-mill.

Fiske's humor may have been less than overpowering, but his focus on sordid details rather than historical panoramas marked an important coming of age in the American interpretation of its past. His prefatory remarks, echoing Browne's disclaimer in *Yusef*, signaled an intention to describe foreign lands as they might have appeared to the eye of an unromantic American:

> I shall endeavor ... to keep wide open my eye financial, agricultural, commercial, architectural, legal, critical, metaphysical, and quizzical. I shall also take a bird's eye view of the feathered tribes, cast a sheep's eye at the flocks and herds, and obtain dissolving views of the beet sugar crop and salt mines.... No rouge will be laid on the face of the old lady, and no artificial helps resorted to, to improve her beauty; no milliner's fripperies, trinkets, and jewels, but a simple dress. Mine shall be a "plain, unvarnished tale:" no quips and quiddities, sly innuendoes and oddities of language to disturb the digestion of an after dinner reader.

In June 1867, ten years after the publication of Fiske's book, Mark Twain boarded the *Quaker City* and followed an almost identical route toward the East, determined, like his predecessors, to dispense with the conventional picturesque mode and to report his experience in a language and from a perspective that Americans could understand. Like Paulding's Jonathan Peabody and Haliburton's Sam Slick before him, Mark Twain's narrator arrives in the Old World with only a yarn spinner's shrewdness to compensate for an abundance of ignorance. But that small advantage is decisive in establishing the perspective of Twain's American innocent abroad. The narrator is aware that many experiences escape his unrefined appreciation, yet he neither apologizes for his rough humor nor makes pretenses toward understanding what is alien to his sensibility. He recognizes himself as a greenhorn in matters involving European standards of taste and sophistication, yet he is always ready to strike back by exploiting the credulity of foreigners. His intention, like Fiske's, is "to suggest to the reader how *he* would be likely to see Europe and the East if he looked at them with his own eyes instead of the eyes of those who traveled in those countries before him."

Albert Bigelow Paine noted that Twain's correspondence from Europe and the Holy Land "preached heresy—the heresy of viewing revered landmarks and relics joyously, rather than lugubriously." In fact, the author's favorite strategy in the series of letters he sent to the *Daily Alta California* and to two New York newspapers between 1867 and 1868 was to view his subject matter both lugubriously and joyously, so that his humor tended to operate in the contrast between competing points of view. In a typical passage from the original series of letters, the narrator presents an exaggeratedly luxuriant image of Lake Como, explicitly mimicking the picturesque mode of landscape description: "Last night the scenery was striking and picturesque. On the other side crags and trees, and snowy houses were pictured in the glassy lake with a wonderful distinctness, and streams of light from a distant window shot far abroad over the still waters. After several more lines of indulgent scene painting, the narrator declares, "but enough of description is sufficient, I judge." Feeling he has perhaps gone too far in his praise of Lake Como, he shifts his focus to America with a digressive comment on the "wonderful translucence of Lake Tahoe," and a different sort of scene painting ensues:

> I speak of the north shore of Tahoe, where one can count the scales on a trout at a depth of a hundred and eighty feet. I have tried to get this statement off at par here, but with no success; so I have been obliged to negotiate it at fifty per cent. discount. At this rate I find some takers, perhaps you may as well receive it on the same terms—ninety feet instead of a hundred and eighty.

The narrator's juxtaposition of these two images is significant, for his sudden willingness to negotiate the claim about Tahoe's translucence punctures the romantic picture of Como as well. Moving rapidly from lugubrious description to joyous heresy, as Paine might have put it, the narrator establishes an ongoing contrast between different ways of assessing and reporting experience. Twain employs essentially the same joke in a later episode, again echoing James Hall's 1828 account of an interpretive bartering session in which competing storytellers figure truth as a relative commodity. After a lengthy account of his ascent of Mount Vesuvius, the narrator proposes an interpretive joint venture as the only hope of affording a local legend whose extravagance is too dear:

> It is said that during one of the grand eruptions of Vesuvius it discharged massy rocks weighing many tons a thousand feet into the air, its vast jets of smoke and steam ascended thirty miles toward the firmament, and clouds of its ashes were wafted abroad and fell upon the decks of ships seven hundred and fifty miles at sea! I will take the ashes at a moderate discount, if any one will take the thirty miles of smoke, but I do not feel able to take a commanding interest in the whole story by myself.

Each of America's early yarn-spinning ambassadors, from Peabody to Dunn Browne, had played some version of this game, mingling wide-eyed reverence with a native genius for subversive, irreverent talk. Fiske was particularly adept at juxtaposing panoramic descriptions with sordid particulars, a tactic already standard in more "serious" travel correspondence dating from the first part of the nineteenth century. Nevertheless, familiar as many of its comic devices must have seemed in 1869, readers greeted *The Innocents Abroad* with unprecedented enthusiasm. Other writers knew all too well how to employ the Vesuvius brand of understatement as a way of qualifying their exaggeratedly luxurious descriptions; what separated *Innocents* from its prototypes was Mark Twain's refusal to stop at the sort of contrast suggested by mere understatement—his insistence, in other words, on dramatic confrontation in favor of verbal contrast.

Twain had learned from "The Jumping Frog" and other early pieces that the narrative interest of tall humor stems primarily from the interpretive drama that surrounds the performance of a tale. Thus on his return to America in 1868, he began revising his *Alta* letters in an effort to dramatize the often static comedy of the original correspondence. It was a step that other humorists, J. Ross Browne most notably, had omitted, yet one that proved decisive as a means of organizing what Bruce Michaelson has called Twain's "pleasure tour through modes of narration." Like earlier humorous correspondents, the narrator of *The Innocents Abroad* moves rapidly and unexpectedly from one voice to another—from sentimentalism to parody, from patriotism to anti-Americanism, from silliness to sober observation. Yet in each of his guises, the narrator remains a player in the tall tale's interpretive game, and Twain's ability to give that game dramatic expression lends the book a measure of coherence that is lacking in Browne's *Yusef* and other comic travelogues of the period. Michaelson aptly describes *Innocents* as "a stylistic experiment with the principle of improvisatory play." Insofar as all improvisation is to some extent governed, the rules of that play are the rules of the tall tale's rhetorical drama, which Twain's revisions enact at every opportunity as a way of steering his "pleasure tour" toward its appointed destination.

The Vesuvius and Tahoe passages survived Twain's reworking of the *Alta* letters, yet many of the changes he undertook in preparing a manuscript for book publication reflect a conscious effort to dramatize his humorous material. The most important single change involved a shift in the narrative situation. The third in his series of fifty letters to the *Alta*, for example, begins with a description of the Moroccan port of Tangier, which the author praises with faint damnation: "This is jolly! This is altogether the infernalest place I have ever come across yet. Let those who went up through Spain make much of it—these dominions of the Emperor of Morocco suit me well enough." When he revised the passage for book publication early in 1868, Twain made only minor changes: "This is royal! Let those who went up through Spain make the best of it—these dominions of the Emperor of Morocco suit our little party well enough" (57). The substitution of "royal" for "jolly," and the omission of the slang "infernalest," may be understood simply as part of the author's stated attempt to "weed [the letters] of their ... inelegancies of expression" as a concession to eastern readers. With the more significant insertion of "our little party," on the other hand, Twain intended to prepare a dramatic context for ensuing episodes. Much like the fictive mother of the 1861 letters from Nevada, "our little party" functions throughout *The Innocents Abroad* as a portable audience, a travelling yarn-spinning community whose exchange of yarns and interpretations allows Twain to locate his narrator's verbal pranks in a situational context. The doctor, Dan, Jack, and the Youth, together with the narrator and occasional others, perform yarns, pranks, and deceptions for the entertainment of the group, and they respond as a "community of knowers" to the sanctified fictions they encounter in Europe and the Holy Land. The "I" that reports its impressions of Tangier in the *Alta* letter becomes one of "the boys" in *The Innocents Abroad,* and while the revision has little effect on the descriptive quality of the passage, its effect on subsequent episodes is significant. With Twain as its spokesman, this small community of experienced raconteurs assesses the validity of traditional European fictions with standards imported from America.

Twain was deliberate about replacing the *Alta* narrator's individual perspective with the group perspective of the book, even when such revisions contributed nothing to the humor or elegance of a passage. A sentence in the New York *Tribune* letter of November 9, 1867, for example, originally read: "The real name of this place is Cesarea Phillippi, but I call it Baldwinsville because it sounds better and I can recollect it easier. In his revision, Twain transferred the joke a few miles to the east, attributing the wisecrack to "our little party" instead of to himself: "We rested and lunched, and came on to this place, Ain Mellahah (the boys call it Baldwinsville)" (347). The author's justification for inserting "the boys" here and in similarly curious revisions throughout the book emerges only in the longer episodes, where "our little party" comes to life and significantly alters the direction of Mark Twain's humor. In the *Alta* letter of September 22, 1867, for example, the narrator offers the following description:

> Speaking of barbers reminds me that in Europe they do not have any barber-shops. The barbers come to your room and skin you. (I use that term because it is more correctly descriptive than shave.) They have a few trifling barber-shops in Paris, but the heaviest establishment of the kind only boasted three barbers. There, as everywhere else in Europe, as far as our experience goes, they put a bowl under your chin and slop your face with water, and then rub it with a cake of soap (except at Gibraltar, where they spit on the soap and use no bowl, because it is handier;) then they begin to shave, and you begin to swear; if you have got a good head of profanity on, you see the infliction through; but if you run out of blasphemy, there is nothing for it but to shut down on the operation until you recuperate."

This is Mr. Twain of the *Alta* letters at his best, skillfully employing understatement and metaphor in a good-natured attack on the quality of European services. The narrator of *The Innocents Abroad* describes two shaving episodes, both of which focus more intensely on an actual event. The second episode, which takes place in Venice, is particularly worthy of comparison with the *Alta* version:

> The boys sent for a barber.... I said, "Not any for me, if you please."
>
> I wrote on. The barber began on the doctor. I heard him say:
>
> "Dan, this is the easiest shave I have had since we left the ship."
>
> He said again, presently:
>
> "Why, Dan, a man could go to sleep with this man shaving him."
>
> Dan took the chair. Then he said:
>
> "Why, this is Titian. This is one of the old masters."
>
> I wrote on. Directly Dan said:
>
> "Doctor, it is perfect luxury. The ship's barber isn't anything to him."
>
> My rough beard was distressing me beyond measure. The barber was rolling up his apparatus. The temptation was too strong. I said:
>
> "Hold on, please. Shave me also."
>
> I sat down in the chair and closed my eyes. The barber soaped my face and then took his razor and gave me a rake that well-nigh threw me into convulsions. I jumped out of the chair: Dan and the doctor were both wiping blood off their faces and laughing.
>
> I said it was a mean, disgraceful fraud. (173)

Whereas the humor of the *Alta* letter is generated by Mr. Twain's versatility as a descriptive narrator, capable of working up "a good head of profanity," the book relies for its effect on a game of credulity involving several characters. In *The Innocents Abroad*, the shaving experience has become less a subject for comic description than the pretense for narrating a brief encounter between gullible and conspiring members of "our little party." As in an earlier story, which pitted the experienced Simon Wheeler against a naive and indignant Mark Twain, it is the relationship between antagonists that generates the humor of the episode.

The difference between the comic method of the letters and that of the book is even more pronounced in the scenes that describe the harassment of Italian guides. In the sixth Alta letter, dated July 16, 1867, Twain relates his experience with a Genoan guide who claims to be one of only three citizens of that city who can speak and understand English. The guide leads his patron to the birthplace of Christopher Columbus, where Twain spends fifteen minutes "in silent awe before this inspiring shrine." Only later does the guide mention that it was not exactly Columbus but Columbus's grandmother who was born there. The purported linguist then conducts the narrator to the municipal palace, where three of the explorer's letters are displayed. When asked if Columbus wrote them himself, the guide answers, "Oh, no." The narrator becomes frustrated:

> I began to suspect that this fellow's English was shaky, and I thought I would test the matter. He showed us a fine bust of Columbus on a pedestal, and I said, "Is this the first time this person, this Columbus, was ever on a bust?" and he innocently answered, "Oh, no." I began to think, then, that when he didn't understand a question, he just answered, "Oh, no," at a risk and took the chances. So I said, "This Columbus you talk so much about—is he dead?" And the villain said quietly, "Oh, no!" I tested him further. I said, "This palace of the Dorias which you say is so old—is it fifty years old?" "Oh, no." "Is it five hundred?" "Oh, no." "It's a thousand, though, ain't it?" "Oh, yes." So his plan was to answer, "Oh, no," twice, always, and then, "Oh, yes," by way of a change. All the information we got out of that guide we shall be able to carry along with us, I think.

The guide's method of concealing his ignorance of English wins a few laughs in this passage, yet when Twain revised the episode for *The Innocents Abroad*, he again shifted the emphasis of his humor from language to drama. As Leon T. Dickinson has remarked in his important study of the book, the humor of the revised version no longer focuses on the guide's ignorance of English, "but rather [on] his consternation in the face of the questions put to him" by the boys. The chief inquisitor is not Mark Twain but the doctor, a consummate yarn spinner and grave humorist who, like the ideal teller described in "How to Tell a Story," "does his best to conceal the fact that he even dimly suspects that there is anything funny" about his statements. The doctor's skill is indeed considerable, according to the narrator's account, for he "can keep his countenance, and look more like an inspired idiot, and throw more imbecility into the tone of his voice than any man that lives" (209–10). Thus the episode with the Genoan guide becomes something more like a tall-tale encounter than a game of words and misunderstanding when the doctor decides to entertain his friends by fooling the unsuspecting European with his deadpan sincerity. Intending to exploit the same American fascination with Columbus that had cost Mark Twain fifteen minutes of wasted awe in the *Alta* letter, the guide leads the boys on a relic hunt:

> "Come wis me, genteelmen! Come! I show you ze letter-writing by Christopher Columbo! Write it himself! Write it wis his own hand! Come!" ...
>
> We looked indifferent—unconcerned. The doctor examined the document very deliberately, during a painful pause. Then he said, without any show of interest:
>
> "Ah—Ferguson—what—what did you say was the name of the party who wrote this?"
>
> "Christopher Columbo! Ze great Christopher Columbo!"
>
> Another deliberate examination.
>
> "Ah—did he write it himself or—or how?"
>
> "He write it himself! Christopher Columbo! His own handwriting, write by himself!"
>
> Then the doctor laid the document down and said:
>
> "Why, I have seen boys in America only fourteen years old that could write better than that."
>
> "But zis is ze great Christo—"
>
> "I don't care who it is! It's the worst writing I ever saw. Now you mustn't think you can impose on us because we are strangers." (210)

The irony of the doctor's last statement lies in the fact that the guide is actually the stranger in this encounter, and his failure to recognize the doctor's deadpan attitude provides entertainment for the boys, who are cultural insiders despite the fact that they are on foreign soil. The humor of the episode results not from the guide's poor English, as in the letter, but from the dramatic consequences of his failure to understand the doctor's tone. As in the shaving scene, the revised version places the original verbal comedy in a situational context that is patterned after a tall-tale performance. The credulity of cultural outsiders like the Genoan guide and, later, the American Pilgrims aboard the ship becomes a rallying point for the boys throughout the book. They repeatedly challenge outsiders with the doctor's brand of veiled absurdity, and those "tests," as the narrator calls them, allow Twain to dramatize the encounter between Old and New World perspectives as he had not done in the original correspondence.

In his addition of new episodes to the book, Twain pursued the same priority of dramatization over description, and again the tall tale provided a

rough dramatic principle. In several scenes, including one that did not appear
in the letters, the narrator parodies his own credulity, which is rooted in an
inherited assumption of European superiority in matters of taste and
refinement. In his effort to appear sophisticated by European standards, the
narrator falls victim to a shop girl's straight-faced flattery:

> It seemed a stylish thing to go to the theatre in kid gloves, and we
> acted upon the hint. A very handsome young lady in the store
> offered me a pair of blue gloves. I did not want blue, but she said
> they would look very pretty on a hand like mine. The remark
> touched me tenderly. I glanced furtively at my hand, and
> somehow it did seem rather a comely member. I tried a glove on
> my left hand and blushed a little. Manifestly the size was too
> small for me. But I felt gratified when she said:
> "Oh, it is just right!" ... "Ah! I see you are accustomed to
> wearing kid gloves—but some gentlemen are so awkward about
> putting them on."
> It was the last compliment I had expected. I only understand
> putting on the buckskin article perfectly.... She kept up her
> compliments, and I kept up my determination to deserve them or
> die.
> "Ah, you have had experience! [A rip down the back of the
> hand.] They are just right for you—your hand is very small—if
> they tear you need not pay for them. [A rent across the
> middle.] ..."
> I was too much flattered to make an exposure and throw the
> merchandise on the angel's hands. I was hot, vexed, confused,
> but still happy; but I hated the other boys for taking such an
> absorbing interest in the proceedings. (55–56)

The girl's flattery is not a tall tale, but rhetorically it works the same way. The
narrator's vanity and credulity cause him to misinterpret her affected
sincerity, and again the performance offers priceless entertainment for the
boys. As before, they play the part of cultural insiders, although it later turns
out that the inside knowledge that allows them to appreciate the ruse has
been won at a cost. After Dan and the doctor soliloquize about the
importance of refinement and experience in a gentleman, the narrator learns
that the boys have already attempted to buy kid gloves and that they, too,
have suffered humiliation as a result of their vanity. In the end, their mutual
victimization draws the members of the "little party" closer together and

helps to define their peculiarly American values against those of Europe: "We threw all the purchases away this morning. They were coarse, unsubstantial, freckled all over with broad yellow splotches, and could neither stand wear nor public exhibition. We had entertained an angel unawares, but we did not take her in. She did that for us" (57).

Actually, the boys perform a twofold function in the book. Together with enabling the author to dramatize the verbal humor of the letters, they implicitly supply the reader with a consistent perspective toward that humor. In his preface to *The Innocents Abroad*, Twain declares that his reflections of travel intend "to suggest to the reader how *he* would be likely to see Europe and the East if he looked at them with his own eyes" (15). James M. Cox has pointed out that Twain's comment expresses the veiled assumption that "as long as the narrator is honest, there is no real distinction between the narrator and the reader. The narrator's feelings and vision stand for the reader's own." In fact, however, the narrator's gullibility and romanticism frequently inject ironic distance between his perspective and that of the reader. Thus when Mark Twain suddenly adopts the role of naive victim, as in the kid-glove scene, the reader shares a laugh with the boys at his expense. "Our little party" functions throughout the book as an ideal inside audience, capable of inviting and sustaining the reader's sympathy whether Twain's narrator is playing the role of spokesman or victim in the group's entertainment.

Elaborating on this question of the narrator's flexible role, Forrest G. Robinson voices a traditional concern about the book when he writes of Twain's narrator that "sudden shifts of tone betray a marked ambivalence about America, and a conspicuous incapacity to sustain a tone of humorous impersonation." Robinson is right to observe a conspicuous lack of stability in the narrator's tone, for *The Innocents Abroad* is indeed a "pleasure tour through modes of narration," and Twain seems just as comfortable playing the innocent as the old timer. Yet the tall tale effectively structures this conspicuous instability by establishing, instead of a consistent narrative tone, a stable rhetorical game in which the narrator consistently participates. Whether the mode of narration is innocent or experienced, sentimental or parodic, the game unfolds among its players in essentially the same way.

The narrator's "marked ambivalence about America" also operates within the larger consistency of the tall tale's rhetorical encounter. Robert Regan has written that it was only toward the end of the journey, in September 1867, that Twain finally discovered "the theme that was to constitute the bedrock of *The Innocents Abroad*." In his thirty-seventh letter to the *Alta*, according to Regan, in which the correspondent describes the hypocritical piety of the *Quaker City's* pilgrims, "Mark Twain for the first time winnows chaff from wheat, separates 'pilgrims' from 'sinners,'" and thus settles on "the theme of his first great work." "Without foreshadowing," Regan continues, "a dramatic antagonism made its appearance." Whereas guides were easy prey because they failed to understand "our little party's" sense of humor, the *Quaker City's* American pilgrims came to represent a more formidable opposition to the attitudes expressed by the narrator and his friends. The pilgrims not only fail to appreciate the narrator's humor; they reject it with a self-righteousness that he never observes in even the most repellent foreigners. Their narrow and inflexible vision of truth leads them on more than one occasion to "commit a sin against the spirit of religious law in order that they might preserve the letter of it." Citing scriptural authority, the pious tourists cruelly misuse their horses rather than risk breaking the Sabbath, and later they desecrate sacred shrines in order to collect reminders of their journey through the Holy Land (323). Zealously determined to parade their piety before the world, they embody the hypocrisy of what Twain elsewhere deemed "the most malignant form of Presbyterianism,—that sort which considers the saving of one's own paltry soul the first and supreme end and object of life."

As he revised the *Alta* correspondence for publication, Twain sought to project his new theme by juxtaposing the interpretive assumptions of the pilgrims against those of "our little party," a plan that required some important changes. In the original letters, for example, a character named Mr. Blucher had served as the vernacular foil for Mr. Twain's romantic and picturesque idiom. Blucher appears frequently in the *Alta* correspondence, where he characteristically interrupts the narrator's ornate descriptions with a contradictory horse-sense comment or a deflating observation, much as the crude Mr. Brown repeatedly interrupts the romantic Mr. Twain in the author's Hawaiian letters. Yet as the revision began to take shape, Twain recognized the possibility of incorporating a larger theme by dissolving the Twain–Blucher character axis, and as a result Mr. Blucher is almost entirely absent from the text of *The Innocents Abroad*. Blucher's irreverence and the narrator's original romanticism converge in the perpetually shifting attitudes of the boys, who encounter a new kind of foil in the sanctimonious pilgrims. While "our little party" engages in hard interpretive bargaining over the plausibility of every secondhand report of experience, the *Quaker City's* pilgrims cannot make sense of the narrator's willingness to negotiate over belief, for they deny the existence of any gray area between truth and lie. Franklin Rogers points out that the confrontation between the self-proclaimed sinners and their pious antagonists is only partially dramatized, yet the nascent conflict represents Twain's first extended treatment of what would become his greatest theme: the pragmatic and commonsense values of a vernacular community, whose natural idiom is the tall tale, confront the rigid beliefs of a society that sanctions conventional myths with the stamp of absolute truth.

The contest between rival approaches to interpretation and experience is waged with exemplary valor by both parties on the banks of the Jordan River. The pilgrims are determined that their experience of the sacred river conform strictly to the expectations they have transported all the way from America. Hence after a cold night in the bushes at the river's edge, they strip naked and wade into the freezing water, singing hymns. Mr. Blucher's cynical idiom is audible in the narrator's account of the adventure.

> But they did not sing long. The water was so fearfully cold that they were obliged to stop singing and scamper out again. Then they stood on the bank shivering, and so chagrined and so grieved that they merited honest compassion. Because another dream, another cherished hope, had failed. They had promised themselves all along that they would cross the Jordan where the Israelites crossed it when they entered Canaan.... While they did it they would picture to themselves that vast army of pilgrims marching through the cloven waters, bearing the hallowed Ark of the Covenant and shouting hosannahs and singing songs of thanksgiving and praise. (430)

Finally, to the narrator's evident disappointment, Jack rescues the shattered hopes of the party by leading the way across the river "with that engaging recklessness of consequences which is so natural to youth" (433). The narrator observes that, henceforth, the real danger will issue less from the rushing Jordan than from the current of sanctimonious rhetoric that is likely to flow from the lips of the victorious pilgrims. They succeed in experiencing the Jordan River according to the clichéd expectations with which they came, and it is the cliché rather than the experience that they will carry home to America.

The narrator, of course, arrives in the Holy Land with similarly unrealistic expectations, although unlike the pilgrims he does not regard them as inviolable. His description of the same river combines a pilot's interest in detail and a yarn spinner's knack for hyperbole:

> When I was a boy I somehow got the impression that the River
> Jordan was four thousand miles long and thirty-five miles wide. It
> is only ninety miles long, and so crooked that a man does not
> know which side of it he is on half the time. In going ninety miles
> it does not get over more than fifty miles of ground. (433)

The narrator repeatedly laments the fact that "travel and experience mar the
grandest pictures and rob us of the most cherished traditions of our
boyhood," but his lament is insincere (433). He actually revels in a process of
sudden displacement, whereby expectations vie with experience in an
unending series of inversions. His allegiance lies neither with "the most
cherished traditions of ... boyhood" nor with the reality that undermines
them; rather, his interest is in a perpetual sequence of contrasts that he
guarantees by exaggerating both the memory and the experience in his
narration. In the book's first shaving scene in Paris, for example, the narrator
elaborately describes the expectations instilled in his mind by secondhand
reports about the luxury of Parisian barber shops.

> From earliest infancy it had been a cherished dream of mine to be
> shaved some day in a palatial barber shop in Paris. I wished to
> recline at full length in a cushioned invalid chair, with pictures
> about me and sumptuous furniture.... At the end of an hour I
> would wake up regretfully and find my face as smooth and as soft
> as an infant's. Departing, I would lift my hand above that barber's
> head and say, "Heaven bless you, my son!" (84)

This illusion is promptly deflated by the "reality" of a Parisian shave,
although the narrator's description of the event is no less extravagant than
the false expectations it displaces.

> I sat bolt upright, silent, sad, and solemn. One of the wig-making
> villains lathered my face for ten terrible minutes and finished by
> plastering a mass of suds into my mouth. I expelled the nasty stuff
> with a strong English expletive and said, "Foreigner, beware!"
> Then this outlaw strapped his razor on his boot, hovered over me
> ominously for six fearful seconds, and then swooped down upon
> me like the genius of destruction. The first rake of his razor
> loosened the very hide from my face and lifted me out of the
> chair. (85)

As James M. Cox has explained, "the 'reality' which deflates the expectation is clearly not actuality, but an extravagant invention which, poised against the clichés, displaces them." The narrator's "old dream of bliss," like the other misconceptions he and the boys carry to Europe, turns out to have been a fraud, and his description of a razor-wielding "genius of destruction" thus supplies a preferable, although no less outrageous, fiction. It is a preferable fiction because, like a yarn, the narrator's account of his Parisian shave disparages illusion in favor of self-conscious fantasy. Whereas the pilgrims successfully blind themselves to experience by sanctifying false expectations, Twain's narrator acknowledges the Parisian fraud for what it is and answers with an aggressive invention of his own.

As the shaving episode makes clear, Twain's narrator is committed to a series of exaggerated poses, and his unpredictable movement from one to another generates much of the book's comedy. Forrest Robinson describes this "spastic lurching" between states of innocence and experience as a symptom of Twain's profound ambivalence, noting that the narrator of *The Innocents Abroad* possesses "a consciousness irremediably at odds with itself, moving at great speeds between mental states, struggling quite in vain to find a comfortable point of vantage on a deeply unsettling experience." Robinson continues: "The failure to achieve this equipose between opposites and incompatibles registers in the book's characteristically nervous, at times even frantic rhythm, and in its gathering inclination to locate the source of its painful frustration not in experience but in consciousness itself." Robinson's psychoanalytic insight is acute, but his assumption that Twain's unstable narrator must be in search of "equipose" turns the book's humorous strategy into a symptom of mental unrest. Twain was quite as capable as Robinson of finding a "comfortable point of vantage" from which to describe his unsettling experience in a Parisian barber's chair, but such a description would have been far short of humorous. In his narration of the event, he chose to exaggerate both the expectation and the experience because effective humor always moves "at great speeds between mental states," and it does so precisely in order to prevent the reader from settling upon a "comfortable point of vantage." The "painful frustration" that Robinson observes in the text may in fact issue more from the critic than from the humorist, for Twain's game of juxtaposition *requires* a "divided consciousness" and a "frantic rhythm" for its effect.

Robinson and many other readers are right to notice that Twain's incessant movement between different narrative poses compromises the book's unity and coherence. At his best, however, Twain organizes the sometimes "spastic" interplay of voices in *The Innocents Abroad* by enacting the tall tale as a dramatic and rhetorical principle. In his revision of the *Alta* letters, he invented characters and episodes that enabled him to embed the verbal juxtapositions of the letters in a series of situational contexts based on the tall tale's pattern of interpretive challenge and response. Members of the narrator's "little party" gallop through foreign lands delighting in "splendid lies" and disparaging "disgraceful frauds" as they go, bargaining over the relative truth of every report and accepting the visible world as the only reliable standard. The tall tale did not resolve the contradictions inherent to the narrator's game of exaggerated contrasts, but it gave his many poses a coherent dramatic principle, a way of connecting with one another. The narrative consciousness of *The Innocents Abroad* is indeed divided, as the book's readers have always understood, but the tall tale's interpretive game allowed Twain to enact those divisions, enabling him to convert them into a form of play.

NEIL SCHMITZ

Mark Twain's Civil War: Humor's Reconstructive Writing

Humor, at its best, forgives and resolves a grievous wrong. It admits it, full measure, receives it, and expresses the immediate experience in humorous language. With verbal dexterity, in some comical voice, it economizes pain's impact. It speaks beautifully in Huck Finn's report of Buck Grangerford's death: "It made me so sick I most fell out of the tree. I ain't agoing to tell all that happened—it would make me sick again if I was to do that. I wished I hadn't ever come ashore that night, to see such things. I ain't ever going to get shut of them—lots of times I dream about them."[1] Humor doesn't deny, or defend; it transacts, it negotiates. Buck is dead, but there's Jim and the blessed raft, safety, survival. The Civil War section of the *Adventures of Huckleberry Finn* ends with Huck's euphoria, the sensation of escape, river and raft sweeping Huck away from the combat zone, ends with Huck's ecstatic rediscovery of Jim, the good food, the great stories. "You feel mighty free and easy and comfortable on a raft" (HF 155). Briefly Huck sails free of the unreconstructed South. Its fight is not his fight. He's not a Grangerford, doesn't see himself in their narrative. His is the new narrative of the new (reconstructed) South, the solution for a still-dumbfounded postbellum Southern writing, very shaky in its postwar fiction, its plots, its speeches.

In 1865 the principal Confederate armies, everywhere either hemmed

From *The Cambridge Companion to Mark Twain*, Forrest G. Robinson, ed. © 1995 Cambridge University Press.

in by General U.S. Grant or pursued by General W.T. Sherman, began to suffer major desertion. Manpower shortages were so critical, the Confederate government, in March 1865, too late, began to emancipate slaves for military service. There were casuistical Confederates (Jefferson Davis, Robert E. Lee, Judah Benjamin, Davis's secretary of state) who could parse the irony, but for most Southerners the decision was lunacy, and open admission that the South had lost the argument, lost the right to be at war. Slavery was the "chief stone of the corner," Alexander Stephens, Jefferson Davis's vice-president, had said in 1861. "Be it good or bad, [slavery] has grown up with our society and institutions, and is so interwoven with them, that to destroy it would be to destroy us as a people." This was the hard core of John C. Calhoun's Southern doctrine, the compact center of Southern ideology. "I hold," said Calhoun, "that in the present state of civilization, where two races of different origin, and distinguished by color, and other physical differences, as well as intellectual, are brought together, the relation now existing in the slaveholding states between the two, is, instead of an evil, a good—a positive good."[2] Hard-pressed by Grant and Sherman, unable to see God's favor in the turn of events, the cause seemingly fatally compromised (there was an argument for a selective Confederate emancipation), the Confederate South in 1865 could no longer convincingly assert its nationalist project. What was the expense of life and treasure for? R.M.T. Hunter, Davis's first secretary of state (1861–2), wrote, "I do not see, but I feel, that there is a righteous God in Heaven, who holds our destinies in his hand, and I do not believe He will allow us to be cast down and the wicked to prosper." But He did visibly seem to do so. "What have we done that the Almighty should scourge us with such a war?" General Josiah Gorgas asked in his diary. "Is the cause really hopeless? Is it to be abandoned and lost in this way?"[3] Everywhere there was isolation, stupefaction, silence. "We are shut in here," Mary Chesnut wrote, "turned with our faces to a dead wall. No mails. A letter is sometimes brought by a man on horseback, traveling through the wilderness made by Sherman. All RR's destroyed—bridges gone. We are cut off from the world—to eat out our own hearts."[4]

Substantially revised in the postwar period, 1881–4, but never brought into final book form, Chesnut's Civil War diary, even in its several modern editions, remains a mélange of contradictory thought and feeling. It contains many great lines and passages, but nothing ever adds up, gets larger or deeper, escapes the frame of the daily narrative. It is this massive unfinished text that is the consummate work of revisionary Confederate literature, not the massive finished apologetics of Jefferson Davis's *The Rise and Fall of the Confederate Government* (1881), of Alexander Stephens's *Constitutional View of the Late War Between the States* (1868–70). Chesnut freely expresses what they rigorously exclude in their text-based analyses, the real burden of Confederate nationalism, and does so early on, March 18, 1861.

> I wonder if it be a sin to think slavery a curse to any land. Sumner said not one word of this hated institution which is not true. Men and women are punished when their masters and mistresses are brutes and not when they do wrong and then we live surrounded by prostitutes. An abandoned woman is sent out of any decent house elsewhere. Who thinks any worse of a negro or mulatto woman for being a thing we can't name? God forgive us, but ours is a monstrous system and wrong and iniquity.

Unlike Harriet Beecher Stowe, whom she read with hateful admiration, Chesnut couldn't locate a motive, moral, or plot for this antislavery position in her daily narrative. It was, after all, the damage slavery did to the marriages of respectable Southern white women that principally appalled her. "Thank God for my countrywomen," she writes in this same entry, "—alas for the men! No worse than men everywhere, but the lower their mistresses, the more degraded they must be." She didn't see the self-centeredness of her antislavery position in the sixties, and didn't see it in the eighties. "My Molly," her personal slave, exits the diary in June 1865, saying, "Never lef' Missis for no husband an' children in this world."[5] "My Molly" says it all. This Confederate trope, Confederate Southern writing won't surrender.

What was her politics? What is the vision that informs her daily narrative? Chesnut scrupulously reported her reading: *Uncle Tom's Cabin*, Emerson, European histories, English and French literature. Whatever slavery was, monstrous or beautiful, the early narrative of Confederate nationalism brought to mind great histories, epic deeds. "While I was cudgeling my brain to say what kind of men we ought to choose," she writes in 1861, "I fell on Clarendon, and it was easy to construct my man out of this material." Many Confederates in 1861–2 looked into the *History of the Rebellion and the Civil Wars in England* (1702–4), pondered the mix of identifications: Cavalier/Puritan, tyranny/rebellion, Charles I/Cromwell. What story—English, biblical, classical—explained Southern defeat in 1865? At the end Chesnut was reading Byron's *Childe Harold's Pilgrimage*; Carlyle's *The French Revolution*, especially chapter 4, "The Loser Pays"; Sylvio Pellico's *Le Mie Prigioni* (1832), a political prisoner account; and Thomas Hood's "The Bridge of Sighs" (1844). In the C. Vann Woodward 1981 edition of

Chesnut's diary, Mary Chesnut says finally, "Forgiveness is indifference. Forgiveness is impossible while *love lasts*." She quotes Hood: "Make no deep scrutiny / Into our mutiny—."[6]

As Chesnut toiled over her diaries in the early 1880s, wanting dramatic coherence and intensity, wanting, but failing, to find a witty, far-seeing Cassandra in her text, the figure of conceptual order, a supple reconstructed Southern humorous writing came suddenly into the field and produced the first significant Southern reading of the Civil War. George Washington Cable's *The Grandissimes* (1880), Joel Chandler Harris's *Uncle Remus: His Songs and His Sayings* (1881), Mark Twain's *Adventures of Huckleberry Finn* (1884), Thomas Nelson Page's *In Ole Virginia* (1887) are interested in forgiveness, accept the humiliation and subjection of the Confederate South, undertake a therapy of disclosure, offer effective strategies of displacement and insulation, do the work of humor. Confederate generals surrendered to Grant and Sherman. These Southern writers surrendered to Harriet Beecher Stowe. Uncle Tom was the opportune figure, his text, his speech, the place where the unspeakable (trust) could be entertained, the impossible (love) regarded. "My Molly" is fairly silent in Confederate writing, restricted in her speech. Uncle Tom speaks volumes, is the fount of story. He was the site of knowledge, where the deepest South revealed itself. Harris had put it together beautifully, the mis-en-scène, the words:

> One night, while the little boy was watching Uncle Remus twisting and waxing some shoe-thread, he made what appeared to him to be a very curious discovery. He discovered that the palms of the old man's hands were as white as his own, and the fact was such a source of wonder that he at last made it the subject of a remark. The response of Uncle Remus led to the earnest recital of a piece of unwritten history that must prove interesting to ethnologists.
>
> "Tooby sho de pa'm er my han's w'ite, honey," he quietly remarked, "en, w'en it comes ter dat, dey wuz a time w'en all de w'ite folks 'uz black—blacker dan me, kaze I done bin yer so long dat I bin sorter bleach out."[7]

All the principal Southern humorists (ethnologists of color and color differences) knew how brilliant this was, this kind of writing with its tender exchanges, how appropriate the form and language. Here was a resource, fresh, interesting, extensive, a history not yet written, the turn Chesnut could not make, to My Molly, her subjectivity, her history.

In the 1880s, Mark Twain and Cable toured together, giving readings and lectures. Harris would have toured with them, but he had a fear of public speaking. When Page toured, he, too, wanted Uncle Remus in the act, and couldn't get him. All were variously published in the same powerful Northern journals and magazines, often in the same issue. Harris and Page remained within the conceit of the sentimental, were formally and tonally reassuring whatever the grief their fiction bore. Page was the most sedative of the humorists. "Dem wuz good ole times, marster—de bes' Sam ever see! Dey wuz, in fac'! Niggers didn' hed nothin' 't all to do—jes' hed to 'ten' to de feedin' an' cleanin' de hosses an' doin' what de marster tell 'em to do; an' when dey wuz sick, dey had things sont 'em out de house, an' de same doctor come to see 'em what 'ten to de white folks when dey wuz po'ly."[8] The stories his black storytellers typically tell are about their beloved masters and mistresses, "Marse Chan" and "Meh Lady: A Story of the War" in *Ole Virginia*. In Harris's text, the fable's frame, Uncle Remus's tender care of Miss Sally's seven-year-old boy, held the turbulent feelings set forth in the stories. "Food-sharing, sex-sharing—the Remus stories read like a catalogue of Southern racial taboos, all standing on their heads," Bernard Wolfe tells us in his superb 1949 essay on Harris. "It was the would-be novelist in him who created Remus, the 'giver' of interracial caresses, but the trained journalist in him, having too good an eye and ear, reported the energetic folk blow in the caress."[9] Mark Twain and Cable set Stowe's figure and conceit at risk in different ways, confronted larger issues in their fiction. In *The Grandissimes*, where it is 1803–4, the lynching of a black woman, Clemence, is briefly described in cold documentary prose.

Of these writers, Mark Twain is the most problematic, the most distanced from the New South championed in Henry Woodfin Grady's *Atlanta Constitution*, a New South that still venerated its Confederate fathers, still insisted: "The South has nothing for which to apologize." Grady's famous 1886 speech, "The New South," given at a banquet in New York, spelled out the New South's perfect understanding of the prime dictate of Unionist discourse. It listened, this triumphant Unionist discourse, to Southern protestation, and then it asked: "But what of the negro?" The New South, Grady assured his public, understood what was to be done. "Our future, our very existence depends upon our working out this problem in full and equal justice." It affirmed the Unionist discourse of Lincoln and Sherman, their definitive versions. "We understand that when Lincoln signed the emancipation proclamation, your victory was assured, for he then committed you to the cause of human liberty, against which the arms of man cannot prevail—(while those of our statesmen who trusted to make slavery the corner-stone of the Confederacy doomed us to defeat as far as they could, committing us to a cause that reason could not defend or the sword maintain in the sight of advancing civilization).” The New South went this far into Unionist discourse, but had its reservations, its obstinacies. At certain critical instances, the Confederate and Unionist narratives were still in conflict. The “late struggle between the States was war and not rebellion, revolution and not conspiracy.” As Grady had it, the “new South presents a perfect democracy, the oligarchs leading in the popular movement.” There were problems and paradoxes everywhere in Grady’s speech, as there were in the New South itself. How does oligarchical democracy so perfectly work? What now was the status of black people in the New South? Of Harris’s Uncle Remus and Page’s Sam, the black men the New South chose to recognize and celebrate, it said: “To liberty and enfranchisement is as far as the law can carry the negro. The rest must be left to conscience and common sense.” Harris wrote for the *Atlanta Constitution*, was its principal editorial writer. Why couldn’t Harris do public readings of his Uncle Remus stories? In *Life on the Mississippi* (1883), Mark Twain saw through Harris’s shyness, saw the whole rich irony of the New South’s situation in Unionist discourse, of its humorous transactions in dialect poetry.

> [Harris] deeply disappointed a number of children who flocked eagerly to Mr. Cable’s house to get a glimpse of the illustrious sage and oracle of the nation’s nurseries. They said:
> "Why, he’s white!"
> They were grieved about it. So, to console them, the book was brought, that they might hear Uncle Remus’s Tar-baby story from the lips of Uncle Remus himself—or what, in their outraged eyes, was left of him. But it turned out that he had never read aloud to people, and was too shy to venture the attempt now.[10]

Mark Twain, it might be said, was the Southern humorist gone over, not just a deserter, a dissenter, but a literary scalawag, a Southern writer in Unionist discourse and narrative. Chapter 6 in Louis Budd’s *Mark Twain: Social Philosopher* (1962) is entitled “The Scalawag.” As Budd has it, this heavy term (its modern cognates are “quisling,” “collaborator”) aptly characterizes Mark Twain’s political practice in the postwar period. There he was, at all those postwar Grand Army of the Republic banquets, happily toasting Union generals. The *Notice* posted at the head of *Huckleberry Finn* evokes Civil War/Reconstruction orders, the bills put up in the courthouse squares of occupied Southern cities and towns. “Persons attempting to find a moral in it will be banished; persons attempting to find a plot in it will be shot." For all its Southern speech, this text is in Unionist discourse. It abjures Sir Walter Scott, professes Uncle Tom.

How did Mark Twain get here, and how secure, how satisfying, is Huck's position? As late as 1954, the New South was still warily regarding Mark Twain. In his compendious *The South in American Literature, 1607–1900* (1954), Jay B. Hubbell, deriding Mark Twain's Scott thesis, argued that "Mark Twain had been out of touch with Southern life so long that, like many Northern travelers and historians, he had come to look for some simple formula which would explain the many differences between the two sections." As for Mark Twain's Jim: "There is in his picture of slavery a little too much of the old abolitionist legend of the Deep South."[11] I count as the classic texts in Mark Twain's Civil War writing "A True Story" (1874), *Life on the Mississippi* (1883), *Huckleberry Finn* (1885), and "The Private History of a Campaign That Failed" (1885). Mark Twain's reconstructive humorous reading of the Civil War gets essentially done in these texts, which were published in important national magazines—the *Atlantic Monthly*, the *Century Illustrated Monthly Magazine*—and immediately entered the major discursive networks in American literature. "An Adventure of Huckleberry Finn: With an Account of the Famous Grangerford–Shepherdson Feud" appeared in the November 1884 issue of the *Century*, which had just begun its monumental series, *Battles and Leaders of the Civil War*. Readers turned past Huck's account of Buck Grangerford's death, past E.W. Kemble's illustration, "Behind the Woodpile" (Grangerford farm boys shooting at Shepherdson farm boys), to find Warren Lee Goss's mud gritty "Recollections of a Private" and its illustration, a mounted federal cavalryman. It put Mark Twain figuratively right in the thick of things, though up a tree, onlooking, *hors de combat*.

To enter the cultural debate over the remembrance and meaning of the Civil War, to ponder the responsibility of the South for the Civil War, Mark Twain had bravely to come forward and admit he had no right to speak about such matters. He had spent the Civil War in Nevada, a sometime employee of the federal government, most of the time advancing his career as a comic journalist. What was he doing at all these military banquets, loving the toasts, the banter, the badinage, the blue coats and brass buttons? Mark Twain's love for the company of old soldiers betrayed him. His voice in this assembly of speakers, he realized, was "a sort of voice,—not a loud one, but a modest one; not a boastful one, but an apologetic one."[12] As early as 1877, in the Putnam Phalanx Dinner Speech, delivered in Hartford, Mark Twain had begun to address, humorously, at once the painful issue of his desertion and the present problem of his right to speak about the Civil War. "I did not assemble at the hotel parlors today to be received by a committee as a mere civilian guest; no, I assembled at the headquarters of the Putnam Phalanx, and insisted upon my right to be escorted to this place as one of the military guests. For I, too, am a soldier! I am inured to war. I have a military history."[13] This, too, was a sort of voice, facetious, protected.

"Putnam Phalanx" is the first draft of "The Private History of a Campaign That Failed," a suspiciously breezy first draft oozing anxiety. There is no traumatic shooting in this first piece. It is Ben Tupper, not young Samuel Clemens, who boyishly rationalizes his desertion: "Gentlemen, you can do as you choose; as for me, I've got enough of this sashaying around so's 't you can't get a chance to pray, because the time's all required for cussing" (MTS 108). And there was, too, as Justin Kaplan taught us in *Mr. Clemens and Mark Twain* (1966), the complex issue of Mark Twain's relation to U.S. Grant, the question "why a former Confederate irregular should be publishing, and ostensibly making a good deal of money doing so, the *Personal Memoirs* of the commander of all the Union armies."[14] In 1887, two years after the publication of the "Private History," addressing the Union Veterans Association of Maryland, Mark Twain was at his boldest: "You Union veterans of Maryland have prepared your feast and offered to me, a rebel veteran of Missouri, the wound-healing bread and salt of a gracious hospitality" (MTS 219). Tom Quirk and Richard E. Peck have written excellent essays on the relation of *Huckleberry Finn* to the "Private History." "This moving tale of Clemens shooting a stranger," Peck writes, "is, if you like, a lie, a most useful lie because it pulls into focus all the fragments comprising `The History' in a dramatic conclusion that accounts for (and `justifies'?) Clemens' desertion on grounds that it represented a moral act."[15] Yet there is a difference between young Samuel Clemens's retreat from his wartime duty in the Marion Rangers, his desertion of the cause of Confederate nationalism, and Huck's flight. *Huckleberry Finn* is not only about running away, it is also about the fright and guilt of changing sides.

In these Civil War texts, "A True Story," *Life on the Mississippi*, *Huckleberry Finn*, and "Private History," Mark Twain looks for ways to break out of the Southern imaginary (William Gilmore Simms, Sidney Lanier) into a Northern real (William Dean Howells, U.S. Grant), to break its narcissistic Sir Walter Scott trance, to open his text to the real, to difference, to the most radical of alterities. "Sir Walter," Mark Twain wrote in *Life on the Mississippi*, "had so large a hand in making Southern character, as it existed before the war, that he is in great measure responsible for the war. It seems a little harsh toward a dead man to say that we never should have had any war but for Sir

Walter; and yet something of a plausible argument might, perhaps, be made in support of that wild proposition."[16] The Scott chapter is entitled "Enchantments and Enchanters." As Mark Twain saw it, there was no longer a usable Southern patriarchal literary tradition, a Confederate narrative. There was just the biracial Southern narrative Harriet Beecher Stowe had mothered in American literature, its complexities, its dreads, its horrors. Huck is in Unionist discourse, but only because where Jim is going, what Jim wants, is the Ohio, not the Mississippi. Such is the breakthrough of *Huckleberry Finn*, its stroke of genius. With Huck, Mark Twain sort of deserts Tom Sawyer, sort of chooses Jim. Mark Twain is a Southern writer in Unionist discourse, happily at work within its tenets, but always revising its terms, exploring its tolerances, its shortcomings, its practical meaning. Huck's speech is equivocal. His narrative isn't yet committed to a direction, isn't totally invested in a denouement. Hence we see in Mark Twain's Civil War writing this ongoing literary phenomenon, narratives interrupted, invaded, silenced. Huck is always on the move, now in Tom's story, then in Jim's, just as Tom and Jim come upon Huck's story and try to determine it. Huck's narrative is afloat, in passive suspense. Whose story is told here? Huck's? Tom's? Jim's? Humor reaches here its purest liquidity, its supplest resilience. What does Huck's speech do? It registers, it goes on.

All this discourse shifting and story breaching in *Huckleberry Finn* is remarkably foretold in "A True Story," which warns us about reading Jim as Uncle Remus, seeing in him what Misto C sees in Aunt Rachel: "She was a cheerful, hearty soul, and it was no more trouble for her to laugh than it is for a bird to sing."[17] The interlocutor is a Northern liberal gentleman who didn't request the story he receives, doesn't even want to hear it. "Why, I thought—that is, I meant—why, you *can't* have had any trouble. I've never heard you sigh, and never seen your eye when there wasn't a laugh in it" (TS 60). The title, "A True Story, Repeated Word for Word as I Heard It," still marks his incredulity and denial, as a Northerner, of any involvement or responsibility for Aunt Rachel's "trouble." He is here only as a scene setter, as asking the provocative question, as putting into play the decisive term, "trouble." It is in fact the outrageous ignorance/innocence of the interlocutor's casual remark that abruptly cuts Aunt Rachel's uproarious laughter off. "Aunt Rachel, how is it that you've lived sixty years and never had any trouble?" It is the lie of the euphemism that gives Aunt Rachel her sudden stab of pain, that snaps into sharp focus her relation to Misto C and his family, her alienated difference. "Trouble" is Misto C's cloaking term for slavery, his denial of its experience and its consequences. *How is it you're so merry—you who were once a slave? Slavery could not have been that bad since it has left you the joyous creature you are*. As the sketch begins, Aunt Rachel is "sitting respectfully below our level, on the steps,—for she was our servant, and colored." Into the narration of her story, word for word as he heard it, the interlocutor intrudes only once more, to reset the scene of narration. "Aunt Rachel had gradually risen, while she warmed to her subject, and now she towered above us, black against the stars" (TS 60). It has been an after-dinner sit on the porch, summertime, twilight, the company has been teasing Aunt Rachel, entertained by the rich exuberance of her Negro mirth, and then that explosively wrong phrase is uttered, "and never had any trouble." "Has I had any trouble? Misto C—, I's gwine to tell you, den I leave it to you" (TS 59–60). After Aunt Rachel towers, black against the stars, the interlocutor disappears. Aunt Rachel has the closing, the conversion of Misto C's term. "Oh, no, Misto C—, I hain't had no trouble. An' no *joy!*" (TS 63). This sentence is like a freeze-frame, Misto C's term in a wreckage of negatives.

To this extent, "A True Story" prefigures certain transactions in *Huckleberry Finn*, especially those in the pre-Cairo chapters. Jim will also speak up here, emerge in his threatening difference and counter Huck vigorously. "Doan talk to me 'bout Sollermun, Huck, I knows him by de back" (HF 95). "A True Story" thus redirects Southern writing, turns comic dialect sketch into serious testimony, a survivor's tale told in "'arnest," and does so with artful tact, inscribing the narrator's flawed appropriation, even though Aunt Rachel gives her story to him, leaves it with him. In that framework, Mark Twain's "A True Story" testifies to the literary value of Aunt Rachel's testimony. It realizes, as it were, that all the emergent complexities of African-American experience, the riches of its oral tradition, *His Songs and His Sayings* (Harris's subtitle), are properly the resources of Southern literature, as long as the Anglo-American writer inscribes Misto C. Liberated, enabled, this Southern writing already occupies in 1874 the fictive space Toni Morrison has come to define in *Song of Solomon* (1977) and *Beloved* (1987), African-American family history at the critical juncture of emancipation.

What are the familial traces? What are the documentary texts? In "A True Story," there is just a saying. A grandmother born in Maryland, a proud woman, would say: "I wa'nt bawn in de mash to be fool'd by trash. I's one o' de old Blue Hen's Chickens." And a scar, to recognize. Aunt Rachel's son, "my little Henry tore his wris' awful, and most busted his head, right up at de top of his forehead, an' de niggers didn't fly aroun' fas' enough to 'tend him" (TS 60). The grandmother angrily declares her saying, clears the kitchen, bandages the child's wounds. The family is sold at auction, broken up. Aunt Rachel loses her husband and her seven children. "— 'an six of 'em

I hain't set eyes on ag'in to dis day, an' dat's twenty-two years ago las' Easter" (TS 61). When the Civil War comes, African-Americans begin searching for each other, children for parents, parents for children. Henry, who had run North and prospered, "sole out an' went to whar dey was recruitin', an' hired hisse'f out to de colonel for his servant; an' den he went all froo de battles everywhah, huntin' for his ole mammy" (TS 62). Saying and scar are finally matched, mother and son, a family line established, but there are ominous complications. A "*nigger* ridgment" on guard at the mansion where Aunt Rachel manages the kitchen holds a dance in that kitchen. Henry doesn't recognize his mother, treats her insolently, "smilin' at my big red turban, and makin' fun," has an attitude not unlike Misto C's, whereupon Aunt Rachel indignantly uses the grandmother's saying. In the rapture of the reunion, Aunt Rachel briefly exults: "Lord God ob heaven be praise', I got my own ag'in!" But what then? Where is she now? Where is Henry? "A True Story," as we've seen, abruptly closes.

"A True Story" gives us summarily an African-American account of the American midcentury, the 1850s, the Civil War, the Reconstruction. The three actions in *Huckleberry Finn* refer to these periods in Southern history. In the first section, chapters 1–16, written largely in 1876, runaway Huck suddenly finds himself in a slave narrative, a secondary character, reluctantly, anxiously, aiding and abetting Jim's flight to freedom in Illinois. We are here in actual time, in the 1850s. The middle section, chapters 16–22, written in 1879–80, begins with the Grangerford–Shepherdson feud, the chapter Mark Twain purposefully dealt into the series, *Battles and Leaders of the Civil War*, and ends with the humiliating overthrow of the king and the duke. The final section, chapters 31–43, written in 1883, concerns setting free an already freed Jim, symbolically enacts the Reconstruction as a nightmarish agony. For us the problem is the middle section, its gunfire, its bands and mobs of men. In this section we come upon the South as a place, a people, a nationality. Of the sections, it is the riskiest. It exposes Huck up his tree, keeps him in constant jeopardy, puts him in that hard place where he must finally choose sides. At these points, *Huckleberry Finn* intersects with *Life on the Mississippi*, with Mark Twain's reminiscences of his Civil War experience: "Putnam Phalanx," "Private History," "An Author's Soldiering." Complexes of pacifist/bellicose feeling swirl through the middle section of *Huckleberry Finn*. What is courage? The Grangerford episode seems to say one thing, the Bricksville episode another, the Wilks episode still another.

"The new South is simply the old South under new conditions."[18] In its ideological negotiation with the North, Grady's New South insisted that it be allowed to sanctify the memory of the old regime. "The sign of nobility in her families for generations to come will be the gray cap or the stained coat, on which, in the ebb of losing battle, God laid the sword of his imperishable knighthood." The New South would be progressive, would be in Unionist discourse, but it wouldn't recant, wouldn't criticize the fathers. "Slavery as an institution cannot be defended—but its administration was so nearly perfect among our forefathers as to challenge and hold our loving respect."[19] There is a lot of bad faith oozing in Grady's formulations; "its administration" simply lies on the page, blatant, palpable. The Confederate fathers "administered" slavery, and did the work of it so well as to "hold our loving respect." Could one retain Confederate articles, Confederate tropes, in Unionist discourse, perhaps even revise Unionist discourse, end the insistence of its punishing question: "But what of the negro?" In its early going, Grady's New South, Harris its principal writer, struggled with this question, worked in a humorous mode to resolve it. The human slaves and masters in Page's *Old Virginia* are the very Brers in Harris's *Uncle Remus*. Slavery is foregrounded, sentimentalized. The newspaper that brings the tragic news of Lincoln's assassination to old Colonel Cameron in D.W. Griffith's *Birth of a Nation* (1915) is the *New South*, the name boldly printed. Griffith's film epic, which beautifully illustrates the jam and the jar of the two narratives, Confederate and Unionist, is at its most gloriously appropriative creating a Confederate Lincoln, a Lincoln sort of compelled to sign the Emancipation Proclamation.

Bad faith in *Huckleberry Finn* is rankest in the middle section. In the Old South you can't live without it, Huck discovers, offering that knowledge to us as a truism. "If they wanted us to call them kings and dukes, I hadn't no objections, 'long as it would keep peace in the family; and it warn't no use to tell Jim, so I didn't tell him. If I never learnt nothing else out of pap, I learnt that the best way to get along with his kind of people is to let them have their own way" (HF 165). Forrest G. Robinson writes, in *In Bad Faith: The Dynamics of Deception in Mark Twain's America* (1986), a dark Melvillean reading of *Huckleberry Finn*, "Bad Faith rules, by necessity, in all human affairs." Huck's phrase, "no use," is particularly telling. "Perhaps Huck's decision not to tell is the reflex of his fear that Jim will react to the truth by running away; perhaps, too, it expresses a fatalistic surrender to the inevitable failure of the quest. Whatever the case, the 'no use' that Huck appeals to cannot possibly speak for Jim, even though in declining to share what he knows Huck does just that."[20] No use, *now*. We are in and out of faiths, and narratives, in *Huckleberry Finn*. Jim, too, is withholding information. He has not told Huck that the reason for his flight no longer exists, that the cruel, murderous Pap Finn who is after Huck is dead. In the

Old South of *Huckleberry Finn*, in the New South of *Life on the Mississippi*, everywhere, even among the best of friends, there is, at times, serious bad faith, significant withholding.

In what ways does the middle of *Huckleberry Finn*, so heavily freighted with Civil War experience, the bad feeling of that bad faith, humorously resolve its subject? Bad acting, always before us, is a major trope. The circus gives us good acting, we briefly see it, the fake drunk is a real acrobat, Huck is amazed, and then it is gone. The king and the duke, fabulators, mythologists, confidence men, bad actors, are in specific relation to those other two bad actors, Colonel Grangerford and Colonel Sherburn. These rule Huck's world, shore and river, in the middle section. Colonel Grangerford commands foolhardy courage, life-wasting bravery. Colonel Sherburn confronts riotous bravado, personal cowardice. They wear the planter's white suit, the white suit that would in time become Mark Twain's signature suit. When Colonel Sherburn speaks, Mark Twain forces his way into Huck's text. It is the worst moment in *Huckleberry Finn*. Suddenly there is ugly writing, conflicted feeling, unresolved thinking, a spew of angry statements. It is as if Colonel Sherburn were addressing the Marion Rangers of "Private History." "But a mob without any *man* at the head of it, is *beneath* pitifulness. Now the thing for you to do, is to droop your tails and go home and crawl in a hole" (HF 191). Buck Grangerford, on the other hand, is ready to die, and his father is too. "I don't like that shooting from behind a bush," Colonel Grangerford tells thirteen-year-old Buck. "Why didn't you step into the road, my boy?" (HF 145). This is bad acting, as is the shooting of Buck floundering in the river, unable to defend himself, unarmed, in the open. But it is the king and the duke, the doctors of divinity and literature, who are always before us in the middle section, who deliver, at once lunatic and fraudulent, the ongoing dominant discourse.

In *Life on the Mississippi* Sir Walter Scott is the name of that discourse, of its romantic *a priori*, its faux medievalism. Scott enchains Southern thinking, Southern imagining, "with decayed and swinish forms of religion; with decayed and degraded systems of government; with the sillinesses and emptinesses, sham grandeurs, sham gauds, and sham chivalries of a brainless and worthless long-vanished society" (LM 241). He "made every gentleman in the South a major or a colonel, or a general or a judge, before the war," created "rank and caste down there, and also reverence for rank and caste, and pride and pleasure in them" (LM 242). He is the progenitor, the forefather, his faux medievalism the enabling mythos, its theology, its poetry. He is the killer of Southern writing. There is strenuous pursuit of Sir Walter Scott in *Life on the Mississippi*. Mark Twain stresses his radical disaffiliation.

Chapter 46, "Enchantments and Enchanters," is the hottest chapter in the book, and still seething. Here, too, Mark Twain curiously inscribes the feminine, puts a mark on the manliness of Southern chivalry. "Take away the romantic mysteries, the kings and knights and big-sounding titles, and Mardi Gras would die, down there in the South. The very feature that keeps it alive—girly-girly romance—would kill it in the North or in London" (LM 241–2). In *Huckleberry Finn* the Duke of Bridgewater has about him a certain effeminacy, a certain intonation. Rehearsing the king as Juliet, the duke says: "You mustn't bellow out *Romeo*! that way, like a bull—you must say it soft, and sick, and languishy, so—R-o-o-meo! that is the idea; for Juliet's a dear sweet mere child of a girl, you know, and she don't bray like a jackass" (HF 177). It is there in the way the duke calls Looy the Seventeen by his familiar name, Capet, a misnomer, of course. The duke's carpetbag is much more interesting than the king's, which yields, besides clothes, only a "ratty deck of cards." The duke's bag is packed with convenient wonders, posters, costumes, wigs, theatrical face paint. The interesting question of how this squirmy bad acting relates to the straight bad acting of the Grangerfords and Sherburns Mark Twain merely exposes.

On board the raft, the king and the duke immediately establish rank and caste, place and position. Like Sir Walter Scott, they are blissfully blind to the plights of Huck and Jim. The king's first move as the executor of the Wilks estate is to sell the slaves, "two sons up the river to Memphis, and their mother down the river to Orleans" (HF 234). The duke's line: "jour printer, by trade; do a little in patent medicines; theatre-actor—tragedy, you know; take a turn at mesmerism and phrenology when there's a chance; teach singing-geography school for a change; sting a lecture, sometimes." The king's line: "I've done considerable in the doctoring way in my time. Layin' on o' hands is my best holt—for cancer and paralysis, and sich things; and I k'n tell a fortune pretty good, when I've got somebody along to find out the facts for me. Preachin's my line, too; and workin' camp-meetin's; and missionaryin' around" (HF 160–1). Mark Twain's critique of the patriarchal orders in Southern society is encompassing, though differently established. Huck merely registers the moral idiocy of the honor-bound colonels, the casualties of their disastrous leadership, then turns from them, to Jim and the raft, to a circus. He promptly sees through the king and the duke, discounts their fictions, despises their bad acting. Sir Walter Scott is a sunk concern in *Huckleberry Finn*.

In the Wilks episode, the sides are perfectly clear. Huck and Jim have come together on the issue of the king and the duke, shared their detestation of the "rapscallions." Yet Colonel Sherburn is still at large in the text, fearless, contemptuous, a figure not wholly in the brackets of censure, his speech not completely in Sir Walter Scott. He has killed a man with cool dispatch. He stares down Buck Harkness in the crowd, chooses Buck to confront individually. His challenge is—personal cowardice. He cocks his gun. Here's another Buck to be shot. "The crowd washed back sudden, and then broke apart and went tearing off every which way, and Buck Harkness he heeled it after them, looking tolerable cheap" (HF 191). Huck witnesses, makes the barest commentary: "I could a staid, if I'd a wanted to, but I didn't want to" (HF 191). Sherburn is not mentioned again in the narrative. The Colonel, so to speak, goes unanswered—until, that is, Mark Twain's ingeniously worked-out formal response in the "Private History" appears in the *Century*, speaks modestly, humorously, among the war papers in its ongoing Civil War series.

Humor works very hard in this reminiscence. The text argues that it is autobiographical, to be held to the rules of evidence, but does so teasingly, is facetious from the start. There is still something smarmy about the "Private History," something totally unconvincing. It wants to make a pacifist argument (Huck's), wants to represent all the deserters, the Bull Run runners, the rabbits, the Buck Harknesses, the Hucks. It wants to show that Mark Twain left the war because, like Huck, he was horrified by killing, hated killing, but it can't finally face down its Colonel Sherburn, the grimly fearless, coolly self-controlled U.S. Grant. It turns abruptly from the pacifist pieties given over the corpse of the slain stranger to glorify Grant and the killing power of well-trained modern troops. The narrator exits with a nonsequitur, humorously put, cowardly speech par excellence, spoken from the safety of the subjunctive: "I could have become a soldier myself, if I had waited. I had got part of it learned; I knew more about retreating than the man that invented retreating" (PH 123). It echoes Huck's "I could a staid, if I'd a wanted to, but I didn't want to," but differently, is apologizing where Huck is not, is obsequious where Huck is simply decisive. In the text generally, extenuators and specifiers are not always immediately detectable. Here Mark Twain explains his family's relation to slavery: "I said, in palliation of this dark fact, that I had heard my father say, some years before he died, that slavery was a great wrong, and that he would free the solitary negro he then owned if he could think it right to give away the property of the family when he was so straitened in means" (PH 207). "Then" is the fixer in that sentence. The father in fact once dealt in slaves. As for the lugubrious death scene, Mark Twain scholarship has yet to corroborate its actual happening.

"In confronting that past in which the nation had reached its limits and been rent asunder, Mark Twain reached the limits of his humor, which is to say he reached the threshold of his disillusion." James M. Cox's reading of the situation in *Mark Twain: The Fate of Humor* (1966) still stands. "In *Huckleberry Finn* [Mark Twain] had come as near—and as far—as he was ever to do in reconstructing the Civil War past. The 'Private History' marked a second effort to encounter that past, but it was a smaller, safer effort."[21] Humor doesn't pull it off in the "Private History," is uncertain in its focus, doesn't admit the pain, evades it, puts into play the defense of the dead stranger, prevaricates, is contradictory. In *Huckleberry Finn*, Mark Twain's humor works purposefully. Huck says: "I reckon a body that ups and tells the truth when he is in a tight place, is taking considerable many resks; though I ain't had no experience, and can't say for certain; but it looks so to me, anyway; and yet here's a case where I'm blest if it don't look like the truth is better, and actuly *safer*, than a lie" (HF 139). Such is the difference between Huck Finn and Mark Twain. Huck never signed up, never pledged allegiance to Confederate nationalism. He is its witness, the doings of Sir Walter Scott, of the king and the duke. In the middle section, Huck has already, to some extent, gone over into Jim's narrative. Jim tells him the pitiful story of his deaf child, 'Lizabeth. He has a son, we learn, Johnny. This brief story from Jim's family history is beautifully arresting, and not at all self-serving. Huck will side, too, with Mary Jane Wilks and work to restore the African-American family the king has so callously broken up. This is where he comes into Unionist discourse, specifically into the allegiances of the Stowe variant. Huck signs up for women and blacks. Confiding in Mary Jane, spelling out a very complicated anti-king and duke strategy, Huck manfully swears his oath: "I don't want nothing more out of you than just your word—I'd druther have it than another man's kiss-the-Bible" (HF 239).

Apart from the problematic "Private History," Mark Twain's only other Civil War narrative is in *Life on the Mississippi*, "Vicksburg during the Trouble." Distinctly anti-Confederate, the chapter begins citing the euphemistic term "Trouble," uses the form of the dialect sketch again to do something like a documentary interview. There is no glorification of Confederate heroism here. Under bombardment, frantic women and children scurry for the cave shelters, "encouraged by the humorous grim soldiery, who shout 'Rats, to your holes!' and laugh" (LM 195). A civilian survivor of the siege, a married man, the father of children, remembers, in a flat prosaic voice, the awful tedium, and terror, of bomb-shelter life. He speaks, like Huck, in the language of reportage, seeing it all as it is, marking the absurdities. His wife, Maria, is caught outside as a bombardment begins. "When she was running for the holes, one morning, through a shell shower, a big shell burst near her and covered her all over with dirt, and a piece of iron carried away her game-bag of false hair from the back of her head. Well, she stopped to get that game-bag before she shoved along again!" (LM 196). Humor works very hard here, telling these funny truths. Another time a shell burst interrupts the narrator's inviting a friend to share a drink of rare whisky in his shelter. "A chunk of it cut the man's arm off, and left it dangling in my hand. And do you know the thing that is going to stick longest in my memory, and outlast everything else, little and big, I reckon, is the mean thought I had then? It was, `the whisky is *saved!*'" (LM 197). In "Vicksburg during the Trouble," humor is almost exhausted, almost becomes the steeled irony of Stephen Crane and Ernest Hemingway, yet not quite, because it is the victim, the survivor who speaks, not the interlocutory observer. "We always had eight; eight belonged there. Hunger and misery and sickness and fright and sorrow, and I don't know what all, got so loaded into them that none of them were ever rightly their old selves after the siege. They all died but three of us within a couple of years" (LM 196).

Mark Twain admires the National Cemetery outside Vicksburg, a "Mount Auburn" cemetery, modern, its grounds "tastefully laid out in broad terraces, with winding roads and paths; and there is a profuse adornment in the way of semitropical shrubs and flowers; and in one part is a piece of native wild-wood, left just as it grew, and, therefore, perfect in its charm" (LM 198). He particularly admires the touch of that remnant piece of wild-wood, "left just as it grew." There is no question here of Mark Twain's chosen side, his respect for the reach and power of the national government, its situation of this National Cemetery, its management of it. "The government's work is always conspicuous for excellence, solidity, thoroughness, neatness. The government does its work well in the first place, and then takes care of it" (LM 198). Unionist discourse empowers him, braces its monuments with metal, lets him interview outside the National Cemetery, an "aged colored man," another survivor of the siege. He

> showed us, with pride, an unexploded bombshell which had lain in his yard since the day it fell during the siege.
> "I was a-stannin' heah, an' de dog was a-stannin' heah; de dog he went for de shell, gwine to pick a fuss wid it; but I didn't; I says, 'Jes' make youseff at home heah; lay still whah you is, or bust up de place, jes' as you's a mind to, but *I's* got business out in de woods, I has!" (LM 198)

Unionist discourse was multifarious, supple, differently interested, competent in diverse speech. When "a Southerner of genius writes modern English," Mark Twain insisted, "his book goes upon crutches no longer, but upon wings; and they carry it swiftly all about America and England, and through the great English reprint publishing-houses of Germany—as witness the experience of Mr. Cable and 'Uncle Remus,' two of the very few Southern authors who do not write in the Southern style" (LM 243).

Life on the Mississippi is a charter for a new postwar Southern writing, *Huckleberry Finn* its first local masterpiece. Such writing abjures Sir Walter Scott, professes Huck and Jim. But what happens to Harris, to Cable? Only Page, the most apologetic, the most reverential, always lapsing into Sir Walter Scott, is fairly productive in that Southern writing. After *Huckleberry Finn*, nothing of comparable measure, until Griffith's *Birth of a Nation* (1915), which returns the Confederate relics, the Confederate tropes, to American literature, brings formally to a close Mark Twain's radical program in the 1880s, his humorous resolution of the Civil War.

NOTES

1. Mark Twain, *Adventures of Huckleberry Finn*, ed. Walter Blair and Victor Fischer (Berkeley: University of California Press, 1985), p. 153. Hereafter cited parenthetically in the text as HF.

2. *Works of John C. Calhoun*, 6 vols., ed. Richard Cralle (New York, 1854–7), vol. 2, p. 627.

3. Richard Beringer, Herman Hattaway, Archer Jones, and William N. Still., Jr., *Why the South Lost the War* (Athens: University of Georgia Press, 1986), p. 352.

4. *Mary Chesnut's Civil War*, ed. C. Vann Woodward (New Haven, Conn.: Yale University Press, 1981), p. 830.

5. Ibid. pp. 29, 39, 829.

6. Ibid., pp. 7, 836.

7. Joel Chandler Harris, *Uncle Remus: His Songs and His Sayings* (New York: Shocken Books: 1965), p. 163.

8. Thomas Nelson Page, *In Ole Virginia* (New York: Scribner's, 1887), p. 10.

9. Bernard Wolfe, "Uncle Remus and the Malevolent Rabbit: 'Takes a Limber-Toe Gem-mun fer ter jump Jim Crow,'" in *Critical Essays on Joel Chandler Harris*, ed. R. Bruce Bickley, Jr. (Boston: G.K. Hall, 1981), pp. 74–5.

10. Henry W, Grady, *The New South* (New York: Bonner's, 1890), pp. 320, 316, 315, 320, 318, 316, 244.

11. Jay B. Hubbell, *The South in American Literature, 1607–1900* (Durham, N.C.: Duke University Press, 1954), pp. 832–3.

12. Mark Twain, "A Private History of the Campaign That Failed," in *Selected Shorter Writings*, ed. Walter Blair (Boston: Riverside Editions, 1961), p. 206. Henceforth cited parenthetically in the text as PH.

13. *Mark Twain Speaking*, ed. Paul Fatout (Iowa City: University of Iowa Press, 1976), p. 106. Henceforth cited parenthetically in the text as MTS.

14. Justin Kaplan, *Mr. Clemens and Mark Twain* (New York: Simon & Schuster, 1966), p. 274.

15. Richard E. Peck, "The Campaign That ... Succeeded," *American Literary Realism, 1870–1910* 21.3 (Spring 1989): 10. See also Thomas Quirk, "Life Imitating Art: *Huckleberry Finn* and Twain's Autobiographical Writings," in *One Hundred Years of Huckleberry Finn: The Boy, His Book, and American Culture*, ed. Robert Sattelmeyer and J. Donald Crowley (Columbia: University of Missouri Press, 1985).

16. Mark Twain, *Life on the Mississippi* (New York: Hill & Wang, 1968), p. 243. Henceforth cited parenthetically in the text as LM.

17. Mark Twain, "A True Story, Repeated Word for Word as I Heard It," in *Selected Shorter Writings*, ed. Blair; p. 59. Henceforth cited parenthetically in the text as TS.

18. Grady, The New South, p. 146

19. Ibid., pp. 148-9.

20. Forrest G. Robinson, *In Bad Faith: The Dynamics of Deception in Mark Twain's America* (Cambridge, Mass.: Harvard University Press, 1986), pp. 240, 139.

21. James M. Cox, *Mark Twain: The Fate of Humor* (Princeton, N.J.: Princeton University Press, 1966), p. 197.

JOHN CARLOS ROWE

How the Boss Played the Game:
Twain's Critique of Imperialism in
A Connecticut Yankee in King Arthur's Court

> Shall we bang right ahead in our old-time, loud, pious way, and commit
> the new century to the game; or shall we sober up and sit down and think
> it over first? Would it not be prudent to get our Civilization-tools
> together, and see how much stock is left on hand in the way of Glass
> Beads and Theology, and Maxim Guns and Hymn Books, and Trade Gin
> and Torches of Progress and Enlightenment (patent adjustable ones,
> good to fire villages with, upon occasion), and balance the books, and
> arrive at the profit and loss, so that we may intelligently decide whether
> to continue the business or sell out the property and start a new
> Civilization Scheme on the proceeds?
>
> Mark Twain, "To the Person Sitting in Darkness,"
> *North American Review*, February 1901

Twain is famous for his jeremiads against European imperialism and the fledgling efforts of the United States at colonial expansion in the Philippines. As scholars have pointed out, most of Twain's anticolonial zeal dates from the late 1890s and early 1900s, provoked by such international crises as the Spanish-American War (1898), the Boxer Rebellion in China (1900), and the Boer War in South Africa (1899–1902). Twain's rage over U.S. annexation of the Philippines in "To the Person Sitting in Darkness" (1901) and "A Defense of General Funston" (1902), the cruel despotism of Belgium's

From *The Cambridge Companion to Mark Twain*, Forrest G. Robinson, ed. © 1995 Cambridge
University Press.

Leopold II in the Congo Free State in "King Leopold's Soliloquy" (1905), and Czar Nicholas II's exploitation of Russians, Poles, and Finns in "The Czar's Soliloquy" (1905) belongs to the historical period in which "imperialism" had entered the popular vocabulary as a term of opprobrium.[1]

Powerful as Twain's anticolonial writings from this period are, they seem to be different from the more ambivalent sentiments regarding the uses and abuses of "civilization" Twain had articulated as late as 1897 in *Following the Equator*. Despite frequently expressed sympathies with native peoples throughout his global lecturing tour, Twain also appears to acknowledge the inevitability of Euroamerican hegemony over the modern world. Richard Bridgman concludes in *Traveling in Mark Twain* that such a destiny did not in 1897 disappoint Twain: "For all the abuses of conquest that Twain had documented and lamented, his conclusive feeling was that 'all the savage lands in the world are going to be brought under the subjection of the Christian governments of Europe. I am not sorry, but glad.' He was not being ironic. He believed, he wrote, that India demonstrated that after much bloodshed the result would be 'peace and order and the reign of law.'"[2]

To be sure, Twain was powerfully impressed by historical events, from the Spanish-American War to the Russo-Japanese War, that underscored the brutality of Euroamerican colonialism and foreshadowed the violence of the First World War. Yet these historical events alone were not the primary reasons for the changes in Twain's views on colonialism from *Following the Equator* to the anti-imperialist tracts he wrote between 1898 and 1905. What Bridgman confidently decides to be Twain's preference for imperial order, British India over the "misrule" of the Thugs, for example, by no means applies generally to Twain's often contradictory attitudes in this travel book regarding the uses and abuses of Western civilization both at home and abroad. The strict periodization of the "anti-imperialist" Mark Twain of the fin de siècle as distinct from the apparently patriotic and nationalist Twain of the 1870s and 1880s, has prevented us from recognizing how anticolonial and anti-imperialist attitudes inflect virtually all of Twain's writings.[3]

One of Twain's most obvious literary treatments of imperialism, indeed one of the most obvious in nineteenth-century literature in general, is *A Connecticut Yankee in King Arthur's Court*, but it is not customarily approached in terms of its serious reflections on imperialism. One reason for this neglect is that *Connecticut Yankee*, published in 1889, belongs to the decade preceding Twain's overt "change of mind" about the dangers of colonialism and imperialism. Another reason, of course, is the formal distraction of the historical romance. Arthurian England "invaded" by a nineteenth-century Yankee does not seem to be a fictive *donnée* likely to encourage discussion of the dangers of Euroamerican colonialism in the modern period. Yet more familiar literary indictments of Western imperialism, such as Conrad's *Heart of Darkness* (1899), often recall the colonial origins of the European colonizers, as Marlow does at the beginning of his tale: "'Imagine the feelings of a commander of a fine—what d'ye call 'em—trireme in the Mediterranean, ordered suddenly to the north.... Imagine him here—the very end of the world, a sea the colour of lead, a sky the colour of smoke.... Sandbanks, marshes, forests, savages—precious little to eat fit for a civilised man, nothing but Thames water. No Falernian wine here, no going ashore.'"[4] At times, such invocations of Roman conquerors work to rationalize European or American ventures abroad, either by connecting the modern nations with a great tradition or by encouraging resignation to the "inevitability" of men's will to conquest and expansion.[5] In other cases, previous colonial projects are recalled to remind us that history repeats itself primarily when we refuse to acknowledge the fundamental theft involved in colonization. Melville's *Typee* (1846) makes frequent reference to Roman generals and legions in Europe, and *Benito Cereno* (1856) revives the imperium of the Holy Roman emperor both in Europe and in the New World to warn us that the nominally democratic United States is following the lead of the European imperium against which it claimed to have rebelled.[6]

The most convincing argument for excluding *Connecticut Yankee* from a consideration of Twain's anti-imperialism is the relative novelty of the terms "imperialism" and "anti-imperialism" in the United States at the end of the 1890s, primarily as a result of the public debates over the Spanish-American and Philippine-American Wars. Rudyard Kipling's poem "The White Man's Burden" (1899), in which Kipling specifically urges the United States to assume its "responsibilities" in the Philippines as the European powers had done elsewhere, is often considered a sort of historical marker for the infection of public discourse in the United States with the jingoism of conservative European imperialists.[7] In the 1896 presidential campaign, William Jennings Bryan ran on a free-silver platform and, after his defeat by McKinley, served as colonel of a Nebraska regiment of volunteers in the Spanish-American War. In the 1900 campaign, Bryan combined free-silver with anti-imperialism to challenge McKinley once again, recognizing that the incumbent president was closely associated with expansionist foreign policies.[8]

This sort of historical specificity regarding the popular use of the terms "imperialism" and "anti-imperialism" in political debates in the United States seems to be reinforced by Twain's own statements regarding the "change" in his position on our foreign policies between 1898 and 1902. In his 1947 essay, "Mark Twain and Howells: Anti-Imperialists," William Gibson restricts his consideration of Twain's anti-imperialism to this period in large part because of Twain's public declarations that he has changed his mind about U.S. expansionism after our betrayal of Aguinaldo and the Philippine people's revolution. Responding to a *Chicago Tribune* reporter's statement in 1900, "'You've been quoted here as an anti-imperialist,'" Twain replied, "Well, I am. A year ago I wasn't. I thought it would be a great thing to give a whole lot of freedom to the Filipinos, but I guess now that it's better to let them give it to themselves."[9] Gibson and others have pointed out that Twain, like Henry Adams, supported our foreign policy in the nominal "liberation" of Cuba from Spain, but changed his mind about U.S. foreign policy when it shifted from one of aiding republican movements to annexing foreign territory, as it did, however "accidentally," at the end of the Philippine-American War.[10]

Twain's public statements about his "change of mind" belie, however, the continuity of his thinking about imperialism from *Connecticut Yankee* to his overtly anti-imperialist satires of the period 1898–1905. His ambivalence regarding Euroamerican imperialism is also quite consistent throughout his career, as I shall argue *Connecticut Yankee* demonstrates. What appears at times to be Twain's equivocation regarding the changing foreign policies of the great powers can usually be attributed to his strong and consistent conviction that *all* people throughout history are prone to conquer and colonize their neighbors. As he writes in *Following the Equator*:

> All the territorial possessions of all the political establishments in the earth—including America, of course, consist of pilferings from other people's wash. No tribe, however insignificant, and no nation, howsoever mighty, occupies a foot of land that was not stolen. When the English, the French, and the Spaniards reached America, the Indian tribes had been raiding each other's territorial clothes-lines for ages, and every acre of ground in the continent had been stolen and restolen five hundred times.[11]

The only solution to this vicious historical cycle of conquest and exploitation seems to be the emancipation that Twain identified with the American and French Revolutions, both of which turned crucially on war and conquest in the interests of the people's rule. Twain's problem throughout his writings, whether he is questioning domestic politics or foreign policies, is finding a standard for judging correctly the degree to which republican aims and their emancipatory struggles can be distinguished from the tiresome old business of conquest by kings, priests, and tycoons.

It is just this division between the republican sentiments of Hank Morgan and his bid for despotic power in sixth-century England that organizes the dramatic action and social criticism of *A Connecticut Yankee in King Arthur's Court*. In the course of negotiating this fundamental division in his protagonist's character, Twain anticipates most of the anti-imperialist views he would make so explicit in his satires between 1898 and 1905. In exposing the ways that the usual tyrants would learn to disguise themselves as bearers of enlightenment and thus emancipation from both despotic rule and the drudgery of everyday labor, Twain anticipates the more modern critique of neoimperialist strategies of "winning hearts and minds" in the course of shaping consumers—the sort of neoimperialism we associate with today's global corporations, proper heirs both of Hank Morgan's late-nineteenth-century capitalist feudalism and of the Euroamerican colonial "missions" into the earth's "hearts of darkness."

For all this modernity, however, Twain's anti-imperialism remains fully grounded in older definitions of imperialism as "the personal sovereignty of a powerful ruler over numerous territories, whether in Europe or overseas."[12] What Twain likes to call the "game" in his anti-imperialist writings remains much the same as it has been for centuries. In "To the Person Sitting in Darkness," Twain writes: "The Blessings-of-Civilization Trust, wisely and curiously administered is a Daisy. There is more money in it, more territory, more sovereignty, and other kinds of emolument, than there is in any other game that is played. But Christendom has been laying it badly of late years."[13] In *Following the Equator*, his metaphor for the masquerade of colonial exploitation as "enlightenment" is clothing, in terms of what has been hung out to dry on the clothesline, stolen wash, and "fashionable" dress of the day:

> In one hundred and fifty years England has beneficently retired garment after garment from the Indian lines, until there is hardly a rag of the original wash left dangling anywhere. In eight hundred years an obscure tribe of Muscovite savages has risen to the dazzling position of Land-Robber-in-Chief; she found a quarter of the world hanging out to dry on a hundred parallels of latitude, and she scooped in the whole wash.[14]

In his attacks on Chamberlain's conduct in the Boer War and McKinley's annexation of the Philippines, Twain equates these democratic leaders with the German kaiser and Russian czar in their willing deception of the people they represent and conquer: "We all know the Business is being ruined. The reason is not far to seek. It is because our Mr. McKinley, and Mr. Chamberlain, and the Kaiser, and the Tsar and the French have been exporting the Actual Thing *with the outside cover left off*. This is bad for the Game. It shows that these new players of it are not sufficiently acquainted with it" ("Person" 2.95). In *A Connecticut Yankee*, he anticipates this indictment of imperialism by showing how despotism secures its power by controlling people's attitudes and values, either by encouraging their superstitions, as the Church and Merlin do, or by manipulating public opinion, as Hank and Clarence do with their weekly newspaper. When Twain writes in 1901 that "Mr. Chamberlain manufactures a war out of materials so inadequate and so fanciful that they make the boxes grieve and the gallery laugh" ("Person" 295), we are reminded that the "theatricality" of the publicity used by Chamberlain to disguise the real motives of the Boer War is anticipated by the "theatricality" of Hank Morgan's republican postures in *Connecticut Yankee*.

Numerous scenes of such political "theater" are enacted by the Boss, from the eclipse and the restoration of the holy well to his penultimate "duel" with the Knights of the Round Table. I want to focus now on that "duel" both to typify Twain's treatment of political theatricality in *Connecticut Yankee* and to connect it with one of the most legendary "events" of nineteenth-century British colonialism: "Chinese" Gordon's death at the hands of the Mahdi and his "dervishes" in Khartoum. In chapter 39, Twain deliberately confuses the contemporary Western street fight, the "last-stand" of the heroic frontier officer overwhelmed by "Indians" or "natives," the Southern duel of honor, and the chivalric jousting tournament. Calmly standing before the charge of mounted knights in full armor, Hank uses his Colt "Dragoon" revolvers to demonstrate his military power. Shooting Sir Sagramour out of his saddle, he calmly fires nine more shots and kills nine more of the five hundred knights massed against him. This scene obviously anticipates the genocide at the end of the narrative, as well as the failure of Hank's revolution, "trapped" as it is both by its own fortifications and by its own perverse logic. Hank's "bluff" in facing down five hundred knights with two Colt revolvers holding twelve cartridges is the sort of scene repeated countless times in the dime novels of Western adventure and in the "heroic" exploits of British and European adventurers in exotic colonial sites. Not only is Chinese Gordon's tragic bravura recalled ironically here, but the equally legendary stand of General Custer at the Little Big Horn in 1876 echoes through the scene for the contemporary reader.

Twain "conceived, composed, and finally revised *Yankee* during five years of intermittent work between December 1884 and September 1889."[15] One of the most celebrated events of European colonialism in that period was the death of Charles George Gordon, "Chinese Gordon," on January 26, 1885, in Khartoum, Sudan, where he had returned in February 1884 to put down the rebellion led by the Moslem leader, Mohammed Ahmed (the Mahdi), whose forces had destroyed British General William Hicks's Egyptian force of ten thousand. Like the final battle between the Church's knights and the Boss's boys, the fabled end of Chinese Gordon, besieged by the rebels at Khartoum, was the result of a religious "revolt." Like Hank Morgan's, Chinese Gordon's "progressive reforms" in Egypt and North Africa had helped "precipitate the inevitable disaster," as Lytton Strachey would put it in his apt conclusion to *Eminent Victorians* (1918), "The End of General Gordon."[16] Among the reforms Gordon had accomplished while serving as governor of the equatorial provinces of central Africa (1873–80) was the "suppression of the slave trade," which is the first reform Hank Morgan makes after he has made public his revolution against knight-errantry, following his shooting of ten knights out of their saddles in chapter 39.

Contemporary accounts of Chinese Gordon's death at Khartoum are typically legendary; not surprisingly they range from saintly forbearance to martial valor. Strachey's account captures just this legendary quality of the "progressive" European colonizer sacrificing himself in the cause of Civilization:

> Another spear transfixed him; he fell, and the swords of the three other Dervishes instantly hacked him to death. Thus, if we are to believe the official chroniclers, in the dignity of unresisting disdain, General Gordon met his end.... Other witnesses told a very different story. The man whom they saw die was not a saint but a warrior. With intrepidity, with skill, with desperation, he flew at his enemies. When his pistol was exhausted, he fought on with his sword; he forced his way to the bottom of the staircase; and, among a heap of corpses, only succumbed at length to the sheer weight of the multitudes against him. (EV 190)

Strachey concludes that these contradictory accounts of Chinese Gordon's end typify just what he represents in the European imperial project at the end of the Victorian age: "But General Gordon had always been a contradictious person—even a little off his head, perhaps, though a hero; ...

At any rate, it had all ended very happily—in a glorious slaughter of 20,000 Arabs, a vast addition to the British Empire" (EV 192).

Chinese Gordon's "contradictions" are, of course, just what subsequent literary representations of the Eurocolonial adventurer would stress, as Conrad's Kurtz and even his narrator, Marlow, attest. In a similar manner, Hank Morgan combines contradictory impulses favoring emancipation of the people from their slavery and the conventional conqueror's desire for absolute power.[17] Interpreted in this way, the Yankee "Boss"—Gordon assumed the title "Gordon Pasha"—can be linked with the imperialist projects of European monarchs and the Church's missionaries, but in a manner that is at once notably farsighted for 1889 and curiously archaic. Interpreting the Yankee entrepreneur and his alter ego, the Barnum-like promoter, as a version of the frontier military or political representative of imperial power—Custer or Gordon—Twain makes the equation between capitalist expansion and Euroamerican imperialism that does not enter the public debate until several decades later. On the other hand, Twain's apparent equation of the frontier hero, colonial adventurer, and capitalist entrepreneur with the feudal despot seems to ignore the important changes that had occurred in the intervening thirteen centuries, especially in terms of how these different fictions are marketed and consumed.

In connecting Morgan with Gordon, capitalism with political imperialism, Twain seems to anticipate early modern critics of capitalism such as Lenin, who in *Imperialism, the Highest Stage of Capitalism* (1916) argued that capitalism had entered its "last" phase in the imperial expansion that had temporarily saved the industrial nations, only to plunge them into the sort of world conflict (the First World War) that would ensure their final collapse.[18] There is little evidence in *Connecticut Yankee* that Twain fully comprehends what the shift from the older forms of political imperialism to the newer modes of economic domination involves. All the evidence works in the contrary direction to argue that Twain hopes to show that the Yankee capitalist is simply a revival of the feudal monarch, who claims his power either by force of arms or by theatrical display of "divine right." Rather than viewing the new modes of economic and political power—what Lenin considered the inevitable expansion of capitalism by whatever means—as significant transformations of such older modes of domination as hereditary wealth and title, Twain treats capitalism as simply a repetition in different dress of the same old story of the will to power of the "damned human race." Despite much attention to economics in *Connecticut Yankee*, the actual *theory* of political economy is quite simple and involves little transformation of economic conditions from Arthur's sixth-century Britain to Morgan's nineteenth-century America. Hank does attempt to "enlighten" the feudal peasantry regarding their rights to their own labor power and to explain how wages for such labor must be determined in relation to prices, endorsing a "free-trade" economic philosophy that, while lost on the serfs he lectures, appears to be Twain's answer to imbalances of international power occasioned by older forms of political imperialism.

In chapter 33, "Sixth Century Political Economy," Hank uses the differences of wage-price ratios in the several tributary kingdoms of Arthur's disunited England to condemn protected trade and endorse free-trade economies in ways unmistakably relevant to the late nineteenth century and the increasingly global economy stimulated in large part by imperialism. At the end of the elaborate banquet that Hank has staged to help Marco impress his neighbors, but that ends up merely glorifying the disguised Boss, Hank assumes his willful place as ruler by lecturing the peasants while Arthur "went off to take a nap." The substance of his lesson is the promise of free trade: "At first glance, things appeared to be exceeding prosperous in this little tributary kingdom—whose lord was King Bagdemagus—as compared with the state of things in my own region. They had the 'protection' system in full force here, whereas we were working along down towards free trade."[19] Morgan's endorsement of free trade is preparatory to his pitch for trade unions and the rights of the worker to "take a hand in fixing his wages himself"—the familiar late-nineteenth-century bid for "free labor" (CY 330). Whatever doubts we may have about Morgan representing Twain's views elsewhere, there can be no such doubt here. In his March 22, 1886, address to the Monday Evening Club of Hartford, "The New Dynasty," Twain lends powerful support to the cause of organized labor, and he does so by linking exploited workers with such "victims" as "the nations of the earth":

> Now so far as we know or may guess, this has been going on for a million years. Who are the oppressors? The few: the king, the capitalist, and handful of other overseers and superintendents. Who the oppressed? The many: The nations of the earth; the valuable personages; the workers; they that MAKE the bread that the soft-handed and the idle eat.[20]

Henry Nash Smith argued many years ago that Twain's analysis of economics in *Connecticut Yankee* is one of the several failures of the book, attributable to Twain's inability to provide the "concrete detail" for a "complex of institutions that had previously been little more than a vague abstraction for him."[21] Twain's problem in representing modern economic theories is not, however, his confusion over the "concrete detail," but his endorsement of a "progressive" free-trade theory that was already showing in the 1880s its adaptability to the new modes of imperial domination. Since the seventeenth century, free-trade advocates had argued that tariffs and economic parochialism only "wasted" economic energies that should be used to increase the world's wealth. "Free-trade" theory is central to enlightenment political economies, and Adam Smith's *Inquiry into the Nature and Causes of the Wealth of Nations* (1776) is the classic text, especially in its advocacy of the coordination of free trade with what might be termed a global "division of labor," or specialization by region or nation in modes of production best suited to it.[22] Hank Morgan and Twain clearly agree that free trade will help maximize the wealth of a united "England," bring an end to its sixth-century division into many "tributary kingdoms" (i.e., "colonies"), and do so by awakening serfs (i.e., "workers") to their rights over their own labor and thus to their roles in negotiating appropriate wages for that labor.

If this is the "enlightenment" that Hank Morgan brings to the "colony" of sixth-century England, it is nonetheless a wisdom that did not prevail in the course of early modern imperial expansion. Insofar as Twain links "free trade" and "trade unionism" in chapter 33, we may conclude that *Connecticut Yankee* deals with the important relationship between domestic and international economies, between the rights of labor in the United States and the rights of colonized peoples in the various Euroamerican empires Twain would satirize so explicitly between 1898 and 1905. What Twain does not take adequately into account in *Connecticut Yankee* or in his later anti-imperialist writings is what subsequently came to be termed "free-trade imperialism." Mommsen traces "free-trade imperialism" to a "pioneer study" in 1953 by Ronald Robinson and John Gallagher, "The Imperialism of Free Trade."[23] As Mommsen summarizes their argument:

> By developing the theory of "informal empire" Robinson and Gallagher broke decisively with the tradition which defined imperialism exclusively in terms of formal territorial colonial rule, and instead emphasized the importance of imperialist factors of a non-governmental character. The true motive force of Victorian expansion was economic, and the imperialists were at first content to exercise informal control from a few coastal stations. Political methods were in the main used only to open up previously closed markets to the ostensibly free operation of Western competitive capitalism.... The usual summing up of the

policy of the free trade empire as 'trade, not rule' should read 'trade with informal control if possible; trade with rule when necessary.'"[24]

Robinson and Gallagher's theory of "free-trade imperialism" was developed in light of the process of decolonization taking place in the years following the Second World War. Twain could hardly have been farsighted enough to "predict" the neocolonial dangers that could be seen as still operative even as former colonies were being granted their nominal "independence" in this much later process of decolonization.

What Twain *does* anticipate, even as he relies on an older theory of imperialism, is the degree to which capitalism will be involved in global domination and the reinscription of the old evils of the "damned human race" in the new texts of economic and technological exploitation and control. When Hank Morgan does begin to play the "Game" on his own, making public his revolution against knight-errantry and the Church, his admirable social reforms are explicitly linked with his own colonial practices:

> Slavery was dead and gone; all men were equal before the law; taxation had been equalized. The telegraph, the telephone, the phonograph, the type-writer, the sewing machine, and all the thousand and handy servants of steam and electricity were working their way into favor. We had a steamboat or two on the Thames, we had steam war-ships, and the beginnings of a steam commercial marine; *I was getting ready to send out an expedition to discover America*.
>
> (CY 228, my emphasis)

The Boss's ultimate revolution, "a rounded and complete governmental revolution without bloodshed ... a republic," to be declared "upon Arthur's death," seems to accord well with Twain's advocacy in his anti-imperialist satires of republican revolutions in colonized countries like Cuba and the Philippines (CY 229). But the failure of the Boss's project—a failure that in the context of the historical romance occasions thirteen centuries more of despotism, slavery, and suffering—is already inscribed in the reforms of which he is so proud.[25]

Cataloging the weaknesses of *Connecticut Yankee*, Henry Nash Smith adds Twain's "meager" development of the "theme of technological advance": "Despite Mark Twain's occasional efforts to give fictional substance to the Yankee's mechanical prowess, he actually performs no constructive feat except the restoration of the holy well; and it will be recalled that the technology of this episode does not go into repairing the well, but into the fraudulent display of fireworks with which he awes the populace."[26] Actually, Twain provides considerable details about the technologies he considers basic to Morgan's capitalist and free-trade economy. In addition to Hank's talents with munitions (including fireworks, of course), he is adept at the new modes of transportation and communication he introduces into sixth-century England ostensibly to end feudal provincialism and encourage national unity, secretly to secure his power and influence. What his various mines and factories serve is, after all, the development of the telegraph lines, newspaper and publishing enterprises, and steam-powered transport that enable him to "unite" and, of course, thereby rule an "England" soon to become the "British Empire," as Hank prepares to "send out an expedition to discover America."

I cannot review here all that has been written about Twain's own contradictory attitudes toward the new technologies, except to point out how perfectly *Connecticut Yankee* expresses those contradictions. This is not to claim that Twain took no intellectual position on the new technologies of "electricity and steam," or that he condemned them in print while hypocritically trying to develop and market the Paige typesetter and other inventions in which he invested. Twain's views in *Connecticut Yankee* about the role of capitalism in the old styles of political imperialism may be somewhat archaic, but he understands quite clearly that *control* not only of the means of communication but also of the *technology* of such communicative instruments would become increasingly crucial factors in determining social, political, and economic power in the modern age.

If the republican revolutions he supported in his anti-imperialist writings were to succeed, they would have to take into account the new modes of communication and transport—modes of "colonization" that extended from everyday life at home and in the workplace to the most distant and exotic "foreign territory." Yet *how* the "people" were to control these means of communication eludes Twain in *Connecticut Yankee*, as well as in his anti-imperialist satires. The Boss's vocational training schools (boy and man factories) and his normal schools ("Teacher-Factories") are unsatisfactory solutions in two respects. First, he provides little insight into the curricula and pedagogy of these schools—that is, their basic modes of production. Second, Warner and Twain had already exposed in *The Gilded Age* the vulnerability of such educational institutions to control by the usual political despots and confidence men.[27] Among those educated by the Boss and his new social system, only Clarence displays the independence of mind, healthy disrespect for authority, and creative imagination required to control the new technologies rather than simply "operate" the machines. Clarence's qualifications for such authority are already apparent when Hank Morgan first meets him. With the exception of his quick aptitude for technical training, Clarence gains little from the modern education provided by the Boss. There is little evidence that the boys and teachers "trained" under the new educational regime have learned anything beyond the mere manufacture and operation of the new technologies; they are still profoundly dependent on the ruler, who has simply exchanged his crown or miter for the scientist's laboratory coat.

The failure of conventional education often signals in Twain's writings the alternative of Twain's special brand of satiric "instruction." Twain's subtle, artistic solution to the despair his own social criticism encourages is to teach the reader how to expose truth behind the ceaseless lies of those in power. In his anti-imperialist writings, he teaches us to recognize the "Actual Thing" those in power have for millennia tried to "sell" to "the Customer Sitting in Darkness" as "Civilization." In place of that false "enlightenment," Twain offers the "many" who are "oppressed" the means to bring their own light into the shadowy game played by those in power ("Person" 295). He knew quite well how to teach us to subvert the pretensions of language and other signs of power that allow kings to assume their arbitrary powers.

Yet the new technologies of communication that were already replacing the dominant medium of print and the new modes of transportation that were drastically changing global geography and commerce in the 1880s were far more difficult to comprehend and control than even the infamously deceptive language of power and pretense that Twain had learned to subvert with such genius. At the end of *Connecticut Yankee*, Hank Morgan is trapped within Merlin's Cave by the very military technology he has employed to defend his forces and annihilate knight-errantry. Electrocuting, drowning, and machine-gunning "twenty-five thousand men," the Boss enacts in the sixth century the special horrors of modern, mechanized warfare as they were revealed in the unequal battles between European imperial powers and preindustrial peoples: "Within ten short minutes after we had opened fire, armed resistance was totally annihilated, the campaign was ended, we fifty-four were masters of England! Twenty-five thousand men lay dead around us" (CY 440). Terrible as the cost of this imbalance of power between colonizers and colonized would be throughout the Victorian period, Twain's criticism hardly begins to address what were already becoming the new means of economic imperialism that would employ in far subtler and more pervasive ways the new technologies Twain treats here as mere instruments of military conquest.

During the week of waiting for the Battle of the Sand-Belt to begin and then as he convalesces from his wound, Hank Morgan "was writing all the time ... turning my old diary into this narrative form," writing letters to Sandy, and later bringing the story we are reading to the abrupt end requiring Clarence's P.S. (chapter 44) and Twain's "Final P.S." (formally beyond the "End of the Manuscript") (CY 426). From the site of feudal superstition and tyranny to the site of modern technological terror, the Cave continues to function, as it had in *The Adventures of Tom Sawyer*, as Twain's metaphor for the cultural unconscious. Throughout his career, Twain himself always tried to write himself out of that Cave, but something always seemed to block the entrance. In *Tom Sawyer*, it is the corpse of Injun Joe; in *Connecticut Yankee*, it is the disease-breeding mass of rotting corpses that hang from or float in the Boss's fortifications.

Twain imagines at the very end that he *has* escaped the Cave, insofar as the Boss's manuscript is both protected and "postscripted" by Clarence, then "framed" by the modern storyteller, "M.T," who in turn leaves this fictive history to the reader. Such literary circulation is often Twain's answer to the determinant power structures he so abhorred, and the collaborative project of "writing" our own history offers a charming, if sentimental, answer to the question of how the true republic should employ technology in the interests of democratic representation. Yet even as Twain wrote *Connecticut Yankee*, the neoimperialist policies that would lead the United States from the Philippines to Vietnam and the Persian Gulf were already being developed in the marketing strategies of global capitalism and the technologies of the telegraph and steamship.

The formal political empires of the nineteenth-century European powers metamorphosed at the turn of the century into the "informal imperialism" that combines "commercial penetration and political influence" so characteristic of the First World's global power in our own age.[28] Crucial to what some have termed the contemporary process of *recolonization* under the conditions of "informal" or "new" imperialism is control of the means of communication and thus representation.[29] Twain imagines in *Connecticut Yankee* that the bodies heaped at the mouth of the Cave, like the colonial atrocities exposed by "that trivial little kodak" in King Leopold's Congo Free State, will at last become visible as the "Actual Thing." In our own age, Third and Fourth World peoples and countries are increasingly rendered "invisible," even as their everyday fields of vision are saturated by the consumer products and media technologies of the First World.[30] This commercial and technological penetration of every corner of the globe, which at the same time renders invisible the others so dominated, begins with the well-intentioned republican and progressive rhetoric epitomized by Hank Morgan and historically performed by turn-of-the-century diplomats, like John Hay, secretary of state in the McKinley and Roosevelt administrations (1898–1905). In his 1901 address, "American Diplomacy," Hay endorses the free-trade philosophy that Twain himself appears to endorse in *Connecticut Yankee*: "We have kept always in view the fact that we are preeminently a peace-loving people; that our normal activities are in the direction of trade and commerce; that the vast development of our industries imperatively demands that we shall not only retain and confirm our hold on our present markets, but seek constantly, by all honorable means, to extend our commercial interests in every practicable direction."[31] With little variation, perhaps a few more rhetorical "flowers" and many more printer's errors, this might have been published in Camelot's *Weekly Hosannah and Literary Volcano* under the Boss's byline.

In *Connecticut Yankee*, Twain warns the reader that the United States is already following the lead of the European imperial powers, a message he would repeat with growing volubility in the anti-imperialist writings from 1898 to 1905. Twain did not understand, however, what he had himself written, or perhaps what had been telegraphed by the cultural unconscious that worked so fantastically through Twain: that the very medium which he had protected so jealously for its capacity to resist tyranny and build republic consensus had already been invaded, if not conquered. Unable to explain how the nineteenth-century "man of letters" might leap into the communications expert—both spin doctor and computer scientist—of our post-modern age, Twain could only condemn the instrumentality of the new technologies and the repetition of the older forms of despotism under the conditions of modernity. In this respect, his critique of Euroamerican imperialism failed to account for the transformation from the nineteenth-century modes of political domination to twentieth-century modes of commercial and technological domination. Yet by imagining in *Connecticut Yankee* the curious intersection of feudal modes of domination with the progressive claims of nineteenth-century capitalism—the uncanny resemblance of Merlin and Morgan—Twain sent yet another of his prophetic warnings from the mouth of the Cave.

NOTES

1. Wolfgang Mommsen, *Theories of Imperialism*, trans. P.S. Falla (Chicago: University of Chicago Press, 1980), p. 4: "It was Disraeli's opponents, especially Gladstone, who used the opprobrious term 'imperialism' to describe his policy of external aggression inspired

by domestic motives," in response to the British foreign policies announced in Disraeli's famous Crystal Palace Speech of 1872.

2. Richard Bridgman, *Traveling in Mark Twain* (Berkeley: University of California Press, 1987), p. 143. Bridgman goes on to acknowledge that if "these hopeful sentiments ... represented Mark Twain's best judgment as he came to the end of his last extensive journey, in fact he would shortly be obliged to repudiate them, and did, with unparalleled indignation, in a series of critiques of imperialist policy" (pp. 143–4).

3. William Gibson, "Mark Twain and Howells: Anti-Imperialists," *New England Quarterly* 20 (December 1947): 470, tries to reconcile Twain's anti-imperialism with his general criticism of America's failure to realize its democratic and republican promise: "Throughout the Gilded Age, Twain and Howells were aware of the problems implicit in democratic government in the United States, and critical of what they held its shortcomings to be, but at no time were they more jealous of its preservation than at the end. At the turn of the century they attacked imperialism as Emerson and Thoreau had attacked slavery. Like Emerson and Thoreau before them, they also wrote in a major tradition in American letters."

4. Joseph Conrad, *Heart of Darkness*, ed. Robert Kimbrough (New York: Norton, 1971), pp. 5–6.

5. Yeats, Pound, and Eliot helped revive classical traditions in the early modern period, even as they ironized their sources, blasted traditionalists, and claimed avant-garde status for their new "classicism." There is nevertheless a certain cultural narrative linking Victorian "medievalism" with early modern "classicism" that becomes more readable if we understand its function to be the reconsolidation of the cultural resources of the European and American nation-states as they shifted from political to economic and cultural modes of colonial domination in the same historical period.

6. See my "Imperialism at Home and Abroad in Melville's *Typee*," in *National Identities and Post-Americanist Narratives*, ed. Donald E. Pease (Durham, N.C.: Duke University Press, 1994), and "Romancing the Stone: Melville's Critique of Ideology in *Pierre*," in *Theorizing American Literature*, ed. Bainard Coward and Joseph Kronick (Baton Rouge: Louisiana State University Press, 1991), pp. 195–232, for a more detailed discussion of Melville's anticipation of early modern critiques of the role of the United States in colonial expansion.

7. Rudyard Kipling, "The White Man's Burden: The United States and the Philippine Islands," *Rudyard Kipling's Verse* (Garden City, N.Y.: Doubleday, 1940), pp. 321–3.

8. At the beginning of the Spanish-American War, McKinley claimed not to have known the location of the Philippines within two thousand miles. To this day, standard reference books, like the *Encyclopedia Americana*, treat our annexation of the Philippines as an "accident" of history, thus thrusting us unwillingly and unexpectedly into the role of imperial power. McKinley assumed this role quite well, but Twain makes clear in "To the Person Sitting in Darkness" (1901) that McKinley was following quite consciously the European plan.

9. As quoted in Gibson, "Mark Twain and Howells," p. 446.

10. See my "Henry Adams and Imperialism," in *New Essays on Henry Adams's "Education*," ed. John Carlos Rowe (New York: Cambridge University Press, forthcoming).

11. Mark Twain, *Following the Equator: A Journey Around the World*, 2 vols., in *The Writings of Mark Twain* (New York: Collier, 1899), vol. 16, pp. 298–9.

12. Mommsen, *Theories of Imperialism*, p. 4.

13. Mark Twain, "To the Person Sitting in Darkness," *Selected Shorter Writings of Mark Twain*, ed. Walter Blair (Boston: Houghton Mifflin, 1962), p. 295. Henceforth cited parenthetically in the text as "Person."

14. Twain, *Following the Equator*, vol. 16, p. 299. Western political analysts had worried about the unpredictable role Russia would play in the struggles for territory among the European imperial powers since the Russo-Turkish War of 1877–8, during which Russian troops had driven as far as Constantinople in their support of the Serbs and Bulgarians. The new threat posed by Russia to the established nineteenth-century European empires, especially in Asia Minor and the Far East, explains in part Twain's begrudging endorsement of the rule of British order and law elsewhere in *Following the Equator*. Like other Westerners, Twain tended to demonize the colonial and expansionist policies of non-Euroamerican powers, as his reference to Czar Nicholas H's descent from "an obscure tribe of Muscovite savages" indicates.

15. Robert Hirst, "Note on the Text," *Connecticut Yankee*, Mark Twain Library, (Berkeley: University of California Press, 1983), p. 477.

16. Lytton Strachey, *Eminent Victorians* (New York: Weidenfeld & Nicolson, 1988), p. 149. Henceforth cited parenthetically in the text as EV.

17. There are many parallels between Hank Morgan and Chinese Gordon. Although he died representing the British government, Gordon was a new kind of foreign adventurer and diplomat, who served rulers other than Victoria, but always (it would appear) with the larger interests of the British Empire in mind. He had served the Khedive Ismail of Egypt before returning to Africa, and he had been invited by King Leopold II to serve as his representative in the Congo Free State (an assignment Gordon declined). In a similar fashion, Hank Morgan serves Arthur, even as the Boss knows that his best interests lie in serving the higher authority of modern U.S. interests—both commercial and political. Gordon's disdain for British bureaucracy and his insistence on accomplishing tasks on his own is another quality he shares with Hank (as well as with later figures, like T.E. Lawrence, who modeled themselves after his overtly anti-imperialist cosmopolitanism). In the final siege of Khartoum, Gordon ordered the cellar of the palace to be loaded with gunpowder, so "that the whole building might, at a moment's notice, be blown in the air," anticipating the Boss's and Clarence's plans to blow up their factories should they fall into the hands of the Church and the Boss's earlier "demonstration" of his power by blowing up Merlin's Tower (EV 188). Finally, Gordon's one constant in all his adventures was a curious sense of missionary zeal, that he was doing "God's" work. One of Hank Morgan's major projects—and differences from Mark Twain—is his plan to begin the Reformation "early," substituting the Protestant Church for Catholicism.

18. V. I. Lenin, *Imperialism, the Highest Stage of Capitalism*, in *Collected Works* (London: International, 1964), vol. 22, pp. 185–91.

19. Mark Twain, *A Connecticut Yankee in King Arthur's Court*, ed. Allison R. Ensor, Norton Critical Edition (New York: Norton, 1982), p. 323. Henceforth cited parenthetically in the text as CY.

20. Mark Twain, "The New Dynasty" (March 22, 1886), in ibid., pp. 284–5.

21. Henry Nash Smith, *Mark Twain's Fable of Progress: Political and Economic Ideas in "A Connecticut Yankee"* (New Brunswick, NJ.: Rutgers University Press, 1964), p. 100.

22. See Adam Smith, *Inquiry into the Nature and Causes of the Wealth of Nations* (1776; New York: Random House, 1937), pp. 440–65, for the classic discussion of advantages of

free trade and the division of international labor (book 4, "Of Systems of Political Economy," chap. 3).

23. Ronald Robinson and John Gallagher, "The Imperialism of Free Trade," *Economic History Review*, 2d ser., 6 (1953): 1–25. See Mommsen's discussion of Robinson and Gallagher in *Theories of Imperialism*, p. 87–90.

24. Mommsen, *Theories of Imperialism*, p. 88.

25. The failure of Hank Morgan's revolution is anticipated in Twain's "The Great Revolution in Pitcairn," which was first published in *Atlantic Monthly* 43 (1879): 295–302, and included by Ensor in "Backgrounds and Sources" in his Norton Critical Edition of *Connecticut Yankee*. Not only does "The Great Revolution in Pitcairn" suggest that Americans, like Hank Morgan and Butterworth Stavely, are just as prone to imperial power as the British and Europeans, it also establishes the continuity of Twain's anti-imperialist thinking from the 1870s to the early twentieth century.

26. H.N. Smith, *Mark Twain's Fable*, p. 86.

27. See my discussion of Twain's critique of American higher education in *The Gilded Age* in "Fatal Speculations: Murder, Money, and Manners in Twain's *Pudd'nhead Wilson*," in *Mark Twain's "Pudd'nhead Wilson": Race, Conflict, and Culture*, ed. Forrest G. Robinson and Susan Gillman (Durham, N.C.: Duke University Press, 1990), pp. 137–46.

28. Mommsen, *Theories of Imperialism*, p. 89.

29. Bernard Nietschmann, "The Third World War," *Cultural Survival Quarterly* 11 (1989) 6.

30. In ibid., p. 3, Nietschmann provides a helpful definition of Fourth World nations as "the nation peoples and their countries that exist beneath the imposed states.... Fourth World nations may be surrounded, divided or dismembered by one or more international states. The Fourth World encompasses most of the world's distinct peoples, about a third of the world's population and approximately So percent of the land area." These "nation peoples" are notoriously "invisible," because of their relation to "one or more international states."

31. John Hay, "American Diplomacy," *Addresses of John Hay* (New York: Century, 1907) p. 122.

JOSEPH L. COULOMBE

The Eco-Criticized Huck Finn: Another Look at Nature in the Works of Mark Twain

Among the many divergent readings of *Adventures of Huckleberry Finn*, Huck himself is often interpreted as an innocent youth more in touch with the natural world than his nineteenth-century culture. Although taught the biases of his age, he ultimately rejected its restrictions (the argument goes) by embracing nature and its liberating ethics. His final statement about "lighting out for the territory" to escape "sivilization offered the quintessential formulation of Huck's desire for freedom away from the constraints and abuses of civilization. The trend is one of the most enduring in Twain criticism and features Huck as the quasi-romantic hero of the realist novel, a child of nature who found independence on the river and in the woods.[1]

Although reading *Huckleberry Finn* as a battle for Huck's soul between nature and civilization is a compelling approach to the novel, it simplifies Twain's multiple uses of nature and their implications regarding his characters.[2] In fact, he did not equate nature exclusively with purity or innocence. Twain's responses to nature were first documented in his western letters and in *Roughing It*, and they resist easy categorization. His treatment of nature extends well beyond the romantic belief in a benign environment at odds with a corrupt society. Rather, his characterizations of nature range widely—from the pristine and playful to the savage and even sinful. These

From *Mark Twain and the American West*. © 2003 the Curators of the University of Missouri.

depictions are relevant to his literary characters, particularly those linked to the natural world. This chapter will map the relationship of Twain's natural world to his enigmatic title characters in *The Adventures of Tom Sawyer* and *Huckleberry Finn*. By taking an ecocritical approach to Twain—*beginning* with his time in the West—we can further appreciate the ethical complexity of his best-known characters.[3]

Writing for a popular audience, Twain was not averse to making use of conventional tropes, and he capitalized often upon the notion of nature as a region of childlike innocence. It began much earlier than *Huckleberry Finn*, however. In *Roughing It*, for example, Twain described his decision to head west in terms that envisioned the land as a fun-filled playground for adventurous men. His initial perspective emphasized the commonly held view of the frontier as a natural escape from the workaday world of the East. Twain wrote, "There was a freshness and breeziness, too, and an exhilarating sense of emancipation from all sorts of cares and responsibilities, that almost made us feel that the years we had spent in the close, hot city, toiling and slaving, had been wasted and thrown away" (*RI*, 6). In the early chapters of *Roughing It*, the open western land was contrasted to the confining city. The passage anticipated Huck's discomfort with the starchy clothes and regulated thoughts imposed upon him by the Widow Douglas and Miss Watson. He, too, ached for—and gloried in—the freedom of life away from such seemingly unnatural forces.

On the surface, the city offered monotonous conformity, the country unbounded liberty. Such characterizations show Twain shrewdly tapping into the popular nineteenth-century myth of frontier freedom celebrated by diverse writers, poets, pundits, and politicians. According to this perspective, common people were granted a sort of limited nobility if they fully recognized the natural beauty of the unbridled land. Many writers worked within this romantic tradition and glorified nature as a place of spiritual and physical rejuvenation. James Fenimore Cooper was probably the most famous literary example; his character Natty Bumppo was lifted above his low socioeconomic status by his close association with nature. Thomas Bangs Thorpe portrayed the boatman Mike Fink in a similar manner: "Wild and uncultivated as Mike appeared, he loved nature, and had a soul that sometimes felt, while admiring it, an exalted enthusiasm." To Thorpe, the frontier West changed what would be a common man into a great man. In 1856, Charles Wentworth Upham borrowed the trope: "This mode of life, in its perfect freedom and manly excitements and achievements, was favorable in many respects to the development of noble energies and sentiments."[4] These writers were followed by legions of others who flooded the literary marketplace with dime novels that characterized historical figures such as Daniel Boone, Davy Crockett, and Kit Carson as moving westward to escape the entrapments of civilization. Twain's calculated use of the convention demonstrated his knowledge of contemporary reading trends and his desire to produce another best-seller like *The Innocents Abroad*. Although Twain borrowed from the popular mythology, he also presented in *Roughing It* an alternative view of nature that openly contradicted it. Since he had spent three years on the Mississippi River and five years in the far West, his understanding of the frontier myth—and his reaction to nature in general—was not necessarily sugared with visions of physical freedom or spiritual nobility. Rather than viewing nature as entirely positive and purifying, he often depicted it as threatening, dangerous, even depraved. The rhetorical strategy typically emphasized the gross misconception of his initial expectations and thus the humorous naïveté of young Sam (see chapter 1 for a more complete discussion of this popular interpretation). Rather than sustaining a romantic view of the West as a natural escape, Twain tended toward the opposite. He described the desert as a "harsh reality—a thirsty, sweltering, longing, hateful reality!" (*RI*, 124). Even when he escaped its tedious flatness, he complained of the "barren, snow-clad mountains" (*RI*, 137). Twain's evident disapproval touched upon a wide array of western nature. For example, arriving at Carson City, Nevada, he was nearly carried away in the swirling winds of the Washoe zephyr. On a later excursion to Esmeraldo, flash floods raged through a valley in "the wildest way—sweeping around the sharp bends at a furious speed, and bearing on their surface a chaos of logs, brush and all sorts of rubbish" (*RI*, 198). After being stranded at an inn (housing the bully Arkansas), Twain risked death in the "boiling torrent" to escape claustrophobia, only to become completely disoriented in a blinding snowstorm that killed an acquaintance, the Swede. On another "pleasure trip," he explored the region around Mono Lake, described in *Roughing It* as "a lifeless, treeless, hideous desert" (*RI*, 245). The alkaline lake water was little short of poison. Introducing a boating adventure, Twain wrote: "once capsized, death would ensue in spite of the bravest swimming, for that venomous water would eat a man's eyes out like fire, and burn him out inside, too, if he shipped a sea" (*RI*, 250). Twain evidently saw the natural elements as an array of overwhelmingly dangerous forces pitted against relatively helpless humans. Although he was able retroactively to extract humor from his earlier situations—or to contextualize specific dangers within a conceptual framework of frontier freedom—he often depicted nature itself as something less than a glorious refuge from the constraints of civilization. It had constraints of its own.

The threatening natural environment was emphasized repeatedly in *Roughing It*, and, furthermore, it shaped those who lived in it. Twain's typically humorous treatment did not belie the more sardonic message underneath. For Twain, the land itself was rarely ennobling or inspirational. In *Roughing It*, he used western animals to help characterize the region as tainted. The natural environment seemed to have turned them into distinctly malicious species. Whether it was the jackass rabbit "thinking about his sins" (*RI*, 12), the coyote with its "furtive and evil eye ... deceitful trot ... [and] fraudful smile" (*RI*, 31), Bemis's vengeful and murderous buffalo (*RI*, 42–43), the "creeping, bloody-minded tarantulas" (*RI*, 146), or the "uncommon mean" Mexican Plug (*RI*, 162), the animals of the region possessed personalities that were anything but pure and guileless. Their sinister characteristics—while humorously rendered—emanated from the natural environment that they existed in. To Twain, the West was a perilous place. Its inhabitants might appear innocent and sweet on the surface, but they soon revealed themselves to be ruthless, violent, and false.

Moreover, the humor of his animal anecdotes often sprung from his inability to recognize their danger immediately. For example, his response to the vicious Mexican Plug was much like the city dog's reaction to the coyote. Both he and the dog thought they perfectly understood the western animal; both felt assured that they could overcome the challenge posed by the creature. Both learned otherwise. Rather than glory in preconceived notions, they were forced to recognize an element of wild danger in the natural world around them. By missing the clues, both were beaten. Innocence and simplicity led to defeat, not transcendent success.

The inherent menace and restrictions of the western environment were not always attributes that Twain created retroactively for literary effect. During his five years in Nevada and California, the region often represented a trap to Twain. In his private letters he described feeling "as much like a prisoner as if I were in the county jail" (*MTL*, 1:221). He repeated the sentiment a year later, contrasting the remote Nevada "prison" to the "Paradise" of cosmopolitan San Francisco (*MTL*, 1:256). Unable to pretend that he and other western men enjoyed unrestricted freedom, Twain complained that he felt isolated in a desolate land of sand and sagebrush.

His five years in the West played an integral role in shaping his attitude toward the natural environment. Rather than prompting a rustic nobility or allowing a sublime liberation, the West reemphasized for Twain the importance of money to social freedom and happiness. His complaints about being trapped resulted, in part, from his poverty (an idea that he would invert in *Huckleberry Finn*). During his time in the West, Twain viewed freedom as resulting largely from the financial success won within society. Revising Lionel Trilling's terms, we could argue that the "money-god"—not the "river-god" that the critic identified in *Huckleberry Finn*—allowed individuals the opportunity to escape limiting social expectations.

To this end, Twain sought the limelight and the financial rewards it promised. He wanted the money to return to the East and live a life of financial independence, a life he experienced temporarily as a steamboat pilot on the Mississippi River. These aspirations color his descriptions of nature in *Roughing It*. Even at his most admiring, he was something of a materialist. For example, in *Roughing It*, he raved over the "marvelous beauty" of Lake Tahoe (*RI*, 147), one western place about which he continued to write positively after he left. Nevertheless, his account is not unadulterated appreciation of its splendor. He traveled to Lake Tahoe to claim a timber stand and "become wealthy" (*RI*, 147). This fact, however, gave way in *Roughing It* to a conventional commemoration of the snowy peaks that "fitly framed and finished the noble picture" (*RI*, 152). Twain's description cast the West as a set piece in an art book; his vision was suitably framed, tamed, and ready for distribution. As a professional writer, he knew the conventions that attracted readers, and he worked to fulfill their expectations, if only in part. As a result, *Roughing It* sometimes has the stilted feel of a guide book. In this vein, Twain observed: "The eye was never tired of gazing, night or day, in calm or storm; it suffered but one grief, and that was that it could not look always, but must close sometimes in sleep" (*RI*, 152).

In light of such sentiment, the Lake Tahoe section of *Roughing It* took a peculiar twist. As he and his friend Johnny prepare camp, Twain lit a cooking fire that quickly spread to the surrounding forest. Soon the entire area was a dangerous inferno. Rather than chide himself for his negligence or lament the environmental devastation, Twain wrote, "It was wonderful to see with what fierce speed the tall sheet of flame traveled!" (*RI*, 154). He then described how the fire expanded beyond his vision: "It went surging up adjacent ridges—surmounted them and disappeared in the canons beyond—burst into view upon higher and farther ridges ... till as far as the eye could reach the lofty mountain-fronts were webbed as it were with a tangled network of red lava streams" (*RI*, 156). Twain's seemingly misdirected excitement about the fire undoubtedly reflected the prevailing nineteenth-century view of America as a limitless expanse of wilderness. Since it was unlikely that Twain anticipated the modern practice of using controlled fires to prompt forest regeneration, he probably enjoyed the fire because the natural world signified to him neither a place of spiritual enlightenment nor a region of childlike innocence.

Moreover, in Twain's first account of the fire written to his mother in

1861, he was downright complacent. He wrote, "Occasionally, one of us would remove his pipe from his mouth and say,—'*Superb! magnificent! Beautiful!*'" (*MTL*, 1:124). Twisting romantic conventions, he adopted a sort of gentlemanly pose, leisurely appreciating the fire with pipe in mouth, serene in his ability to recognize its aesthetic allurements. In this case, nature was important for the cultural affect it allowed, an idea he developed further in *Tom Sawyer* and *Huckleberry Finn*. In *Roughing It*, however, the episode's connection of nature, individual perception, and public self-presentation was more explicit than in the letter. Twain wrote, "Every feature of the spectacle was repeated in the glowing mirror of the lake! Both pictures were sublime; both were beautiful" (*RI*, 156). The manmade fire was—if perceived properly—as magnificent as the natural world, if not more so. The fire was not tragic waste; it was terrific entertainment. In fact, Twain seemed to savor his power over nature, as if its typically threatening posture made it an adversary. Not only did he assume control over the environment by setting the fire, but he also exerted mastery over the situation by defining the fire with a comfortable authorial indifference. In both cases, he relished his ability to prevail. This time, anyway, he had won.

Twain's somewhat combative attitude toward the natural environment had its roots in popular nineteenth-century conceptions of the frontier as a place of physical adventure for bold men and of financial gain for enterprising men. According to these views, the natural world represented a battleground that coupled two stereotypically masculine pursuits: monetary wealth and physical prowess. Within these conceptual frameworks, men proved themselves by surviving and overcoming the menacing obstacles of nature, which often seemed determined to resist control, damage human accomplishments, and imperil human life. Thus, nature was more Darwinian than Rousseauian. Rather than a place of simple goodness, it was a site of struggle. Twain sometimes extended the ramifications of this perspective to the anthropomorphic, characterizing "Nature's mood" (*RI*, 156) as purely competitive. Never was this more true than in his efforts to strike it rich in the silver and gold mines of Nevada and California.

Mining was all-out war with nature. Despite the "beggar's revel" of optimism that Twain humorously relates in *Roughing It*, the actual work of digging the mine shafts was mindless and backbreaking. Of this "weariest work," Twain explained that they "could blast and bore only a few feet a day—some five or six" (*RI*, 192). Even dynamiting did not hurry the process much, and Twain inveighed against "that hard, rebellious quartz" (*RI*, 193). As he and his companions struggled to extract even minuscule amounts of silver and gold, the land resisted their efforts. Mining was a losing battle for most men, Twain included, and the battle itself reduced them to mere machines. Twain's description of the experience was eloquent in its opposition to idealized conceptions of people and nature in harmonious union, in which nature supposedly uplifted people to heights of purity and goodness. If anything, he saw the battle with nature as pulling humans down into the depths of hell.

In the sketches he wrote in Nevada and California, Twain used Dante-esque imagery to characterize the inhuman effect of this war on its workers. For example, in "The Spanish Mine" he described descending into the mine shafts with "[a] confused sense of being buried alive, and a vague consciousness of stony dampness, and huge timbers, and tortuous caverns, and bottomless holes" (*ETS*, 1:164). Utilizing images of entrapment and disorientation, the description recalls his private letters comparing Nevada to a prison. In both cases, Twain envisioned his own relation to nature as primarily antagonistic. Rather than perceiving a spiritual connection, he felt an intrinsic hostility toward nature that seemed to spring from his failure to succeed physically and financially within its environment. It is worth noting that Twain never cared much for vigorous outdoor activities, even after leaving the West.

Twain's attitude toward nature, however, was anything but simple. After all, his life amongst natural forces was not without its accomplishments. *Life on the Mississippi*, for instance, emphasized his ability to understand and triumph over nature's challenges. As a pilot, he developed the capacity to read the river and negotiate its treacherous snags and currents. Because his job forced him to look beyond the beauty of nature, the "poetry" of the river was lost to him, and he accepted the adversarial relationship between himself (as a steamboat pilot) and the river. If the swirling currents won, then he lost. Comic precursors of this competitive feeling appeared in *Roughing It* and helped to clarify his literary positioning. For example, he scoffed at the Humboldt River, which was a "sickly rivulet" compared to the Mississippi (and the Erie Canal, Twain pointed out). He wrote, "One of the pleasantest and most invigorating exercises one can contrive is to run and jump across the Humboldt River till he is overheated, and then drink it dry" (*RI*, 184). If the mines defeated Twain, he dominated and destroyed the Humboldt River. The process humorously inflated Twain himself to mythic proportions. He succeeded in meeting and overcoming nature's test, and his personal status stood in implicit contrast to the diminutive river. He became a Paul Bunyan—like superman that easily overcame nature, rather than a child of nature who benefited from a spiritual/emotional union with it.

Twain's description also inverted the conventional depiction of the West as a place where natural objects were so immense that they dwarfed everything else. Usually towering mountains, vast deserts, and raging rivers occupied a position of magnificence in western writing. Twain, on the other hand, presented western nature as minuscule and vulnerable—a mere toy. He repeated the performance in his description of sagebrush, writing:

> Often, on lazy afternoons in the mountains, I have lain on the ground with my face under a sage-brush, and entertained myself with fancying that the gnats among its foliage were lilliputian birds, and that the ants marching and countermarching about its base were lilliputian flocks and herds, and myself some vast loafer from Brobdingnag waiting to catch a little citizen and eat him. (*RI*, 14)

Twain envisioned himself as larger than life—or, at least, larger than certain elements of nature—loafing comfortably in the shade of the sagebrush. The natural world appeared tiny and laughable, while Twain depicted himself as satisfied in his ability to control nature by manipulating his perception of it (a tendency relevant to *Tom Sawyer* and *Huckleberry Finn*). By referencing the childish and irresponsible Brobdingnagians in Jonathan Swift's *Gulliver's Travels*, Twain implicitly linked this passage again to the Humboldt River passage. In both, nature appeared as a plaything. When Twain conceived of himself as a child, he gained power over nature, and he grew accordingly, but when he sought adult financial success and dominance, he was driven to humiliating defeat.

These sections of *Roughing It* anticipated issues central to *Tom Sawyer* and *Huckleberry Finn*. In both novels, Twain created a world inhabited by boys who sought adventure, fun, and freedom in the natural world near their village. Although this world was physically quite different than that in *Roughing It*, Twain made clear in the preface of *Tom Sawyer* that St. Petersburg was "in the West" and that Tom and Huck were "western boys" (*TS*, 33, 58). Likewise, drawing upon his success with *Roughing It*, Twain repeated the popular conception of the frontier West as a place of liberty, and the boys often escaped to nature to avoid the stultifying civilization of St. Petersburg. In fact, Twain made use of romantic traditions more in *Tom Sawyer* than in his previous work, describing Cardiff Hill as "a Delectable Land, dreamy, reposeful, and inviting" (*TS*, 46). Following these cues, critics often view nature in *Tom Sawyer* (like in *Huckleberry Finn*) as largely redemptive. Henry Nash Smith defines the conventional perspective:

"Natural man beleaguered by society, but able to gain happiness by escaping to the forest and the river: this is undoubtedly an important aspect of the meaning that thousands of readers have found in the novel." Tom Towers agrees, "In nature the children intuit a spiritually vital world which seems to oppose that of adult society at every point. The town means restrictive rules and onerous tasks, but nature is the scene of games and leisure and, above all, freedom."[5]

In many ways, *Tom Sawyer* represented a new stage for Twain. He had already established himself as an author. *The Gilded Age* had provided the definitive label for the decade, and "Old Times on the Mississippi River" had impressed the distinguished *Atlantic* audience. He had also—for the most part—successfully overcome the deprecating label "humorist"; or at least he was not so bothered by its low-class implications. He could count the reputable W.D. Howells among his closest friends and advisers. With such backing, Twain time-traveled back to his early childhood in Hannibal, Missouri, retroactively leapfrogging over his late twenty-something years of *Roughing It*. The imaginative foray freed him from many of the self-imposed restrictions and worries that he faced when reconstructing his bohemian years in Nevada and California. Instead, he explored his relatively innocent boyhood years, an age typically romanticized by and for middle-class readers.[6] As in *Roughing It*, Twain sought to capitalize on current trends, and he made occasional use of romantic notions of nature as a moral sanctuary.

Nevertheless, if Twain borrowed from common literary conventions, his attitude toward nature in *Tom Sawyer* also shared important similarities with the negative depictions of nature in *Roughing It*. After all, he did not conceive and write *Tom Sawyer* for children. He wrote Howells, "It is not a boy's book, at all. It will only be read by adults. It is only written for adults" (*MT-HL*, 1:91). Although Howells convinced him to market *Tom Sawyer* as a boy's book, little evidence exists that he substantially revised his treatment of nature and its relation to Tom's character.[7] Instead, nature often failed in the role of benevolent sanctuary that provided refuge from a corrupt world and heightened the noble qualities in the boys. In fact, Twain playfully inverted the conventional dynamic. A brief passage featuring Tom in school offered a window into the larger issues of the novel by presenting nature—like in *Roughing It*—as an entity that was easily trifled with. Rather than resurrecting the lazy Brobdingnag, however, Twain focused on Tom (a giant in his own right), who became baffled by his geography assignment and "turned lakes into mountains, mountains into rivers, and rivers into continents, till chaos was come again" (*TS*, 80). As in *Roughing It*, nature was controlled by people despite its vast proportions; it was vulnerable and toy-like. Of course, the difference was that the seismic shifts result from the earth-shattering confusion of Tom. Nevertheless, the resulting rearrangement suggested a God-like power, and the ensuing "chaos" paralleled visions of the Puritan concept of a second coming, in which Jesus returned to destroy earth, damn the sinful, and save the elect. In this case, Tom was humorously placed in the role of Jesus, albeit a somewhat muddled one. Despite its brevity, Twain's passing joke hinted at the shifting relationship between people, culture, and nature. Rather than nature possessing a transcendent power over people, it seemed to be at the whim of human behavior.

This perspective appears more strikingly when Tom, Huck, and Joe Harper played pirate on Jackson's Island in the Mississippi River. Tom woke before the others and observed "great Nature's meditation" (*TS*, 121). Content to observe, he lay quietly for a while, in what initially appeared as a conventionally romantic scene.[8] Twain wrote, "The marvel of Nature shaking off sleep and going to work unfolded itself to the musing boys" (*TS*, 121). At first glance Tom seemed struck by the power and beauty of nature; it existed entirely outside of him as a source of wonder and purity. Yet two small incidents called attention to a different paradigm at work. First, Tom watched a tiny green worm inch toward him, and he was ecstatic when it crawled over him because he believed that the worm presaged "a new suit of clothes" (*TS*, 121). Tom's joy over this somewhat "civilized" form of wealth illustrates the breakdown of supposed divisions between people and nature. Even though he imagined that the clothes would be a new pirate's outfit, the primary value of being a pirate to Tom was its significance among his fellow youngsters; their envy and admiration made it worthwhile. As a result, nature did not draw Tom away from a corrupt world; rather, it promised him success in that world. In a second incident, Tom whispered to a brown-spotted ladybug: "Ladybug, ladybug, fly away home, your house is on fire, your children's alone" (*TS*, 121). When the bug "went off to see about it," Tom was not surprised because he "knew that this insect was credulous about conflagrations" (*TS*, 122). Here again, Tom understood nature purely in relation to his own whims and moods. Nature did not act upon him so much as he acted upon it. His innocence did not result from nature's goodness; rather, the belief that he could control (or interpret) nature pointed to a preexisting naïveté.

In Tom Sawyer, then, nature was less likely to produce or foster a certain type of person (i.e., spiritual, noble, pure), than to reflect a person's attitude at a particular moment. When Tom woke up to the beautiful morning, the bucolic scene said as much about Tom as about nature. He was excited about his "adventure" away from home, so he felt good about himself, and nature mirrored his positive disposition. Lawrence Buell labels this impulse "homocentrism," and in his discussion of John Muir, he explains how Muir "recreated nature in the image of his desire."[9] The tendency placed humans at the center of the natural world not because people lived in its midst, but rather because nature could only be perceived through the filter of the human mind. Human conceptions and descriptions of nature were necessarily subjective; they could not be objective. In a phenomenological world, nature existed as an exterior exhibition of an interior temperament. The literary convention was popular enough—ranging from Cervantes' *Don Quixote* through the Romantic poets—and suggested the extent to which we anthropomorphized the world. Whereas Buell points out that some nature writers discouraged the tendency toward homocentrism, Twain capitalized upon the trope to create complex characters that extended beyond typical boundaries and encompassed entire worlds.

It is in this spirit that we should understand the reigning paradigm in *Tom Sawyer* and *Huckleberry Finn*. "Nature" and "civilization" might represent antipodal extremes on the surface, but their meanings were anything but black and white. The first mention of "civilization" in *Tom Sawyer* seemed to disparage society as overly refined and dull. Tom and Joe lamented that no true outlaws existed in their day, and they wondered "what modern civilization could claim to have done to compensate for their loss" (*TS*, 91). Their sorrow was exaggerated, misplaced, and comic. Their naive romanticism about outlaws humorously pointed to the fact that civilization had, in fact, provided a great deal of compensation, not least of which was creating a literary tradition of adventure novels that fired the young boys' imaginations. Their perceptions offered a distorted version of society and nature. In their relative innocence, they reveled in their supposed escape to a world (i.e., Jackson's Island) far from the restraints of society. Twain wrote, "It seemed glorious sport to be feasting in that wild free way in the virgin forest of an unexplored and uninhabited island, far from the haunts of men, and they said they would never return to civilization" (*TS*, 117). The glory of their presumed solitude and freedom, however, was an illusion, for they could see St. Petersburg from their island camp. Moreover, they were soon racked by guilty consciences, struggled with bouts of homesickness, and silently said their prayers. They miss "civilization." Or, more accurately, they had never left it. The freedom of their experience had less to do with the "virgin forest" than with their own perceptions. Their innate homocentrism simply allowed them to transform the natural world via their own attitudes and perspectives.

As a result, when the boys were feeling fine, the woods around them seemed to share in their joy. At the high point in their adventure, the boys reigned supreme over Jackson's Island, and, thus, the natural environment also took on a distinctly royal air. Twain described how they marched among "solemn monarchs of the forest," crept under "drooping regalia of grapevines," and scampered through "nooks carpeted with grass and jeweled with flowers" (*TS*, 123). By the end of the day, however, the character of the woods took a distinct turn. No longer regal, it instead appeared solemn, brooding with a "sense of loneliness" (*TS*, 123). These were the same woods; it was the boys who had changed. Their moods defined the natural world in the novel, not vice versa. Earlier, Twain had used the identical method to characterize Tom after his fight with Becky Thatcher. When Tom retired to a "dense wood," Twain wrote: "nature lay in a trance that was broken by no sound but the occasional far-off hammering of a woodpecker, and this seemed to render the pervading silence and sense of loneliness the more profound. The boy's soul was steeped in melancholy; his feelings were in happy accord with his surroundings" (*TS*, 87). Nature and boy were in harmony here, but not because of the shaping force of nature, rather because Twain rendered nature in homocentric terms. As a writer, he constructed nature to reflect the disposition of his characters; thus he gained a degree of ascendancy over nature. Like when describing the fire on the shore of Lake Tahoe, Twain was able to exert some control over the natural world that otherwise seemed determined to disrupt human endeavor.

On the other hand, Twain's anthropomorphic view of nature—particularly its strong link to Tom's character—prompts further investigation. From his descriptions of floods, deserts, and snowstorms in *Roughing It*, we know that Twain clearly grasped the destructive potential of nature, and this sensibility should also act as a critical counterbalance to entirely positive interpretations. Nature was violent and deadly, a fact that Tom himself recognized early in the novel. After Aunt Polly spanked him, he imagined the effect of his death on those who (he believed) failed to appreciate him. Looking into the swirling currents of the river, however, Tom wished that he could drown "all at once and unconsciously so, without undergoing the uncomfortable routine devised by nature" (*TS*, 55). Although he romantically desired the sentimental effect (at least he thought he did), he realistically recognized that nature did not play such games. Death by water was painful and ugly. In this case, nature did not adapt to Tom's boyish perspective; rather, Tom submitted to the awful truth presented by the natural world. Homocentrism, apparently, had its limits.

Twain reinforced the grim reality of the natural processes throughout his narrative. Nature was not merely a happy refuge from a corrupt world. Readers were told that "[g]rass and weeds grew rank over the whole cemetery" and that the tombstones were "worm-eaten" (*TS*, 93). The decaying cemetery evoked a version of nature different from perceptions of the sunny shores and smiling forest of Jackson's Island. While both provided appropriate literary settings for the actions that take place there, the cemetery was more insistently morbid and solemn. Twain amplified this grim conception of nature when he described a raging storm as a "battle" and a "fight." He wrote, "The storm culminated in one matchless effort that seemed likely to tear the island to pieces, burn it up, drown it to the treetops, blow it away, and deafen every creature in it, all at one and the same moment" (*TS*, 137). The storm seemed willfully intent upon damaging the island and the boys. Nature was not a sanctuary; it could not be contained or controlled by an individual's perspective. The natural world was dangerous, a potential enemy.

Nevertheless, the line sometimes appears to blur between Twain's treatment of nature as a violent reality and his treatment of nature as shaped by human perception. This becomes more evident with the introduction of another storm that, while exhibiting vindictive traits, seemed to reflect Tom's understanding of his relation to the cosmos. During this storm, Tom "believed he had taxed the forbearance of the powers above to the extremity of endurance and that this was the result" (*TS*, 166). Here, Tom perceived nature as God's tool of vengeance for his own sinful acts. To fully appreciate the implications of this connection, we should consider Twain's Presbyterian background. Stanley Brodwin writes, "His was a deistic God of immutable law utterly indifferent to human prayer or concerns and therefore wholly unable to provide consolation for suffering and evil."[10] To Twain, God—and therefore (to a degree) nature—represented a dangerous and vindictive entity that would more likely cause pain than offer freedom. In this light, nature appeared shifting and incomprehensible, something like the cave that not only threatened Tom and Becky but also killed Injun Joe: "McDougal's Cave was but a vast labyrinth of crooked aisles that ran into each other and out again and led nowhere. It was said that one might wander days and nights together through its intricate tangle of rifts and chasms, and never find the end of the cave.... No man 'knew' the cave. That was an impossible thing" (*TS*, 196). Vast and unfathomable, the cave—like nature in general— embodied godlike qualities that often made it seem malevolent. When Tom and Becky screamed for help deep in the cave, they heard echoes of "mocking" and "jeering" laughter (*TS*, 211). In their opinion, they elicited no pity or compassion from nature (or God). On the contrary, the natural world seemed ruthless, deceptive, and disdainful—twisting their own hapless cries into horrifying taunts.

These negative characterizations help explain Tom. After all, the novel was an account of *his* adventures; nature was often a reflection of *his* moods. As a result, Tom should not necessarily be viewed as the playful, all-American boy who deserves our complacent commendation. As likable and fun as he could sometimes be, he was also arrogant, selfish, dishonest, and cruel. Some critics have begun to explore the negative side of Tom's character more closely. Elizabeth Peck writes, "While Tom Sawyer is widely recognized as a self-centered schemer, an accomplished strategist, and an egotistical sensation-seeker, his character is seldom viewed negatively." Breaking with this trend, Peck links Tom to the adult society of St. Petersburg and its superficiality. Thomas Maik agrees, arguing that "Tom Sawyer is the main example of hypocrisy at the child's level," a younger version of the duplicitous grown-ups that Twain consistently satirized.[11] While linking Tom to the adult world is a helpful way to explain his negative character traits, it tends to ignore his much vaunted connection to nature. Nature was not innocent or good, and neither was Tom.

In the first chapter he was openly defiant and disrespectful to Aunt Polly. When she caught him stealing jam, he distracted her, jumped the fence, and ran away. His actions come across as more impish than cute. Tom became less likable as he ventured out into the neighborhood. He met a new boy and immediately assumed the role of bully, initiating a dialogue of one-upmanship with the threat: "I can lick you!" (*TS*, 43). Later, readers discovered that "[m]ost of the boys" could claim the "distinction" that Tom had beat them up (*TS*, 140). Moreover, he tortured the cat with a large dose of painkiller, flirted with Amy Lawrence only to spite Becky Thatcher, lied repeatedly to his aunt, browbeat Huck with bookish requirements for being a hermit, and berated Joe Harper for being homesick on their "pirating" adventure.

Worse still, Tom betrayed Huck's confidence when he fingered Injun Joe as the real murderer. Afterwards, Twain wrote, "Huck's confidence in the human race was well-nigh obliterated" (*TS*, 173). Tom comes to symbolize to Huck a world that could not be trusted. Yet, if Huck had suspected the true snobbery at the core of their friendship, he likely would have thought even less of Tom. Tom embodied the worst class prejudices of St. Petersburg. As Twain wrote, "He did not care to have Huck's company in public places" (*TS*, 189). Seeking to maintain his social status, Tom exposed a soul far from the supposedly Edenic world envisioned by many nineteenth-century nature writers. Tom was neither noble nor pure. Rather, he was often vindictive, violent, and obscure—much like the natural world to which he was linked.

A similar paradigm was at work in *Huckleberry Finn*, but Twain's best novel represented a distinct departure from *Tom Sawyer* in more ways than one. Although conceived as a sequel, *Huckleberry Finn* moved beyond its predecessor in practically every way. Twain's choice to have Huck narrate his own story was nothing short of brilliant, especially in terms of his complex relationships to nature and "sivilization." His colloquial dialogue, unschooled opinions, and heart-dictated behavior tend to place Huck outside of the dominant culture, a separation that prompted critics to associate him—again positively—with nature. However, Huck's alliance with the natural world provides readers with conflicting signals regarding his much-celebrated growth and goodness.

Part of the difficulty in understanding Twain's use of nature in *Huckleberry Finn* lay in the fact that he often implied that nature embodied freedom, honesty, and innocence. Consider the opposite: civilization was associated with uncomfortable clothing, early bedtimes, Sunday school, and "Tom Sawyer's lies" (*HF*, 17), and Huck clearly rejected these. Moreover, after escaping from Pap, he found peace and friendship on Jackson's Island, even stating, "A couple of squirrels set on a limb and jabbered at me very friendly" (*HF*, 34). As in Tom Sawyer, the exterior world reflected an interior attitude. The homocentric device was, in fact, more obvious in *Huckleberry Finn* because Huck narrated his own story. When he felt good, he wrote positively about nature.

Yet the opposite occurred also: although Huck was able to view nature through the lenses of his own mood, nature had the ability to change him, and Huck used this knowledge to his advantage. Feeling alone on Jackson's Island, he wrote: "I went and set on the bank and listened to the currents washing along, and counted the stars and drift-logs and rafts that come down, and then went to bed; there ain't no better way to put in time when you are lonesome; you can't stay so, you soon get over it" (*HF*, 36). The natural world appeared to be Huck's companion, soothing him out of his low spirits, and Huck recognized and fostered the connection.

In addition, Huck's positive predisposition toward nature often found poetic expression. His first mention of the Mississippi River—"a whole mile broad, and awful still and grand" (*HF*, 11)—showed a deep appreciation of its power and beauty. Critics have often noted how the river allowed his physical and psychological escape from a hypocritical American society. Huck's most famous passages expostulated glowingly upon the refuge offered by river life. When he fled the Grangerford/Shepardson feud, he wrote, "We said there warn't no home like a raft, after all. Other places do seem so cramped up and smothery, but a raft don't. You feel mighty free and easy and comfortable on a raft" (*HF*, 96). Huck's relationship with Jim offered him a chance to share nature's beauty with a friend more sincere than Tom. Among other things, they floated along naked on their raft, talking about the stars that canvas the night sky.

Significantly, Jim's interpretation of the stars—that they "was made"—presupposed a Creator and a plan, but Huck's interpretation—that they "just happened"—suggested randomness and luck (*HF*, 97). Evidently, Huck believed that the universe evolved into its present form by accident. Despite his closeness to nature, he did not see nature as fully imbued with a special providence that imparted goodness to those within its proximity. On the contrary, the evolutionary flavor of his observation suggested that nature proceeded according to Darwin's theory of natural selection. Thus its inhabitants struggled for survival in a brutal competition. This perspective coincided with Twain's view of people versus nature in *Roughing It*. Nature was less a safe haven of transcendent simplicity than a battleground of competing forces.[12]

Elements of this worldview could be seen even in the famously poetic opening of chapter 19, in which Huck observed the dawning of a new day over the Mississippi River. The passage was both beautifully inspirational and realistically precise. The soft breeze, smiling sun, and singing birds were as pleasant and innocent as the rank fish and the underwater snags were sickening and sinister. Huck simply told readers what he saw, but what he saw reflected his personal philosophy. The new day promised both good and bad. One without the other would be incomplete; Huck was a realist, and realism presupposes a combination of positive and negative. He understood that both nature and society contained mixed elements. As a result, seeing Huck's goodness as entirely nature-centered is inaccurate. More precisely, his character reflected the moral ambiguity of nature.

Twain emphasized the equivocal quality of nature with his depiction of "signs" that foretold human events. To Huck, nature had its sinister portents as well as those that promised something positive. More often, however, as Huck noted to Jim, the signs pointed to negative outcomes, thus highlighting again the largely antagonistic relationship of people and nature that Twain illustrated in *Roughing It*. Huck's superstition constituted Twain's most conspicuous examples of homocentrism and emphasized the impossibility of viewing nature objectively. Huck could only interpret nature through the lenses of his culture, and his pessimistic interpretations of natural signs pointed to an inherent distrust of nature. Nonetheless, Huck believed that the signs themselves actually sought him out. He told, for instance, how "the wind was trying to whisper something to me and I couldn't make out what it was, and so it made the cold shivers run over me" (*HF*, 9). Huck relied upon natural signs to negotiate the murky cultural waters of the Mississippi River valley. The signs themselves represented a body of folk wisdom that he had learned from Jim, Pap, Tom, and others. As a result, this particular connection to nature also linked him to the regional culture. Huck was affiliated with nature, but his connection to nature here took a form that ensured his continuing connection to civilization.

In fact, Huck made a clear choice to associate himself with society as much as nature. He learned to appreciate his schooling, felt pride in his ability to read, and trusted Judge Thatcher with his money. In addition, when Huck left the Widow Douglas, he did not abandon "sivilization" altogether. Rather, he went to sleep in a hogshead. A castaway by choice, Huck found refuge in the cast-offs of society, not in unbridled nature. He was no Natty Bumppo or Daniel Boone, nor did Twain likely intend him to be one. Huck depended upon the small-town frontier culture as much as Tom Sawyer did. Even when Pap kidnapped him, he discovered a relatively satisfying life in the dirt-floor shack, a life that depended upon scavenging on the river and trading in town. Huck said, "It was kind of lazy and jolly, laying off comfortable all day, smoking and fishing, and no books nor study" (*HF*, 24). Huck had not rejected society so much as he chose a level of society that required less work. Far from living in harmony with nature, he and Pap depended upon store-bought corn meal, cured bacon, processed coffee and sugar, manufactured fishing hooks and ammunition, and ready-made axes, saws, and guns. Moreover, his favorite pastime, pipe smoking, paralleled Twain's own habit, cigar smoking, and suggested that Huck was less interested in escaping civilization than engaging in its so-called vices.

In fact, Huck's perception of himself pointed to a future life of (so-called) degeneracy within society, rather than a life of innocence outside. He followed Pap's example regarding theft, justifying his chicken stealing and garden plundering in renegade (and comic) fashion. Likewise, after he pressured Jim to board the floundering *Walter Scott* and they barely escaped with their lives, Huck felt some compunction over the violent thieves still on the boat, writing: "I says to myself, there ain't no telling but I might come to be a murderer myself, yet, and then how would I like it" (*HF*, 61). Whereas many critics see Huck as a simple child who broke from a corrupt society, Huck saw himself as a prospective criminal who might someday prey upon society. Of course, he had likely been fed negative and unfair images of himself by Miss Watson, the townspeople, and Pap, but his poor opinion of himself provides a realistic counterbalance to interpretations of Huck as a pure soul in league with nature against an unscrupulous culture. As Stuart Hutchinson writes, Huck "is not the innocent boy traditionally seen as the central figure of the novel."[13] Despite his ability to win admiration, Huck was a complicated teenager who evades one-dimensional labels. He was simply not as pure and good as many readers would like to think.

Neither was the natural world with which he was connected. When he and Jim met on Jackson's Island, they were immediately threatened with a violent thunderstorm. Hiding in their cave, Huck described how it "rained like all fury" and the lightning struck "as bright as glory" and then left the sky "dark as sin again in a second" (*HF*, 43). The raging storm was described in terms that fluctuated wildly between explicitly moral and religious extremes. If the natural world in *Huckleberry Finn* was an indicator of Huck's character, then it should not be reduced to a single symbol. Like the storm, Huck was given to extremes of good and bad, moments where he fully understood the moral implications of his actions, then times when he seemed to have forgotten what he had learned the day before. For example, after pledging to keep Jim's escape a secret on Jackson's Island, which suggested that Huck respected Jim, he willfully (and dangerously) deceived him, placing a snakeskin in his blanket, and then, perhaps more significantly, failed to admit his "trick." Likewise, Huck coerced Jim onto the *Walter Scott*, an "adventure" that tended to negate the humanistic implications of his warning cry: "They're after us!" Huck learned from Jim that "if he did get saved [from the *Walter Scott*], whoever saved him would send him back home so as to get the reward, and then Miss Watson would sell him South, sure" (*HF*, 64). Sometimes thoughtful and considerate, other times reckless and patronizing, Huck vacillated as unmanageably as the storm, swinging from the "bright as glory" to the "dark as sin" in brief amounts of time.

Twain implicitly compared Huck to elements of nature again when he and Jim were separated in the fog. Despite the loneliness and dread that Huck experienced while lost, he played another prank on Jim and pretended the dangerous situation was all a dream. The scene is often interpreted as pivotal to the novel and integral to the development of their biracial friendship. Many critics have admired how Jim stood up for himself, showing enough human dignity to destroy racial stereotypes, and how Huck apologized, showing his growth toward Jim and away from the racist society. The fog, however, might be seen as an element of nature illustrative of Huck's state of mind. After all, he remained deeply ambivalent about his relationship to Jim. The final statements of the chapter revealed that rather than overcoming racism, he was still wrestling with feelings of white superiority. He wrote, "It was fifteen minutes before I could work myself up to go and humble myself to a nigger—but I done it" (*HF*, 72). Even if readers replaced the derogatory label "nigger" with the common term "negro" (used by adults in *Tom Sawyer*), Huck's ingrained prejudice was evident. Befogged by racist social teachings, his thought process lacked a clear sense of direction. Like Ishmael in Herman Melville's *Moby-Dick*, whom Captain Ahab had confused, and who awakened facing backwards and steering the ship to certain destruction, Huck had also become morally inverted. Unlike Ishmael, however, Huck seemed less able to correct himself. His final statement in the fog episode underscored his faulty self-understanding; he said, "I didn't do him no more mean tricks, and I wouldn't done that one if I'd a knowed it would make him feel that way" (*HF*, 72). If we take his words at face value, Huck had taken another step in his growth toward rejecting society. However, we should probably pay more attention to his double negative—because in the very next chapter Huck decided (temporarily) to betray Jim and even left the raft to perform this duty. Again, the wild shifts of Huck's personality matched the extreme changes in the storm, and both resulted in a befuddled state that approximated the fog. Huck's sudden decision to turn Jim in seemed to result, in part, from Jim's excited talk about freeing his wife and children. Huck could reconcile himself to helping Jim, but he apparently had not decided that the institution of slavery itself was wrong. As soon as his actions extended to other black people, Huck wavered. Ultimately, as James Cox has shown, Huck decided to follow his own self-interest, worrying less about moral scruples and others' problems, and instead "do[ing] whichever come handiest at the time."[14] Like Tom Sawyer, he failed to question or understand many social prejudices until compelled, and then it is not obvious that he answered them satisfactorily.

After writing this passage, Twain set aside the manuscript for three years, apparently unable to reconcile the movement of his two primary characters. When he resumed writing in 1879, he focused less on the relationship of Huck and Jim, and more on the Mississippi River culture. These satiric episodes might seem to reinforce Huck's antipathy toward society and his affiliation with the unrestricted life on the river. Huck, however, became quite comfortable with the Grangerfords as well as with the King and the Duke. Both groups represented the worst elements of "sivilisation," but he did what he could to join and/or appease them. In fact, Huck invited the King and the Duke onto Jim's and his supposed sanctuary and then conceded to their rule: "for what you want, above all things, on a raft, is for everybody to be satisfied, and feel right and kind towards the others" (*HF*, 102).[15] Huck ignored the fact that none of them feel "right and kind" toward Jim. Instead, they tied him up for days at a time, printed an incriminating handbill about him, and then dressed him in a gown and painted him blue.

When another storm came, this natural threat—significantly—did not embody conflicting moral implications. Rather, Huck described the second storm more simply: "it was going to be pretty ugly" (*HF*, 103). With ominously flashing lightning and gusting winds, Huck lay down to sleep on the open raft deck, and "along comes a regular ripper [of a wave], and washed me overboard" (*HF*, 104). Far from enjoying a harmonious union with the natural world, Huck was swept from his would-be sanctuary. He became a partner to the con men, taking part in their money-grubbing shenanigans and, inadvertently, in Jim's return to slavery. It was fitting that Huck assumed the role of Tom Sawyer on the Phelps farm. To most critics, Tom was more obviously a mixture of good and bad, and the "rebirth" (like the "evasion") implied that Huck was tainted also—by his connection to civilization and by his resemblance to nature.

One of the last full depictions of nature in *Huckleberry Finn* revealed Huck's mindset and (perhaps) Twain's intentions. Walking toward the Phelps farm, Huck heard the "faint dronings of bugs and flies in the air that makes it seem so lonesome and like everybody's dead and gone; and if a breeze fans along and quivers the leaves, it makes you feel mournful, because you feel like it's spirits whispering.... it makes a body wish he was dead, too, and done with it all" (*HF*, 173). Huck apparently felt that little sanctuary existed, particularly in nature. The natural world only reflected his own pain, sorrow, loneliness, and danger. His description of nature repeated sentiments that he expressed in the opening chapters. Listening to the woods rustle, the wind whisper, and an owl "who-whoing," Huck admitted: "I felt so lonesome I most wished I was dead" (*HF*, 9). If *Huckleberry Finn* had "a certain formal aptness," as argued by Trilling, then it resulted from Huck's attitude toward and representation of nature.[16] The natural world reminded him that death offered an escape from the constant struggle of life.

Never idealized, nature contained poisonous snakes, destructive floods, and violent storms. Huck's affiliation to nature suggests why he was unable to become transformed into an enlightened boy who wholly transcended his culture and its prejudices. Nature did not change either. In *Tom Sawyer*, Twain described the dripping water in McDougal's Cave:

> That drop was falling when the Pyramids were new; when Troy fell; when the foundations of Rome were laid; when Christ was crucified; when the Conquerer created the British Empire; when

Columbus sailed; when the massacre at Lexington was "news." It is falling now; it will still be falling when all these things shall have sunk down the afternoon of history and the twilight of tradition and been swallowed up in the thick night of oblivion. (*TS*, 221)

Considering the permanence and regularity in nature, we should probably hesitate before linking Huck Finn to nature and then expecting him to change. He was not perfect; he was natural instead.

NOTES

1. Lionel Trilling—identifying the Mississippi River as the "river-god" and Huck as its "servant"—describes how nature "seems to foster the goodness of those who love it and try to fit themselves to its ways" ("The Greatness of *Huckleberry Finn*," 321). Even critics who disagreed with Trilling's assessment agreed with the general paradigm that nature was good. James Cox argues that the "divine Huck" "certainly belongs more to the river than to the society along its bank," thus resulting in his "wholeness of spirit" ("Remarks on the Sad Initiation of Huckleberry Finn," 402). Henry Nash Smith also endorses "the contrast between the River and the Shore," and then defines Huck: "Basically this character is natural man, pure and spontaneously good" ("Introduction to *Huckleberry Finn*," xii). Later critics have generally accepted these early assumptions. Millicent Bell defines "Utopia" as "the condition of the raft afloat upon its mystic river" ("Huckleberry Finn: Journey without End," 258). Roger Asselineau describes Huck as a "crypto-Transcendentalist" and "a true child of nature" who heads West "in search of something beyond a reality he was too pure to endure" ("A Transcendentalist Poet Named Huckleberry Finn," 100, 101, 105). Tom H. Towers writes: "Each time Huck escapes from the greed and violence of society, he is reborn on the river and draws closer to the realization of the natural morality that is eventually his salvation" ("'I Never Thought We Might Want to Come Back': Strategies of Transcendence in *Tom Sawyer*," 512).

2. In a PMLA forum on ecocriticism, Jean Arnold writes, "We must recognize an element of artificiality in this perceived separation, for nature and culture often overlap as twinned processes" ("Forum on Literatures of the Environment," 1090).

3. Lawrence Buell defines ecocriticism as an exploration of "art's capacity to image and to remythify the natural environment" (*The Environmental Imagination: Thoreau, Nature Writing, and the Formation of American Culture*, 31).

4. Jules Zanger noted that when Natty Bumppo "expresses the sentimental or mystical side of his nature, his speech becomes elevated and loses its dialectal characteristics; it approximates, that is, the speech of the aristocratic characters in the novels" ("The Frontiersman in Popular Fiction, 1820–60," 151). On Mike Fink, see Cohen and Dillingham, eds., *Humor of the Old Southwest*, 353. Upham is quoted in Kent Ladd Steckmesser, *The Western Hero in History and Legend*, 29.

5. Smith, *Mark Twain*, 85. Towers, "'I Never Thought,'" 512. Likewise, Henry B. Wonham writes, "In the narrator's vision, Jackson's Island becomes a self-centered fictional world whose remoteness from the limiting conditions of reality suggest a parallel

with Cooper's Lake Otsego and other classic settings of American romance" (*Mark Twain and the Art of the Tall Tale*, 230–31).

6. See Twain's hilarious reactions against such romantic renderings in "Advice for Good Little Boys," "Advice for Good Little Girls," and "The Story of the Good Little Boy Who Did Not Prosper" (in *CTSSE*, volume 1).

7. For a discussion of Tom Sawyer and *Huckleberry Finn* as children's literature, see Alan Gribben's "'I Did Wish Tom Sawyer Was There.'"

8. Greg Camfield and Leland Krauth have both documented Twain's use of sentimental romanticism in his writings.

9. Buell, *The Environmental Imagination*, 194.

10. "Mark Twain's Theology: The Gods of a Brevet Presbyterian," 228.

11. Elizabeth G. Peck, "Tom Sawyer: Character in Search of an Audience," 208. Thomas A. Maik, "The Village in *Tom Sawyer*: Myth and Reality," 206.

12. Robert Sattelmeyer has explored the effect of Darwin's ideas on the composition of *Huckleberry Finn*.

13. Stuart Hutchinson, *Mark Twain: Tom Sawyer and Huckleberry Finn*, 125.

14. Cox, *Mark Twain: The Fate of Humor*, 101.

15. A. E. Dyson argues that the King and the Duke (along with Pap) are "the most decisively evil characters in the book" ("*Huckleberry Finn* and the Whole Truth," 31). Elaine and Harry Mensh write: "The king and the duke are frequently portrayed, whether explicitly or implicitly, as invaders. The reality is quite different: it is Huck who rescues them from the townspeople pursuing them, and then brings them aboard the raft" (*Black, White, and Huckleberry Finn: Re-Imagining the American Dream*, 62).

16. Trilling, "The Greatness of Huckleberry Finn," 326.

Chronology

1835	November 30, Samuel Langhorne Clemens is born in Florida, Missouri to John Marshall Clemens and Jane Lampton Clemens.
1839	The Clemens family moves to Hannibal, Missouri.
1847	John Marshall Clemens dies; Samuel leaves school and begins career as a printer.
1853–1856	Clemens travels as a journeyman printer to St. Louis, New York, Philadelphia, and Iowa.
1857	Samuel is apprenticed to a Mississippi River steamboat pilot.
1858	Youngest brother, Henry Clemens, dies in an explosion on the steamboat Pennsylvania.
1859	Clemens becomes a fully licensed riverboat pilot; steadily employed on the Mississippi.
1861	The Civil War breaks out, ending riverboat travel. Serves briefly in a volunteer Confederate battalion; leaves after a few weeks. Heads for Carson City, Nevada with his brother, Orion, seeking fortune in mining.
1862	Works as a miner and reporter. Adopts the pen name Mark Twain.
1864	Travels to San Francisco, still working as a reporter.

1865	"Jim Smiley and His Jumping Frog" is published, and brings him recognition.
1866	Serves as a correspondent for the *Sacramento Daily Union* in Hawaiian islands. Begins career as lecturer. Leaves California for New York.
1867	Publication of *The Celebrated Jumping Frog of Calaveras County and Other Sketches*. Works as a correspondent in Europe.
1869	Publishes *The Innocents Abroad*. Travels in California and Nevada, moves to New York.
1869–1871	Writes for the *Buffalo Express*.
1870	Marries Olivia Langdon, lives in Buffalo, New York. A son, Langdon, born November 7, but he dies in infancy.
1871	Moves to Hartford Connecticut where he lives and writes for the next sixteen years. Embarks on several business ventures and accumulates debts.
1872	Daughter Susy Clemens is born. *Roughing It* published, secures reputation as America's leading humorist. Travels to England.
1873	*The Gilded Age* (co-authored with Charles Dudley Warner) is published.
1874	Daughter Clara Clemens born.
1876	*The Adventures of Tom Sawyer* is published.
1878–1879	Travels through Europe with his family.
1880	Daughter Jean Clemens born. *A Tramp Abroad* is published.
1881	*The Prince and the Pauper* is published.
1882	Travels on the Mississippi.
1883	*Life on the Mississippi* is published.
1884	*Adventures of Huckleberry Finn* is published.
1889	*A Connecticut Yankee in King Arthur's Court* is published.
1890	Mother dies.
1891	Leaves Hartford for a decade, travels through Europe with his family.
1892	*The American Claimant* is published. Disastrous investment in typesetting scheme.
1894	*Pudd'nhead Wilson* is published.

1895–1896	Twain files for bankruptcy and departs on a worldwide lecture tour to pay off debts.
1896	Daughter, Susy, dies of meningitis. *Personal Recollections of Joan of Arc* is published.
1897	*Following the Equator* is published.
1898	Finishes paying off debts.
1899	"The Man That Corrupted Hadleyburg" is published.
1900	Moves to New York City; publicly opposes imperialism.
1901	Receives an honorary doctorate from Yale University.
1902	Receives an honorary doctorate from University of Missouri.
1903	Sails for Florence, Italy, with Olivia.
1904	His wife, Olivia, dies in Florence. Twain returns to New York.
1906	Begins working on autobiography. Publishes *What is Man?* privately and anonymously.
1907	Receives an honorary degree from Oxford University.
1908	Moves to last home, "Stormfield" in Redding, Connecticut.
1909	Daughter Jean dies.
1910	April 21, Twain dies, leaving many unpublished papers, among them the incomplete drafts of "The Mysterious Stranger."

Contributors

HAROLD BLOOM is Sterling Professor of the Humanities at Yale University. He is the author of 30 books, including Shelley's Mythmaking (1959), The Visionary Company (1961), Blake's Apocalypse (1963), Yeats (1970), A Map of Misreading (1975), Kabbalah and Criticism (1975), Agon: Toward a Theory of Revisionism (1982), The American Religion (1992), The Western Canon (1994), and Omens of Millennium: The Gnosis of Angels, Dreams, and Resurrection (1996). The Anxiety of Influence (1973) sets forth Professor Bloom's provocative theory of the literary relationships between the great writers and their predecessors. His most recent books include Shakespeare: The Invention of the Human (1998), a 1998 National Book Award finalist, How to Read and Why (2000), Genius: A Mosaic of One Hundred Exemplary Creative Minds (2002), Hamlet: Poem Unlimited (2003), Where Shall Wisdom be Found (2004), and Jesus and Yahweh: The Names Divine (2005). In 1999, Professor Bloom received the prestigious American Academy of Arts and Letters Gold Medal for Criticism. He has also received the International Prize of Catalonia, the Alfonso Reyes Prize of Mexico, and the Hans Christian Andersen Bicentennial Prize of Denmark.

BERNARD DeVOTO won the Pulitzer Prize for nonfiction in 1948 with the publication of *Across the Wide Missouri*. His *Mark Twain's America* remains a central study of Mark Twain.

The American-British poet and critic T.S. ELIOT was one of the most distinguished literary figures of the 20th century. His first book of poems,

Prufrock and Other Observations, was published in 1917, and *The Waste Land*, considered by many to be the single most influential poetic work of the twentieth century, was published in 1922. Eliot received the Nobel Prize for Literature in 1948, and died in London in 1965.

F.R. LEAVIS was a major British literary critic. His works include *The Common Pursuit*, *The Critic as Anti-Philosopher*, *Culture and Environment*, and *Re-evaluation and Development in English Poetry*, and his classic study, *The Great Tradition*.

ROBERT PENN WARREN was an American novelist, poet, and critic. The author of many books, he won the Pulitzer Prize for fiction in 1947 with *All the King's Men* and Pulitzer Prizes for poetry in 1958 and 1978. In 1986, he was appointed as the first poet laureate of the United States.

JAMES M. COX is a prolific essayist. His best known work is *Mark Twain: The Fate of Humor*. He is also the author of *Recovering Literature's Lost Ground: Essays in American Autobiography*.

SHELLEY FISHER FISHKIN is Professor of English and Director of American Studies at Stanford University. She is the editor of the Oxford edition of Twain's work, and her other books include *Lighting Out for the Territory: Reflections on Mark Twain*; *Was Huck Black?: Mark Twain and African-American Voices*; and *From Fact to Fiction: Journalism and Imaginative Writing in America*.

SUSAN GILLMAN is a literature professor at the University of California, Santa Cruz. She received an honorable mention from the Modern Language Association of America (MLA) for her book *Blood Talk: American Race Melodrama and the Culture of the Occult*. She is also the author of *Dark Twins: Imposture and Identity in Mark Twain's America* and coeditor of Mark Twain's Pudd'nhead Wilson: *Race, Conflict and Culture*.

HENRY B. WONHAM is an English professor at the University of Oregon. His books include *Playing the Races: Ethnic Caricature and American Literary Realism*; *Mark Twain and the Art of the Tall Tale*; and *Criticism and the Color Line: Desegregating American Literary Studies* (editor).

NEIL SCHMITZ is Professor of English at SUNY Buffalo, specializing in American literature. His publications include *Of Huck and Alice, Humorous*

Writing in American Literature, and *White Robe's Dilemma: Tribal History in American Literature*.

JOHN CARLOS ROWE teaches at the University of California. His books include *Henry Adams and Henry James: The Emergence of Modern Consciousness*; *Through the Custom House: Nineteenth-Century American Fiction and Modern Theory*; *The Theoretical Dimensions of Henry James*; and *At Emerson's Tomb: the Politics of Classic American Literature*.

JOSEPH L. COULOMBE is Assistant Professor of English at Rowan University in Glassboro, New Jersey. He is the author of *Mark Twain and the American West*.

Bibliography

Anderson, Frederick and Kenneth M. Sanderson, ed. *Mark Twain: The Critical Heritage.* New York: Barnes and Noble, 1971.

Andrews, Kenneth R. *Nook Farm: Mark Twain's Hartford Circle.* Seattle: University of Washington Press, 1950.

Bloom, Harold, ed. *Mark Twain* (Bloom's BioCritiques). Philadelphia: Chelsea House Publishers, 2003.

Brooks, Van Wyck. *The Ordeal of Mark Twain.* New York: Dutton, 1920. Revised edition, 1933.

Budd, Louis J. *Our Mark Twain: The Making of His Public Personality.* Philadelphia: University of Pennsylvania Press, 1983.

———, ed. *Critical Essays on Mark Twain, 1867–1910.* Boston: G.K. Hall, 1982.

———, ed. *Critical Essays on Mark Twain, 1910–1980.* Boston: G.K. Hall, 1983.

Cardwell, Guy. *The Man Who Was Mark Twain: Images and Ideologies.* New Haven: Yale University Press, 1991.

Coulombe, Joseph L. *Mark Twain and the American West.* Columbia, MO: University of Missouri Press, 2003.

Cox, James M. *Mark Twain: The Fate of Humor.* Princeton, NJ: Princeton University Press, 1966.

Cummings, Sherwood. *Mark Twain and Science.* Baton Rouge: Louisiana State University Press, 1988.

DeVoto, Bernard. *Mark Twain's America*. Boston: Little, Brown, 1932.

Dixon, Wecter. *Sam Clemens of Hannibal*. Boston: Houghton Mifflin, 1952.

Doyno, Victor. *Writing Huck Finn: Mark Twain's Creative Process*. Philadelphia: University of Pennsylvania Press, 1991.

Emerson, Everett. *The Authentic Mark Twain: A Literary Biography of Samuel Clemens*. Philadelphia: University of Pennsylvania Press, 1976.

———. *Mark Twain: A Literary Life*. Philadelphia: University of Pennsylvania Press 2000.

Fetterley, Judith. "The Sanctioned Rebel." *Studies in the Novel* 3 (Fall 1971): 293–304.

Fishkin, Shelly Fisher, ed. *A Historical Guide to Mark Twain*. Oxford: Oxford University Press 2002.

———. *Was Huck Black? Mark Twain and African–American Voices*. New York: Oxford University Press, 1993.

Foner, Philip S. *Mark Twain: Social Critic*. New York: International Publishers, 1958.

Gibson, William M. *The Art of Mark Twain*. New York: Oxford University Press, 1976.

Gillman, Susan. *Dark Twins: Imposture and Identity in Mark Twain's America*. Chicago: University of Chicago Press, 1989.

———, and Forrest G. Robinson, ed. *Mark Twain's "Pudd'nhead Wilson": Race, Conflict, and Culture*. Durham, NC: Duke University Press, 1990.

Harris, Susan K. *The Courtship of Olivia Langdon and Mark Twain*. Cambridge: Cambridge University Press, 1996.

Hill, Hamlin. *Mark Twain: God's Fool*. New York: Harper and Row, 1973.

Hoffman, Andrew. *Inventing Mark Twain: The Lives of Samuel Langhorne Clemens*. New York: William Morrow, 1997.

Howells, William Dean. *My Mark Twain: Reminiscences and Criticism*. New York: Harper & Brothers, 1910.

Inge, M. Thomas. *The Humor of the Old South*. Lexington, KY: University Press of Kentucky, 2001.

Jarrett, Gene. "Jim's Humanity Revisited, and Retracing Mark Twain's Evasion in *The Adventures of Huckleberry Finn*." *American Literary Realism* 35, no. 1 (Fall 2002): 1–28.

Kaplan, Fred. *The Singular Mark Twain: A Biography*. New York: Doubleday, 2003.

Kaplan, Justin. *Mark Twain and His World*. New York: Simon and Schuster, 1974.

Kirk, Connie Ann. *Mark Twain: A Biography*. Westport, CT: Greenwood, 2004.

Larson, Thomas. "Our Samuel Clemens: Mark Twain in the Age of Personal Disclosure." *Southern Humanities Review* 38, no. 2. (Spring 2004): 13–53

Lauber, John. *The Making of Mark Twain: A Biography*. New York; American Heritage Press, 1985.

Leonard, James S., Thomas A Tenney, and Thadious M. Davis, ed. *Satire or Evasion? Black Perspectives on Huckleberry Finn*. Durham, NC: Duke University Press, 1992.

Lerer, Seth. "Hello, Dude: Philology, Performance, and Technology in Mark Twain's *Connecticut Yankee*." *American Literary History* 2003 Fall 15 (3) 471–503

Lott, Eric. "Mr. Clemens and Jim Crow: Twain, Race, and Blackface." In *Criticism and the Color Line: Desegregating American Literary Studies*, ed. Henry B. Wonham. New Brunswick, NJ: Rutgers University Press, 1996.

Pugh, Tison. "Dialectical History, White Indians, and Queer Anxiety in Mark Twain's *A Connecticut Yankee in King Arthur's Court*." *Essays in Arts and Sciences* 31 (October 2002): 83–102.

Rasmussen, R. Kent. *Mark Twain A to Z*. New York: Oxford University Press, 1995.

Robinson, Forrest G. *The Cambridge Companion to Mark Twain*. New York: Cambridge University Press, 1995.

———. *In Bad Faith: The Dynamics of Deception Mark Twain's America*. Cambridge, Mass: Harvard University Press, 1986.

Schmitz, Neil. *Of Huck and Alice: Humorous Writing in American Literature*. Minneapolis: University of Minnesota Press, 1983.

———. "Mark Twin in the Twenty-First Century." *American Literary History* 16, no.1. (Spring 2004): 117–126.

Sewell, David R. *Mark Twain's Languages: Discourse, Dialogue, and Linguistic Variety*. Berkeley: University of California Press, 1987.

Skandera, Trombley, Laura E. *Mark Twain in the Company of Women*. Philadelphia: University of Pennsylvania Press, 1994.

Smith, Henry Nash. *Mark Twain: The Development of a Writer*. Cambridge, Mass.: Harvard University Press, 1962.

———. *Mark Twain: A Collection of Critical Essays*. Englewood, NJ: Prentice-Hall, 1963.

Stahl, J.D. *Mark Twain, Culture, and Gender; Envisioning America through Europe*. Athens: University of Georgia Press, 1994.

Trombley, Laura E. Skandera. *Constructing Mark Twain: New Directions in Scholarship*. Columbia, MO: University of Missouri Press, 2001.

Van Doren, Carl. *The American Novel, 1789–1939*. New York: Macmillan, 1940.

Wonham, Henry B. "'I Want a Real Coon' Mark Twain and Late-Nineteenth Century Ethnic Caricature." *American Literature* 72 (March 2000): 117–152.

Acknowledgments

"Introduction to *The Portable Mark Twain*" by Bernard DeVoto. From *The Portable Mark Twain*. © 1946, renewed 1974 by The Viking Press, Inc.

"Introduction to The Adventures of Huckleberry Finn" by T.S. Eliot. From *The Adventures of Huckleberry Finn*. pp. vii–xvi. © 1950 by The Cresset Press.

"Introduction to *Pudd'nhead Wilson*" by F.R. Leavis. Reprinted from *Commentary* (February 1956) by permission; all rights reserved.

"Mark Twain" by Robert Penn Warren. From *Southern Review* 8, no. 3. © 1972 by Robert Penn Warren.

"Life on the Mississippi Revisited" by James M. Cox. From *The Mythologizing of Mark Twain*, Sara deSaussure Davis and Philip D. Beidler, ed. pp. 99–115. © 1984 by The University of Alabama Press. Reprinted with permission.

"Introduction: Mark Twain in Context" by Susan Gillman. From *Dark Twins: Imposture and Identity in Mark Twain's America*. pp. 1–13. © 1989 by The University of Chicago.

"Jimmy: Chapter One" by Shelley Fisher Fishkin. From *Was Huck Black? Mark Twain and African-American Voices*, pp. 1–40. © 1993 by Shelley Fisher Fishkin.

"Joyous Heresy: Travelling with the Innocent Abroad" by Henry B. Wonham. From *Mark Twain and the Art of the Tall Tale* pp. 70–88. © 1993 Oxford University Press. Reprinted by permission of Oxford University Press

"Mark Twain's Civil War: Humor's Reconstructive Writing" by Neil Schmitz. From *The Cambridge Companion to Mark Twain*, Forrest G. Robinson, ed. pp. 74–91. © 1995 Cambridge University Press. Reprinted with the permission of Cambridge University Press.

"How the Boss Played the Game: Twain's Critique of Imperialism in *A Connecticut Yankee in King Arthur's Court*" by John Carlos Rowe. From *The Cambridge Companion to Mark Twain*, Forrest G. Robinson, ed. pp. 175–192. © Cambridge University Press. Reprinted with the permission of Cambridge University Press.

"The Eco-Criticized Huck Finn" by Joseph L. Coulombe. pp. 113–136. From *Mark Twain and the American West* by Joseph L. Coulombe by permission of the University of Missouri Press. © 2003 by the Curators of the University of Missouri.

Index

Characters in literary works are indexed by first name (if any), followed by the name of the work in parentheses.